From Cuba with Love

D1157478

From Cuba with Love

SEX AND MONEY IN
THE TWENTY-FIRST CENTURY

Megan Daigle

UNIVERSITY OF CALIFORNIA PRESS

University of California Press, one of the most distinguished university presses in the United States, enriches lives around the world by advancing scholarship in the humanities, social sciences, and natural sciences. Its activities are supported by the UC Press Foundation and by philanthropic contributions from individuals and institutions. For more information, visit www.ucpress.edu.

University of California Press
Oakland, California

Library of Congress Cataloging-in-Publication Data

Daigle, Megan, 1984– author.
From Cuba with love : sex and money in the twenty-first century / Megan Daigle.
    pages   cm
    Includes bibliographical references and index.
    ISBN 978-0-520-28297-1 (cloth) — ISBN 978-0-520-28298-8 (pbk. : alk. paper) — ISBN 978-0-520-95883-8 (ebook)
    1. Women—Cuba—Social conditions.   2. Sex tourism—Cuba.
3. Political violence—Cuba.   4. Cuba—Race relations.   5. Cuba—Politics and government—1990–   6. Cuba—Social conditions.   I. Title.
    HQ1507.D35   2015
    305.409729109′05—dc23

                                           2014034642

Manufactured in the United States of America

23   22   21   20   19   18   17   16   15
10   9   8   7   6   5   4   3   2   1

In keeping with a commitment to support environmentally responsible and sustainable printing practices, UC Press has printed this book on Natures Natural, a fiber that contains 30% post-consumer waste and meets the minimum requirements of ANSI/NISO Z39.48–1992 (R 1997) (*Permanence of Paper*).

For Chuck, Barb, Allison, and Andy, in the hope
that this helps in some small way to make up for
all the distance

For Andrew, just because

Contents

Illustrations

MAP

Acknowledgments

There isn't space here to thank everyone who has helped me at some stage of this project, but I can at least name a few. To begin: I want to thank my family for their understanding when I came up with this hare-brained idea in the first place. They get it, and I appreciate that.

I could never have predicted, when I arrived there nearly seven years ago, that the Department of International Politics at Aberystwyth University would be such a transformative place for me. The intellectual community I found there was warm, tight-knit, and challenging. I owe a debt of solidarity and a lot of memories to the friends I made in that funny little town at the end of the train line. And of course, the funding: Aberystwyth supported me through this project with an E. H. Carr Doctoral Fellowship and an Overseas Research Scholarship, which together kept me housed, fed, computered, fieldworked, and buried in chapter drafts for three good years.

The Cuba Research Forum at the University of Nottingham also proved indispensable. Its conferences and graduate seminars gave me a place to bring new ideas, vent frustrations, and assemble the building blocks of this book. Tony Kapcia opened doors for me in Cuba, and Kris Juncker provided me with contacts and insight—but more than anything, I thank her for sending me to Marlina.

While I was in Cuba, my way was smoothed by a number of people and institutions: the University of Havana helped me obtain my research permit; the Museo Nacional de Bellas Artes gave me access to *El rapto de las mulatas,* a painting that inspired much of my thinking for this book over the course of many afternoons in the Cuban collection; and the Centro Nacional de Educación Sexual and the Federación de Mujeres Cubanas were both very gracious with their time and resources, allowing me access to archives and granting me interviews.

My Cuban family and friends kept me whole over the course of what turned out to be a difficult field experience. Carmen and her family gave me a place in which to retreat from the world. In a moment when I needed it, Rachael and Tanja showed me the sort of kindness I would expect only from lifelong friends. And Marlina and Rafael truly became my family. With every birthday since, I've looked back fondly on the flowers, fresh fruit, hot coffee, and presents that awaited me the morning of my twenty-sixth. I will never forget their warmth and generosity.

Upon my return from the field, Jenny Edkins and Lucy Taylor prodded me into writing something far more interesting than I otherwise might have done. They supported and defended my work from the beginning, and more important, they encouraged me as a writer of stories—for that, I am extremely grateful. I also want to thank all of those people who gave me feedback on my writing at various stages: Marysia Zalewski, Jenny Mathers, Edith Villegas, Erzsébet Strausz, Maria Stern, Tony Kapcia, and Naeem Inayatullah. Andrew Slack deserves special mention for dropping everything five or six times to read chapters, ponder theory, edit images, and run interference with my nerves. Naomi Schneider, Chris Lura, and Dore Brown at the University of California Press have been nothing but helpful throughout this process, and I also want to thank the Gothenburg Centre for Globalization and Development for giving me the time to dedicate to the final sprint.

Of course, it bears noting that without Andrew Priest, I would have long ago disappeared under a sea of chapter drafts, ramen packages, burnt-out hard drives, and stress. He has been there for me even when there was tennis or snooker on television, and for that, I am so very grateful.

And finally, my biggest thanks are reserved for Yakelín, Nadia, Lili, Ricky, Andre, Ana, Evan, Karla, Olivia, Cristina, Isabel, Raúl, Haydée, Natalia, Mariela, Rigoberto, Taimí, Sarah, Natalia, and Yoaní. I am grateful for their trust and their frankness, for the ways they pushed and challenged me. They are so much the soul of this book, even if many of them may never see it, that it feels absurd to see just my name on its cover. I hope they would be pleased with what I have done here.

A version of chapter 2 previously appeared in the journal *Alternatives: Global, Local, Political* under the title "Love, Sex, Money and Meaning: Using Language to Create Identities and Challenge Categories in Cuba." It appears here, in substantially altered form, with permission that is gratefully acknowledged. I also wish to thank Nicole Mcdougall and Dave Iggers, whose photographs appear in chapter 5, and Professor Agnes Lugo-Ortiz, who provided me with a digital copy of the lithograph *El palomo y la gabilana.*

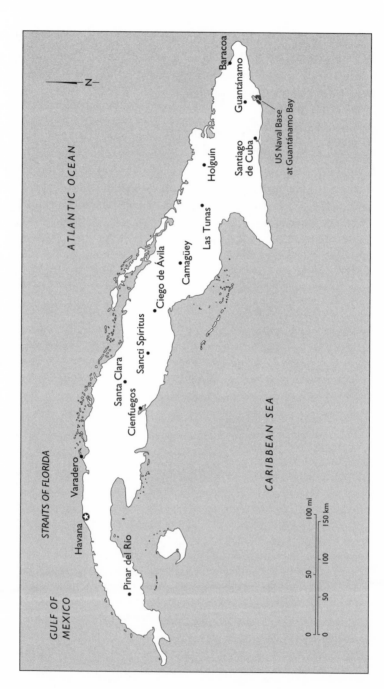

Map of Cuba by Bill Nelson.

Introduction

OCHÚN AND YEMAYÁ

So many Cuban women—most of them, probably—are
descendants of Ochún, the black Virgen de la Caridad del
Cobre. They're good-natured, pretty, sweet, and loyal as long
as they want to be, but they can be cruelly unfaithful, too.
Sensual, lascivious. In time, you begin to recognize them.

Pedro Juan Gutiérrez, *Dirty Havana Trilogy*

There is a place in Centro Habana, just steps from the busy intersection of
Infanta and San Lázaro, called el Callejón de Hamel. A *callejón* is a small
street or an alleyway, but that does not begin to evoke this place. Walking
down Calle San Lázaro, there are no signs to guide the way, but the sounds
of riotous drumming and singing can be heard for blocks. It grows louder
as I turn onto Aramburú, but it is not until I pass under the cobbled gate-
way that stands over the entrance that the atmosphere truly explodes into
life. There are so many people—a great, thronging mass of moving bodies—that for a split second the place itself escapes me. But then it's all
around me: vibrant murals dance up the walls to where urns, manne-
quins, and wrought-iron sculptures stand among the vines that crisscross
overhead. In the mosaic of tiles underfoot, a black doll with straw-colored
hair peers up through a pane of glass set into the ground. The drumming
goes on and on, the divide between dancers and onlookers blurs, and the
music reaches a fever pitch.

Every Sunday afternoon there is a rumba show like this one in the
Callejón de Hamel, but today the party is especially raucous because the
Callejón is marking its twentieth anniversary. Since 1990, the artist
Salvador González Escalona has blanketed the broad alleyway with

Figure 1. Sculptures in the Callejón de Hamel, 25 July 2010. Photo by author.

murals, as well as sculptures made from found materials including scrap metal, toys, tools, and even bathtubs. He maintains a small studio in a room just off the main alleyway, where an assistant sells paintings to tourists for prices far beyond the reach of most Cubans. The people here say that this place was a hub for rumba music in the past, decades ago, but it is González who revived it from years of dormancy and gave it its current brilliant patina. The entire neighborhood became involved in González's project, donating scarce bits of house paint, oil paint, ink, and dye to the effort.

Alongside the art studio, there are elaborate windows through which cans of cold beer are sold. At times, there are also vendors selling fruit smoothies, pork scratchings, CDs of rumba music, and even herbs said to be endowed with magical properties. Indeed, the Callejón has become a hub for the practice of *santería*, a fact that is not unconnected to the Afro-Cuban artists and musicians who congregate here. A syncretic and idiosyncratically Cuban faith, santería is the result of the suppression of the

Figure 2. Murals in the Callejón de Hamel, 25 July 2010. Photo by author.

Yoruba religions of West African slaves and their forced conversion to Spanish Catholicism, incorporating elements of both. It was suppressed as a form of witchcraft during the colonial years and associated with the lowest classes, but since the Revolution it has grown quietly, until its practice was finally decriminalized in the 1980s.[1] Today in Cuba, the names Ochún, Changó, Elegguá, Obbatalá, and Yemayá—some of the most commonly invoked deities, or *orichas,* of the pantheon—are almost ubiquitous in everyday conversation, bandied about as sources of luck and talismans against ill fortune. In an interview, the artist González described his work and its significance in terms of the embeddedness of art, music, and spirituality: "In reality, the Callejón de Hamel is a heavy load of poetic images and sculpture that you have to live through, as you have lived it in the rumba, in all of the goings-on that take place around it. This is, for many, a thing of magic, because it is the result of a conversation with the orishas over a period of many years. It's where you can see the landing of the white dove of Obbatalá that flies and flies and flies until it finds its place here."[2]

Later this same day, there will be what is called a *Changó tambor*, a drum session in honor of Changó, as part of the anniversary celebrations.

Wading into the throng of people, I steel myself for the hands that reach out from every direction, grasping at my wrists and snaking around my waist, trying to draw me in one direction or another. There are other foreigners here—sunburned European faces dotted here and there in the crowd, watching the proceedings hesitantly from the sidelines or awkwardly joining in the dancing—but not so many that I can blend into the background. This is a place where tourists and young Cubans come to meet each other. One of my Cuban friends once told me, on my first visit to this place, that the Callejón serves as a sort of cover story for some foreigners. "They come here to congratulate themselves on being so culturally inclined," he said. "And to meet *mulaticos* and *negritos*, of course, but without having it look like that's what they want."

Over the past fifteen years, the Cuban state has taken an increasingly punitive approach to any kind of romantic or sexual liaison between Cubans and foreigners. In the wake of the Soviet Union's collapse, such encounters and relationships had emerged as viable means of accessing hard currency, consumer goods, travel, and emigration—of gaining admittance to a perceived better life. With the Soviet Union's demise in the early 1990s, Cuba lost its principal source of financial and political support, plunging the country into a profound economic crisis that its government called el Período especial en tiempo de paz—the Special Period in Peacetime. Seemingly overnight, the Cuban economy collapsed by 40 percent.[3] At the same time, the United States solidified its embargo on Cuba, which locals call *el bloqueo*, with the Toricelli Act of 1992 and the Helms-Burton Act of 1996. Thus, throughout the 1990s, and still today for many, Cubans experienced material shortages and grinding poverty that exceeded those seen during the Great Depression in the American Midwest.[4]

It was during this time that the government, as desperate as its citizens for access to hard currency and to the burgeoning underground dollar economy, began to open its doors to mass tourism from Europe and North America. The practice of pursuing relationships with foreign tourists has, since then, become part of a broader set of black- and gray-market activities known locally as *jineterismo*—or jockeying. It has created a tourist-oriented sexual-affective economy, an economy that is not purely *economic* but deals also in affect, love, and solidarity.[5] This is why many of these foreigners, though certainly not all of them, are here today in the Callejón de Hamel.

A number of Cuba's state institutions have gone to great lengths to condemn jineterismo-as-sexual-practice, classing all young women seen out dancing or in the company of foreigners as prostitutes. There have been frequent and repeated mass arrests, and thousands of young women have been sent to what the state calls rehabilitation centers in an attempt to repress what state bodies see as prostitution—a stance that has had profound political implications for young Cubans. As even those engaged in traditional, long-term relationships with non-Cubans are left with the burden of proving the legitimacy of their affection in the eyes of the state, and particularly of the police, in order to avoid arrest and possible imprisonment, an atmosphere of fear has descended, meaning that many are unwilling to speak openly about their experiences. What is more, the supposed prostitutes—*jineteras*, as they are called here—whom the state seeks to address are almost universally understood to be young, attractive, black and *mulata* women,[6] and such a person seen in a heavily touristed zone of the island runs the risk of attracting police scrutiny, if not arrest, based on racist and sexist assumptions about their sexual promiscuity and moral depravity.

The Callejón de Hamel is not a safe haven from this sort of profiling, much as it might appear to be a glinting and euphoric oasis. Several uniformed police officers stand sentinel outside, entering now and then to select black and mulato people for identification checks, arrest, or other forms of surveillance. More than anything, the Callejón de Hamel is an indicator of the complexity of Cuban society in an era of rapid and often unsettling change. The cultural geographers John Finn and Chris Lukinbeal have called this place "essential to the accurate representation of Havana's vibrant Afro-Cuban scene."[7] In the wake of the economic crisis and Cuba's aperture to foreign tourism, Afro-Cuban culture is now studied and celebrated as it has never been before, drawing tourists to witness the appealing exoticism of rumba and santería—what the anthropologist Jafari Allen wryly calls "afro-kitsch."[8]

The Callejón is a nucleus of entrepreneurship where dollars circulate liberally. Its vendors, and González himself, depend on the tourists who flock here to experience uniquely Cuban cultural production. The socialist state machinery, meanwhile, watches over this consumerist heresy and permits it to continue in the name of allying itself with Afro-Cuban cultural expression[9]—and, one could easily argue, to keep the tourists happy and coming back. In this way, the Callejón reveals the impossible position of the Cuban state and its aperture to the foreign international tourism market: it rejects capitalism and consumerism on the one hand, while on the other it lays Cuba out for the delectation of the foreign tourist, making its own deal with the capitalist devil in the name of fiscal solvency.

The role of santería amid all of this commercial ingenuity is also sharply conflicted. Though it is the most popular form of religious expression in Cuba today, its exercise is normally highly secretive. Such a degree of mystery is due both to a history of repression, which gave rise to a tradition of underground observance, and to the perceived need to guard ritual knowledge from the eyes of nonbelievers.[10] In a way, santería is everywhere and nowhere at once in Cuban society, an everyday presence that rarely announces itself too loudly. Thus, day to day in Cuban cities and towns, one sees *santeros* dressed all in white, makeshift shrines to ancestors with offerings of perfumed water in people's homes, caged doves destined for sacrifice, and strings of bright beads here and there whose colors evoke the individual orichas.

Over the course of my time in Cuba, the Callejón de Hamel and the conversations I had there meant that the yellow and gold beads of Ochún around a woman's wrist, or a friend beseeching Yemayá to calm the sea for our trip to the beach, made sense to me. Most Cubans, on opening a bottle of liquor, will always pour the first sip on the ground for the orichas; signs and symbols such as these are nearly ubiquitous. Meanwhile, however, the actual rituals and ceremonies of santería, by which people are initiated to and advance within the faith, are shrouded in secrecy.

So it was that, as I made my way down Calle San Francisco one morning in March, I felt my foot brush against something soft and looked down to find the severed head of a very young goat lying there on the pavement. There must have been a ceremony in that place the night before, under the cover of darkness, and likely in honor of Elegguá, the oricha who governs travelers and crossroads. Outsiders are not meant to witness ceremonies such as these. Santería has few public or permanent churches or temples, since it was practiced clandestinely for so many centuries, though its followers also pay their respects to the Catholic saints, each of which is linked to a particular oricha. In the Callejón de Hamel, however, santería emerges from the shadows for the benefit of foreigners who come to observe ceremonies, partake in drum sessions, and have *babalaos*—the high priests of santería—divine their futures using cowrie shells. The spiritual practice and dogma of santería have become a part of Afro-Cuban folkloric performance.[11] While the santeros of the Callejón certainly do not reveal all their secrets, their complicity with the drive for dollars in places such as these creates santería as a kind of exotic tourist attraction.

This tension is mirrored by the role that sexuality has come to play, both inside and beyond the Callejón de Hamel. Young men and women flock there to mingle with *yumas*, or foreigners,[12] many of whom arrived in Cuba with their ideas about Cuban sexuality already well formed. It is true that desire and sensuality can at times seem to permeate everyday interactions among some Cubans, resulting in a sexualized street culture and a national reputation that extends far beyond the island itself. The Cuban sociologist Abel Sierra Madero describes the Cuban *ambiente* as follows:

> Cuba is a country where people look at one another indiscreetly, impudently and constantly. It's enough just to walk down the sizzling streets at times to seem to feel a sensation of having ardent and libidinous eyes boring into one's back. Between the look and the passing of two bodies there exists a lapse of time, milliseconds in which some flattery or crude word can be spoken: a *piropo*, a sort of fleeting courtship in which desire and lust are given free rein. It's part of our daily life, our idiosyncrasy, and it's the men who traditionally have carried out this element of our culture.[13]

This street culture is mirrored in the Callejón by the courtship narrative of rumba dancing, and of course the presence of the yumas and their dates. This is not the world occupied by all Cubans by any stretch of the imagination, but in spaces of interaction with yumas such as this, it is a world very deliberately inhabited and lived by numerous young Cubans. Many of the young Cubans I encountered here are proud of their country's libidinous reputation; indeed, they would often express disbelief when confronted with a foreigner who might *not* have come to Cuba to take part in this sexual culture—that is, in search of sex with a Cuban.[14] This production of the Cuban as both desirable and sexually energetic has become something of a self-fulfilling prophecy: foreigners come to Cuba for its renowned sensuality, and the Cubans who seek them out become all the more sensual in the knowledge that it is expected of them.

This supposedly distinct Cuban sexuality is epitomized in the bodies of those women who fit an ideal of exoticized Caribbean beauty—the mulata. There is a recurring joke on the island that the beautiful and sensual mulata is Cuba's single greatest invention. This image of Cuban women's allure and availability was reflected on the international scene in 1991, at the very moment of economic crisis, by coverage in both *National Geographic* and *Playboy,* which—in their very different but nonetheless predictable ways—showed Cuba as "a land of dark, sensuous women."[15] These two publications set the tone for a spate of international news coverage that "buzzed with accounts of cheap, sexy, and brown Cuban bodies for sale" in the context of the economic hardship of the 1990s, with reports appearing in everything from the *New York Times* to *Glamour.*[16] Amid devastating shortages, stories were beginning to emerge at home and abroad of attractive young Cubans taking trips to the tourist hubs of Havana, Varadero, and Santiago to meet tourists and returning to their homes in the countryside with cash, clothing, perfume, and even small appliances and building materials. Some women married foreign nationals and emigrated from Cuba entirely; in fact, one of the models who posed for *Playboy* wound up moving to France with the magazine's photographer.[17] So-called jineteras also featured heavily in a new genre of fiction called Cuban Dirty Realism, reflecting both the scale of the sexual-affective economy and the media demand to hear more about it.[18]

Thus, in the Callejón de Hamel, sexuality is like santería: something local, exotic, and fascinating on display for foreigners' enjoyment. It is present in the rumba dancing, certainly, but it is also inscribed on the very bodies of the young Cubans who come here. In the music, the art, the conversations, the lingering looks, and the "authentic" local experience, sexuality is rarely far from the surface in the Callejón. The alleyway is like a microcosm of Cuban street culture: loud, rhythmic, and boisterous, with a friendliness than can verge on the licentious or even, to the unaccustomed, the invasive. On the streets of Havana, old car engines roar, people shout to one another from balconies, and music pours from windows. As a young woman who could only occasionally be taken for Cuban, I never felt like I could fly under the radar; voices called out from every direction, some looking to hawk their wares, but most offering compliments or propositions—the ubiquitous piropo. This culture—with its embedded contradictions of being simultaneously socialist and capitalist, sexually liberal and *machista*, and followers of Catholicism, socialist atheism, and santería all at once—is what makes Cuba a "lively" place to study political and sexual culture.[19]

The jineteras are very much a part of this world. The word itself can sometimes be used as a stand-in for beautiful, sassy, or stylish—both earnest and playfully tongue-in-cheek. More than once, I even heard men call out to female coworkers and friends with an affectionate, *¡Oye, jinetera!*—just as they might otherwise say *preciosa, bonita, mamí.* "From the salsa singers, the cab drivers' quips and the bawdy folk art renderings of *jineteras* I encountered around Havana*,*" writes Coco Fusco, "I got the sense that on the street these women are perceived as heroic providers whose mythical sexual power is showing up the failures of an ailing macho regime."[20] They also have their place in santería: there are those who class jineteras—and mulata women in general—as descendants of Ochún, the Yoruba incarnation of Cuba's patron saint, the Virgen de la Caridad del Cobre. Ochún is the river goddess who governs love, marriage, mirrors, honey, peacock feathers, and all other things of beauty. Others, however, see the jinetera as a daughter of the tempestuous mother goddess, Yemayá, who watches over women and rules the seas.[21] The association of the jinetera with either of these figures, who permeate Cuban culture, is striking in itself.

DEBATING PROSTITUTION IN CUBA

My own position in this project is a complex one. I am a student of Cuban cultural and political life, and not least because of the government's explicit humanist mission and its stated commitment to improve the lives of women, Afro-Cuban people, and, more recently, gay, lesbian, and transgender Cubans. At the same time, I am also invested in struggles against oppression and marginalization, and in modes of resistance that seek a more profound freedom, above and beyond what this—or any—state can offer. Naively, it was the contradictions that drew me to Cuba in the first place: the idea of a self-consciously progressive regime seeking to intervene so forcefully into the sex lives of the very citizens it claimed to have liberated more than thirty years ago—women, and especially Afro-Cuban women. Cuba is certainly not unique as a destination for sex tourism, or even one where the lines between love, sex, and money are so blurry, but this ideological interplay certainly makes it remarkable.[22]

Much has been written, in the media and in academia, about the "glaring ideological contradictions" of resurgent prostitution under socialism.[23] Most commentary seems preoccupied with ascertaining causes and apportioning blame for the phenomenon. Few accounts try to foreground the lived experiences of the young Cubans who are actually involved in sexual-affective economies of tourism, and virtually none depict what the sociologist Heidi Hoefinger calls "the other side of the story—the side which exists in the laughter among friends, in the little joys of daily accomplishments or in the personal satisfaction of helping loved ones."[24] Noelle M. Stout surveys the debate on renewed prostitution in Cuba as follows:

> Cuban scholars and women's rights advocates, charged with the task of explaining the re-emergence of sex tourism, have suggested that *jineterismo* reflects a crisis in values, that sex workers are seduced by superficial desires for commodity goods, and they have supported mandatory rehabilitation for *jineteras*. In response, some analysts in the United States and Europe have characterised Cuban critics of *jineterismo* as unsympathetic to the plight of Cuban sex workers and the realities of poverty they face. More pointedly, a number of foreign analysts have described Cuban women's advocates as stuck in a "Victorian past" by promoting repressive racist and elitist ideologies, defenders of the status quo who falsely claim to champion women's rights, and towing the same party line as right wing Western politicians.[25]

Most of the existing writing on jineterismo fits comfortably into Stout's taxonomy.[26] Socialist feminists, including the women's advocates Celia Sarduy Sánchez and Ada Alfonso Rodríguez, the activist Jan Strout, and the journalists Rosa Miriam Elizalde and Mirta Rodríguez Calderón, are among the former group, concerned above all with the perceived moral crisis that is eroding the foundations of communitarian life in Cuba and replacing it with empty consumerism.[27] Strout argues that jineteras seek the ability to go where they want and purchase what they want, taking advantage of evolving social taboos to reject honest work and de-link love and sex. These women are "unaware," Strout asserts, of the risks of prostitution, in a critique that has been called one of "moral turpitude."[28] The jineteras themselves are portrayed as empowered and able decision makers who have been encouraged to play an equal role in the family, the workplace, and the military for the past fifty years, and who have the benefit of state social resources to equip and assist them, but who choose to turn their backs in favor of shallow materialism.[29] Cuban women's advocates and socialist feminists view the growth of jineterismo as a threat to the hard-won gains of Cuba's women in the decades since the Revolution and in the face of economic hardship that endangers provision of social benefits for all.

This very economic dilemma is what drives Stout's latter grouping. Liberal feminist academics such as Judy Whitehead, Hülya Demirdirek, and Cynthia Pope see Cubans as the victims of hard economic times. The rapidly diminishing value of salaries and systemic shortages of goods have truncated the available range of choices, forcing people to enter the black market in various ways in order to earn hard cash. For example, the anthropologists Whitehead and Demirdirek characterize the moral judgments made by socialists as "elite anxieties" that are "projected onto the bodies and lives of non-elite Afro-Cuban women."[30] While they studiously avoid judging the jineteras for accepting money for sex, Stout observes, they simultaneously chalk those same activities up to the women's helpless victimhood and seem to want to rescue Cuban women from their exploitation.[31]

Amid these competing voices, it is difficult to discern what space remains for the jineteras themselves to define their own position in Cuban society. They do not go far enough in questioning the dominant discourses that frame so-called prostitutes as deviants who either *fail* to be acceptable subjects in their own right—and by *subjectivity,* I mean simply being in the world as the possessor of perspectives, experiences, feelings, beliefs, and desires—or are driven to perversion by circumstances and are thus *failed by* the system. What is at stake, then, is not how certain women come to be labeled as prostitutes or jineteras, or what that labeling does, but rather who is to blame for the rise of jineterismo. Thus most of what has been written about jineterismo functions within the same assumptions as the coverage that has appeared in the media. Amalia L. Cabezas goes much further in her book, *Economies of Desire: Sex and Tourism in Cuba and the Dominican Republic,* questioning the opposition between love and money that is set up by received knowledge on prostitution.[32] In an as yet unpublished thesis titled "(Re)covering Women: The State, Morality, and Cultural Discourses of Sex-Work in Cuba," the anthropologist Alyssa García also explores the historical underpinning of jineterismo as a sexual practice but without in-depth engagement with jineteras themselves.[33]

What is missing seems to be an exploration of jineterismo-as-sexual-practice that acts not just at the level of individual women's lives, but as a potentially political act, starting from the perspectives and identities of the jineteras themselves. Over the course of my time in Cuba, I came to believe that viewing this phenomenon through an explicitly political lens, but *not* one that begins and ends with the state and the Revolution, offers something new to the conversation. Discussions of Cuba and international politics are usually dominated by its fraught relationship with the United States—and, by extension, with underlying commitments to either support or undermine the Revolution or socialism itself. Political life and subjectivity in Cuba are far more complex than this polarized debate will allow. Likewise, histories of Cuba tend to enumerate a list of eras punctuated by an accepted list of nation-building events, whereas I am more interested in subtler processes of articulation and constitution by which Cubans—and especially Cuban women—have been produced as political and sexual subjects. As threads that run through the history of *cubanidad*, these processes predate the Revolution and transcend the successive regimes of the past five centuries. In that light, jineterismo is not a barometer of the strength or weakness of Cuba's model, or of its moral veracity, but a kind of identity formation and ethics of self-creation that goes far deeper than ideology.

The central question that I am seeking to address in this book is, as it turns out, fairly simple: How are bodies governed in Cuba? Or rather, why are *these* bodies—mostly young black or mixed-race women—governed differently and made available for state intervention? This question, together with my own politics, has taken me down a particular path: intersectional, feminist, postcolonial, queer. I am interested in "deconstructing a specific category of woman," in Marysia Zalewski's words, and revealing the ways in which identities are (re)produced, in discourse and in practice, over time.[34] In practice, I have had to be flexible and malleable to circumstances, a choice that I think is reasonable, even essential, when it comes to doing sensitive research like this. Conducting interviews and field research in Cuba presents a special set of difficulties, and these difficulties are magnified a hundred times over when one is concerned with an area of research that the Cuban government finds highly objectionable, as I was.

"ETHICS BOARD" ETHICS VERSUS A PERSONAL ETHICS OF RESEARCH

Moving from these ideas into the "fieldwork, textwork and headwork"[35] of the project proved far from straightforward. Jineterismo was and remains a very sensitive subject for Cuban government institutions. Immediately upon arrival in Havana, in early February 2010, I went to the University of Havana to be registered as a visiting researcher, which was necessary to get my visa. I had been cautioned to be vague about the details of my project—a helpful graduate student in the waiting area had even given me added pointers on ways to frame my work—but I was still not prepared for what happened next: in my meeting, pointing fingers just inches from my nose, I was sternly instructed to abandon all pretense of fieldwork. I could go to libraries and archives, and I could speak to academics, they said, but no one else. I was to do no fieldwork of any kind while in Cuba. "Nada en la calle"—nothing in the street.

Thoroughly chastised, I left the university offices and called the one contact I had in Cuba, a writer who had published several books and had been a visiting scholar at universities in the United States and United Kingdom. At the time, he was a total stranger to me, but over coffee the following day on a hotel terrace near the university, he told me that this is how it always is in Cuba for researchers: you arrive, you swear up and down that you will do no such thing, and then you do it.

So began an uninterrupted six months of observation, archival research, and interviewing in Cuba (but of course, no fieldwork) on the governance of bodies in post-Soviet Cuba. The Biblioteca Nacional José Martí, the library of the Casa de las Américas, and the university libraries furnished me with historical texts and accounts inaccessible outside of Cuba. The archives of the Federación de Mujeres Cubanas (FMC) and the Centro Nacional de Educación Sexual (CENESEX) held more recent policy documents, articles, studies, and congress minutes. Far more of my time, though, was spent observing, listening, talking, and laughing with young Cubans in and around popular nightspots and tourist attractions. I spent my days watching and learning how interactions unfolded among young Cubans, yumas, and the police. By the time I left Cuba, I had conducted over fifty interviews with Cubans who had, or sought to have, relationships with foreigners.

My informants were mostly young women between the ages of eighteen and thirty-five, some (but not all) of whom fit the generally accepted profile of a jinetera. Not all embraced the title of jinetera, but each one had either had or sought sexual-affective liaisons with tourists. I also interviewed a number of young men, self-proclaimed *jineteros* who dated foreign women, whose stories demonstrate how constructions of gender affect the ways in which jineterismo is understood and confronted. The people I interviewed were overwhelmingly heterosexual and cisgendered people who sought foreign partners of the opposite sex. That fact is not intended to diminish or erase the experience of gay, lesbian, transgendered, and queer Cubans, or to define jineterismo "in relation to the sexual preferences of the clients," as Carrie Hamilton cautions.[36] It is rather a reflection of some of the realities of fieldwork and of the evolving direction of the project. First and foremost, though I set out to interview Cubans who engaged in any kind of sexual relations with yumas, I found with time that *pingueros* (young men who date male tourists) rarely appeared in my network. They are, after all, far less numerous than the so-called jineteras and jineteros by virtually all accounts on the ground. Female same-sex desire represents an almost total silence in Cuba's sexual-affective economy, existing as it does in a male-centered machista setting. It is rarely discussed, usually misogynistically dismissed as not *real* sex, and some people I met even denied that lesbian jineteras exist, though there is some evidence to suggest otherwise.[37] In the end, only two of my interviewees professed to be gay or bisexual themselves—either personally or professionally.

Furthermore, the more I learned, the more I realized that what I was studying was the production of the jinetera in the Cuban nationalist imaginary, as well as the violence that this archetype engenders, and this nationalist imaginary functions on a system of compulsory (but raced) heterosexuality. To put it far too simply for the sake of argument, there are only four permissible roles within this system: the black/animalistic man, the white/masculine man, the white/virtuous woman, and the black/sensualized woman. It seemed to me, in conversation with the people I met, that the jinetera had a particular (restrictive, sexualized, archetypal) role written for her in this script, which was used to justify her treatment as a prostitute, whereas gay and transgender Cubans had no place in this script at all. While people who engage in same-sex love and sex in Cuba have had more than their share of discipline at the hands of state institutions, some of which will be discussed in the following chapters, it has been a somewhat different kind of discipline based on their perceived failures as masculine subjects rather than as feminine ones, like the so-called jineteras. It is for this reason that their engagement with foreigners is—like that of heterosexual jineteros—by and large not read as embedded in the same history of imperialism and mulata sensuality. Thus some of my observations will be relevant to the lives of these people as well, as dissident sexual subjects within a strictly gendered setting, but the full range and complexity of their experiences are beyond the scope of this project. While gay, lesbian, transgendered, and queer Cubans are a part of the world I was studying, and will appear in some of the stories that follow, I feel I would be doing them an injustice if I attempted to draw conclusions about their lives or experiences here.

Getting those fifty interviews, as I had expected, proved exceptionally difficult. Even deciding *who* I wanted to interview was not always easy. I quickly learned, as Cabezas had as well, that the "unified object of my research, the 'sex worker,' did not exist, was ambiguous, or at the very least was quite an unstable subject."[38] Sexual-affective relations between Cubans and foreigners are ambiguous, ranging from long-term committed partnerships to fleeting encounters, none of which can be said to be purely transactional, so attempting to determine who is and who is not a jinetera is useless. It is the *idea* of a category of people called jineteras, and the presumption of who fits the bill, that matters. For that very reason, many young women who engage in sexual-affective relationships with foreign men reject the term *jinetera,* creating their own alternative names or eschewing labels altogether. This practice forms the basis for the second chapter of this book. My own understanding of what I was looking for in an interviewee—people who call themselves jineteras? people who have been treated as jineteras by the police? people who look like jineteras?— never truly settled into a single profile.

More to the point, however, was the issue of trust. Few people were eager to discuss such a politically sensitive topic with a stranger, so building rapport with informants was key. Some of my successes came by chance, via conversations I was able to strike up on my own, but the vast majority were the result of a network of contacts built up over time, snowballing into ever more connections and introductions. This strategy brought me into contact with more potential informants and, in turn, provided them with the safeguard of a mutual contact who could vouch for me.

Overall, I managed far fewer interviews than I had originally hoped, and some of my interviews were stilted and uncomfortable, with many awkward silences. I very rarely had the luxury of naming the place and time of an interview. Opportunities were sometimes fleeting and appointments to meet again at a more convenient time were rarely kept, so I had interviews that happened at two o'clock in the morning, that took place inside noisy clubs and bars or on the beach; interviews where I took notes on the backs of maps and bus tickets; and even one where answers came only in the form of nods and shakes of the head. Most of my interviews were between one and three hours long, and due to concerns for my informants' safety some were not audio recorded. The accounts of my interviews in the chapters to come are therefore reconstructions rather than transcripts of every word that passed between us, and I quote them only where I managed to transcribe my informants' words precisely.

As Maria Stern and Lorraine Nencel both observe, learning to understand and interpret silences and exclusions—what was *not* said—became nearly as important as what was said.[39] My curiosity was usually not rewarded with straightforward answers. I learned something new from each person I met, but not in ways that could have been predicted in advance, and I often did not learn what I set out to learn. Circumstances constantly changed, and the meanings of ideas, categories, and words shifted before my eyes. A high degree of flexibility had to be built into my research, both methodologically and conceptually.

This need for flexibility forced me to rebel against the very concept of methodology. My background was in international politics, a discipline more or less closed to nontraditional methods drawn from anthropology or cultural studies. What I had been taught of methodology relied heavily on notions of objectivity, neutrality, and, quite frankly, the ability to predict—and to control—what will happen in the field. I contend that these are impossible (and not necessarily desirable) ideals in the context of an ethnographic, feminist project dealing with marginalized people across lines of race, gender, class, and culture.[40] The experience of ethnographic fieldwork often left me feeling that I was the last person with any sway over the outcome of my work, as I was totally dependent on others who had no obligation to help me. What is more, the differences between me, a white, middle-class, English- and French-speaking young Canadian woman, and my informants, who were mostly young black and mixed-race women who had grown up in Cuba under very different socioeconomic conditions, were significant and certainly influenced our perceptions of one another. We were often close to the same age, but otherwise we looked at one another across a gulf of experience with few commonalities.

These realities of research led me to reassess my ethical relationship to the subjects of my research and standard "ethics board" ethics. I have no doubt as to the ethical integrity of my project, but the practicalities of fieldwork meant that I had to focus on upholding the spirit rather than the letter of ethical regulations, usually in the interest of protecting my informants' anonymity and personal safety. Alan Feldman argues, "In a culture of political surveillance, participant observation is at best an absurdity and at the least a form of complicity with those outsiders who surveil."[41] I could not make use of consent forms in my research, since committing my informants' names to paper would endanger their safety, not to mention likely cause me to lose the interview; however, I had detailed conversations with each one about how I planned to use the interviews and in what forums my work was likely to appear.

To mitigate the risk of police harassment, arrest, and even violence that my informants faced, I did whatever was necessary to make them feel safe and secure speaking to me. I kept absolutely no written record of their real names, became proficient in concealing my documents and files, and did everything I could to keep myself and my interactions with informants off the radar of the police and other state institutions. I also learned strategies for avoiding the gaze of the police while moving through public spaces.

This was another instance where planning and control on my part were often impossible: my informants were much better versed in the methods of Cuban state security, and often I had little choice but to follow their lead in exchange for a "privileged peek backstage" at their lives and worlds.[42]

As important as ethics board ethics was a personal ethics of research. There is a power relationship inherent in interviewing, and particularly in interviewing vulnerable individuals, with one party demanding and the other providing information. This almost unavoidably extractive and "colonial" relationship behooves the ethnographer to be mindful about taking a reflective and self-critical approach to interviewing.[43] It is not enough, as Daphne Patai argues, to assume that a feminist or antiracist standpoint will act as a safeguard against exploiting others: it is a "messy business" from beginning to end.[44] To mitigate these problems as much as possible, I worked with my informants to make our experiences reciprocal and conversational. Many interviewees asked me questions, which I always answered, and these often turned out to be as interesting as the questions I asked them. In James Clifford's words, each of us was (and is) a "speaking [subject], who sees as well as is seen, who evades, argues, probes back."[45] An awareness of the intersubjectivity and impact of race, gender, class, and cultural difference cannot, Nencel notes, "erase the divide" between researcher and researched, but it can help mediate and flag these problems, creating a space for respect, trust, and even humor.[46] In pursuit of a more honest and accurate representation of the field experience, conscious engagement with these issues can only help, even if it can never fully solve them.

Even so, there were moments during my time in Cuba in which I felt some unease with my role or my choices in the field. At times, I was forced to conceal parts of my project from the authorities, to choose my words carefully around neighbors and university staff, or to adapt myself to the expectations of my friends and informants. Vincent Crapanzano discusses the role of researcher as "trickster," where one does not necessarily misrepresent oneself or conceal information but rather molds oneself to suit the needs of the research.[47] I struggled with finding myself occasionally not liking some of my informants, feeling obliged to feign agreement with them, and having to associate with people who treated me poorly or did not respect my boundaries. The researcher in me was in conflict with my various other identities and personae, which do not disappear in the field.[48] I often felt pressure to behave as my Cuban contacts believed I should, whether that meant tolerating sexual propositions from certain contacts with a smile or carrying on drinking when I did not want to do so, because stopping would have seemed rude or out of place. Frankly, I cannot count the number of shots of rum that I poured into the sea when no one was looking.

This uneasiness made me consider the role that I played for my Cuban informants. I often felt cast in a role, as Patai did, but that role changed from time to time.[49] Some of the young people I met forbade me to use their experiences in my writing but still insisted on sharing them with me, while others implored me to write about them. I was at times a friend, a potential benefactor, a naive outsider, a confidante. As a yuma and, in the eyes of most Cubans, a perpetual tourist, I felt forever on the outside—which may have had its advantages at times[50]—and my topic of research marked me out for many as at best peculiar and at worst a "moral transgressor and thus *una mala mujer* [a bad woman]."[51] More than once, I heard reports that male contacts of mine claimed to have slept with me. I found this kind of macho *guapería* distressing in the moment, but with time it became just one part of a landscape of emotions and tensions that simultaneously troubled and constituted my experience of ethnography.

WRITING PROSTITUTE/*JINETERA* LIVES

Maria Stern refers to her interviewees as coauthors of her text, since she consulted them on multiple occasions and got their feedback on the narrative produced by their conversations.[52] This is another area where my research has had to diverge from such an ideal scenario, for both ethical and logistical reasons. Though we spoke for hours on end, many of my informants preferred never to see me again after our interviews, for their own safety and peace of mind. They often had no telephone in their homes, much less access to cell phones or email, so contacting many of them for a second meeting or to send them any of my writing has not been possible. While I maintain contact with some informants, others have more or less slipped into the ether by their own design. The dangers of interpreting and appropriating their lives and experiences are thus very real here. As the orchestrator and manager of the narratives produced by the conversations I had with young Cubans, I felt keenly aware of my precarious ethical position toward the people I met and the stories they entrusted to me. Stéphanie Wahab expresses something similar: "I was acutely aware of what felt like a colonial position I was taking, if nothing else, by virtue of managing their/our words and stories. Furthermore, I dreaded the sensationalising process that occurs once knowledge and experience are uttered and recorded. We were already swimming in sensationalism and sexiness given the topic we were exploring."[53]

The role of the author in ethnographic accounts is one of "both getting out of the way and getting in the way"[54]—far from invisible or neutral (nor should it be), and not always even helpful to the unfolding of the text. But, as Clifford notes, life stories are contingent and allegorical: it is the telling, as my informants told them to me and as I have retold them here, that is the most important.[55] "Ethnographic truths," continues Clifford, "are thus inherently *partial*—committed and incomplete."[56] I do not feel that this text has been of my own making, and I hope that is because my informants' lives have been fairly represented and their voices are here with my own in these pages.

To best portray this experience of ethnography and this commitment to ethical representation, I have written this book loosely chronologically, according to the phases through which my research progressed. I feel that a narrative, chronological structure can provide the most genuine rendering of the Cuban setting and my time there. Ethnographic fieldwork is a process of learning how to do this kind of research: which questions to ask (and which not to ask), how to get interviews, how to understand these people and this scenario. In this way, I can be honest about how fuzzy the line between work and life really was, how personal some of my field experiences were, how my position had an impact on my work, how what I learned at each stage affected what happened later. In short, I do not have to pretend that I knew things at certain stages that I simply did not know yet.

Thus the book begins with an exploration of Cuban identity and the figure of the mulata, both as an emblem for and a specter that haunts Cuban nationalism. Evolving ideas of gender roles, women's sexuality, race, and prostitution are juxtaposed to the dominant narrative of Cuban history. I have attempted to defuse the usual focus on nation-building moments (colonial conquest, wars of independence, and the 1959 Revolution) by drawing attention to the ongoing processes of subject formation that founds Cuba as a nation and Cubans as raced, gendered, sexualized individuals. Cuba's distinct relationship to foreigners and "the foreign" comes through clearly, particularly in the context of the rise of jineterismo, as young women who engage in sex with foreigners are persecuted in the present day.

The second chapter commences the account of my fieldwork. These were my first interviews, the ones that were the most straightforward to obtain and that turned out to be, for the most part, the longest and most detailed, with people who felt most confident and comfortable speaking to me. We talked about their self-perceptions and their feelings about relationships, race, and labels like "jinetera"—what they mean, and also what they do. These conversations help to destabilize jineterismo-as-sexual-practice (and the jinetera) as discursive constructs, and allowed me to delve into practices of categorization and gendered and raced social expectations and their effects on young Cuban women of color.

From there, as my network of contacts grew, I spoke with people who had personal experience of the police practices and other forms of violence that have become standard parts of the world of jineterismo. These opportunities were often fleeting or incomplete, as many of these people feared retribution from any number of sources—state security, individual police officers, employers, or their own partners and families—if they were caught speaking to me. These encounters, along with my observations of policing and other direct forms of repression, form the basis of my third chapter, which deals with everyday practices of repression and resistance. I discuss the violence that acts in, through, and above the law as a conditioning factor in the lives of many young Cubans and the various ways these same people have found of averting and co-opting the gaze of the police through micro-practices of resistance.

The concluding stage of my fieldwork is covered in the fourth chapter, which includes interviews conducted with representatives of some of Cuba's mass organizations that have been central to the state's response to jineterismo. Through these conversations, as well as the resources from their archives, I attempt to piece together a picture of the state-centered

discourse of prostitution that informs the legal and supposedly rehabilitative measures taken against young women perceived as jineteras. Amid
the policy documents, congress minutes, studies, and interviews there
emerges an ideal of socialist womanhood—a New Woman to accompany
Ché Guevara's New Man—and, along with it, a notion of idealized, revolutionary love.

Finally, in the fifth chapter, I endeavor to bring together all of these
strands of thought—the (re)production of women of color as sexual/politi-
cal subjects, their perceived availability for intervention by a variety of
forces, their constitution as failed subjects of revolutionary womanhood
and love—to formulate an understanding of jineterismo-as-sexual-practice as a form of resistance to a power that seeks to forge a productive,
ideologically engaged citizenry. The young women I interviewed in my
investigation of Cuba's sexual-affective economy are actively pursuing a
life completely at odds with the norms and mores of the socialist world in
which they were raised. I argue that this phenomenon, which defies
notions of virtuous sexuality, healthy relationships, and moral conduct put
forward for women by the socialist value set, constitutes a form of aesthetic self-creation, which in itself is a potent form of resistance to subjectifying power. This resistance as a sexual and bodily practice is what
renders the Cuban case relevant to a broader understanding of oppression
and marginality.

Throughout this project, I have developed my interviews in a conversational, almost novelistic style. This approach to writing ethnography is, I
believe, not just a stylistic choice, but an ethical and a political one. I hope
that bringing out the histories and personalities in my work will result in
a more genuine representation of my interviewees' lives and the politics of
their stories. I want my informants to live within the text as true-to-life,
complex characters, as they are in real life. I have written their stories *as*
stories to foreground their personalities and their lived experiences of the
discourses, practices, and systems that I discuss. These vignettes are "fictions"[57]—not in the sense of being untrue but in that they highlight the
constructedness of all life stories, which are more than simple chronolo-
gies. They represent each individual's articulation of self. Or, as Stern
puts it: "A focus on the discursive, constructed character of stories, or
lives, does not deny that people *really* live, experience threat and harm, or

safety and wellbeing, to disclaim that this were so would be silly. We act, experience and live, but the *meaning* we give to our actions is continually constructed within a web of different discourses. Similarly, we as subjects are continually reconstructed or reinscribed through narrative and representation."[58]

Throughout the process of writing, I have often wondered to myself if my informants would recognize themselves in what I have written, if they would be satisfied with it, if they knew that every word—the conflicts, the dismissals and misunderstandings, the silences—would be noted and possibly included in my account.[59] For the most part, I cannot approach these people to ask their opinions on what I have written, but I hope that in continually asking myself these questions, I can go some distance toward challenging and destabilizing the problem of representation.

This project is meant to trouble disciplinary norms. It does not map easily onto the structures and formats to which we are accustomed when we talk about international politics. It is not, to borrow Patti Lather's words, a "comfort text."[60] I have tried to work from the ground up, starting with the stories told to me by the so-called jineteras themselves and building a theoretically informed analysis on that foundation. My intention is not to speak *for* these people, or to simply *apply* theoretical insights, but rather to "weave the insights gained from [theory] through my discussion."[61] I hope that these stories will help illuminate the ways in which sexuality and sexual subjects are produced in interaction with normative ideals in the Cuban setting and thus the effects that this regime of repression directed at jineterismo, and the practices of resistance to it, have had on sexual subjectivity.

The accepted discourse of prostitution is one that creates a category of people as available for intervention, rehabilitation, and practices of violence. It erases the desire and consent of individual women, reducing their motivations to the transactional. By denying any motivation other than selfishness, it also erases those women who are genuinely coerced into sex with tourists by their partners or other intermediaries. The young Cubans I met in my exploration of the sexual-affective economy describe another world where love and money are not mutually exclusive, and where morality and sexuality do not exist in separate spheres. In a system that so explicitly demands all that each has to give, carefully crafting political subjects in the likeness of imagined socialist heroes and in the face of severe austerity, these individuals are finding ways to carve out spaces for themselves—spaces that allow them some measure of freedom, however incomplete, where they can live according to their own priorities and images of the good life.

1 From Mulata to Jinetera

PROSTITUTION AS IMAGE OF THOUGHT

Nations stand up and greet one another.
"What are we?" is the mutual question,
and little by little they furnish answers.

José Martí, *Our America*

I arrived in Cuba with a copy of a United Nations report tucked between the pages of a notebook. The report had been filed by Radhika Coomaraswamy, then the U.N. Special Rapporteur on Violence against Women, after her visit to Cuba in 2000, and I returned to it many times over the course of my time there. Its pages were filled with accounts of an almost Orwellian system of "behaviour modification"—arbitrary arrests, police brutality, and rehabilitation centers for prostitutes and other "at-risk" women where, the Special Rapporteur noted, they are kept "until the dangerousness disappears from the subject."[1] Other interviews and testimonies confirmed that around 1996 police had begun subjecting young women seen walking alone, and especially black and mixed-race women, to spontaneous searches and identification checks in Havana and Varadero. Reports of police violence and arbitrary arrests of young women became increasingly common, as did bribery, extortion, and sexual abuse of detainees.[2] In Varadero, a major enclave of resort tourism, thousands of arrests were made during this time—as many as six thousand in a single year—in the name of "sanitizing" the town.[3] New rules were enacted that prevented Cubans not registered to live or work there from even entering the town and forbade Cubans from riding in private cars with foreigners unless they were licensed taxi drivers. These regulations are still in place today: while working in Varadero, I would meet Cuban friends just outside the town limits for car trips to and from other places.

By 1998 the campaign escalated. With the support of Cuba's organization for women, the Federación de Mujeres Cubanas, a cleanup campaign—or "crusade," to use Fusco's term—began, under the name Operativo Lacra. There were raids on nightclubs and bars, sweeps of entire neighborhoods, and mass arrests of women based on their style of dress, the company in which they were found, their presence in the street at night, and even their skin color. *Guajiras* from the countryside, working-class women, and especially mulatas and other Afro-Cuban women were targeted for surveillance, arrest, forced gynecological examinations, and incarceration, sometimes just while walking home from work or friends' houses.[4] Upon arrest, women were given a *carta de advertencia,* or warning letter; three such cartas led to a summary trial, after which the women were sent to a rehabilitation center for an indeterminate sentence of up to four years. In 2000 the authorities indicated to the U.N. Special Rapporteur—the first to be allowed into Cuba—that they planned to build such centers in each of Cuba's then fourteen (now fifteen) provinces, but in her report Coomaraswamy recommended the closure of the centers because they "violate the rights of prostitutes."[5]

These stories beg two main questions. First, what is so objectionable about these sexual liaisons to the Cuban state? Cuba is ostensibly a country with a progressive attitude toward sexuality, based on the East German model of sex education, and Cuba's sexual culture is very frank and open.[6] What is more, prostitution is not explicitly against any law in Cuba, as I would later be assured by the FMC and the penal code itself, so this campaign against it seemed incongruous to say the least.[7] Second, how did these particular women—young, attractive, black or mixed race—come to be seen in such a way? The reports of arrests suggest that the jinetera must be a signifier for far more than meets the eye. In archives, galleries, and libraries, I pieced together that the story of the jinetera runs parallel to the history of Cuba. The influence of many different forces, often originating far from Cuba's shores—Roman Catholicism, Spanish colonialism, Moorish sexual values, the racial system of the slave economy, socialist ideology, Monroe Doctrine–era American expansionism, even English

Victorianism[8]—is undeniable, but together these elements elaborate an idiosyncratic Cuban ambiente.

In this history, moments of crisis such as colonial conquest, the wars of independence, and the Revolution throw into relief the subtler and never-ending processes of coercive subjection and creative subjectification. Major ideological and political upsets may come and go, but certain over-arching themes persist (and shape the pages to come): the understanding of women of color as sexual and sexualized beings, dating to the colonial period; the establishment of a masculine nationalism, born of a protracted struggle for independence and embodied by the *mambí* and the New Man; and recurring moments of a stringent, moralizing discipline over women's bodies, one which is inflected with both Catholic and, later, socialist ideology. Women and men, black and white, are configured in the national imaginary over time by discourses of race, gender, class, and sex, producing a sexuality and a sexual subject that underpins how we under-stand the jinetera: who she is and what she means for Cuba and for Cubans. In the process, prostitution becomes an *image of thought* that travels to sites of anxiety—be they urban districts, metaphors for imperial-ism, or bodies—in times of crisis and insecurity.

SEX IN THE COLONY: THE PLANTATION, *PUDOR*, AND THE BIRTH OF THE *MULATA*

The history of sexuality in Cuba is inextricably bound up with the island's centuries-long encounter with colonialism—and with the interlocking histories of slavery and machismo that brought indigenous, European, and African together on the island that Columbus named Isla Juana. From the very beginning, as they founded the first colonial cities and sub-dued native resistance, Spanish settlers looked to the native Guanajatabey and Taíno peoples for concubines and sometimes wives. Indigenous women were vulnerable to white settlers' advances and existed, to European eyes, outside the moral codes that governed European behavior. According to testimony from a settler named Juan González de León, dated 12 November 1538, the conquistador Diego Velázquez himself maintained a barracks behind his home where he kept young native

women whom he had selected for his personal use and that of his sol-
diers.[9] The Dominican friar Bartolomé de las Casas, a fervent supporter of
the rights of Cuba's indigenous people, reported to the Spanish royal court
at the time that many native women and girls had died as a result of the
sexual abuse they endured.[10] Particularly in the early years, when
European women were not yet encouraged to move to the colony, systemic
sexual abuse seems to have served as an effective tool of colonial subjugation and certainly contributed to the near-obliteration of the indigenous
peoples from Cuba within a century of contact, alongside European dis-
eases, the privations of slavery, and suicide.[11]

As the indigenous people rapidly disappeared from the island and as
the numbers of Spanish settlers increased, the colony slowly began to
import African slaves to provide labor for its growing plantation system,
first for tobacco and later for sugarcane. The first three hundred enslaved
Africans arrived in Cuba in 1522, but as trade was tightly controlled by
Spain their numbers grew only incrementally at first.[12] The Seven Years'
War, however, brought the British navy to the port of Havana in 1762 and,
with it, dramatic changes to the social landscape. Cuba was surrendered
back to Spain under the Treaty of Paris after only ten months, but in that
time the British had introduced free trade. This triggered an influx of
thousands of slaves, brought in chains from Yoruba-speaking parts of
West Africa to work in the ever-expanding sugarcane plantations. The
island's white *criollo* elite, the descendants of Spanish settlers, began to
enjoy such prosperity as slave owners that the Spanish authorities declined
to reinstate the old regulations. Ships bearing African slaves continued to
pour into Cuba until slavery was finally abolished in the late nineteenth
century, such that by 1817 the population of free and enslaved Afro-Cubans
significantly outpaced the criollos.[13]

From such violent founding moments—the near-extermination and
subjugation of one race, the relocation of a second, and the alienation and
enslavement of a third—the nation of Cuba began to take shape with sexuality at its heart. A significant contingent of Chinese laborers was eventually brought to Cuba as well, but the construction of Cuba's national imaginary had already taken shape around the interplay of indigenous, African,
and European. Colonial sexuality was fraught by anxiety over racial mixing from the very beginning, taking shape as it did under the auspices of a

very powerful Roman Catholic Church, a repressive slave economy, and fears of miscegenation. White criollo elites' preoccupations with racial purity were only exacerbated by the uprising of slaves in the 1791 Haitian Revolution, which sent chills down the spines of the slave-owning classes across the region and inspired a great deal of anxiety over preserving racial lines, and more specifically, the purity of white women.[14]

The first legal restrictions on marriages between people of different racial backgrounds were enacted in 1776. By 1805 those people considered to possess *limpieza de sangre*, or purity of blood, needed licenses to marry according to civil law. In practice, few license applications were refused, but the legislation granted concerned family members the power to challenge in court a couple's intent to marry in the name of upholding social conventions and values, the broader implication being that interracial marriage would weaken the socioeconomic order in the colony.[15] The emancipation of African American slaves in the United States in the 1860s only further inflamed racist nerves, and interracial marriage was legally prohibited in Cuba in 1864.[16]

The burden of *proving* racial purity and sexual morality remained a question that fell to Cuban women, and the outward projection of morality and honour became the central conditioning factor of their daily lives. In Cuba, and across Latin America, the governing principle of acceptable sexuality was *pudor*, an idea that is Spanish in its etymology and its conservatism and that translates as "modesty," "reserve," or even "shame." Women, as the bearers of children and gatekeepers of sexual morality, were required to demonstrate pudor in their dress, manner, choices, and behavior. This was true across much of Latin America at the time, but it has been argued that Cuba saw a more extreme incarnation, manifesting in an even stricter regime of surveillance and control over women's bodies, although this ideal was possible only for the privileged who could afford to totally seclude their women—that is, white families.[17] Day to day, in the interest of preserving their personal integrity, safeguarding bloodlines, and guaranteeing the paternity of children, white women were all but confined to their homes to such an extent that, on arrival in Havana in 1853, the nineteenth-century Colombian traveler Nicolás Tanco Armero made the following remarks: "Where are the women and where can one find them in Havana? . . . If one goes out into the street, they are nowhere to be found; if one goes for a stroll, one hardly sees one or two in carriages; if one draws near to the windows, one finds them deserted. It is the most difficult undertaking in the world, endeavouring to see these daughters of Eve. . . . Where have the women of Havana gone? Why is it so difficult to see them?"[18]

So great was the isolation of upper-class, "pure-blooded" women that they were restricted even from speaking to other people, especially men, when passing through public spaces. Hippolyte Piron observed at the time that women living with such severe restrictions often developed means to communicate using just the movements of their eyes and the flutters of the ubiquitous hand-held fans they carried to ward off the tropical heat. "The language of the fan," Piron wrote, "is one of the most curious things in this country."[19] The sociologist Abel Sierra Madero traces this practice of isolation to the Christian tradition, Moorish influence brought to Cuba from Spain, and even Victorian English values.[20] Virginity and chastity were prized attributes in (white) women, explicitly linked to their personal honor and that of their families, and upper-class white women were confined to private spaces to preserve these characteristics. Only a female sexuality that was chaste, passive, demure, without passion, and easily contained by the restrictive philosophy of pudor was deemed acceptable and proper by colonial ideals.

Meanwhile, the social production of respectable wives and mothers— good women—as lily-white paragons of chastity, passivity, and virtue, uninterested in sex and even frigid, necessarily evokes its other: the bad woman. Afro-Cuban women, whether free or enslaved, were usually obliged to work outside their homes as domestic servants and plantation workers or as seamstresses and laundresses in the cities and thus represented opportunities for sexual adventures for white men in their very accessibility. In contrast to feminine meekness, male sexuality was constructed as insatiable and voracious, in need of an outlet; where virtuous women were meant to see sex as a duty, and an unhappy one at that, men pursued it freely, actively, and without fear of stigma. Their desire to prove their virility through sexual conquest was the other side of the coin of gendered colonial sexuality, and women of color became the objects of male lust, due to their subordinate status as social inferiors to, and frequently as literal possessions of, (white) men. From the earliest days of African presence in Cuba, white men sought out African women for sex on the plantations and in the cities. These encounters, as well as the children they frequently produced, quickly began to complicate easy racial hierarchies and the very idea of racial purity. This intermingling of races created—both literally and figuratively—a central mythic figure in the Cuban imaginary: the mulata.

The mulata is a figure who transcends borders, existing in any locale where slave plantations once were. Her being speaks to the specifically sexual facet of colonial violence, to the frequently intimate nature of the relationship between master and slave, colonizer and colonized. The terms in which they were (and are) described—often the same scales used for grading coffee, tobacco, and sugar[21]—served to further embed them in tropicalist mystique and to commoditize them as objects of (male) pleasure. The product of illicit sex, the mulata was interpreted as the embodiment of sex and sexuality. Moving through the city streets while white women remained chastely at home, the mulata was highly visible and available. She became the quintessential mistress, characterized by innate beauty, sensuality, and licentiousness: born of lust, made of lust. A popular saying, also common in Brazil, highlights this: "White women [are] for marrying, black women [are] for working, and *mulatas* [are] for sex."[22]

In the Cuban colony, though often not presented with much choice, many mulata women were nonetheless savvy actors who navigated a complex economy of desire—of others as well as their own. Individual women of color, living within a racially hierarchical society, frequently found relations of concubinage to their advantage: they were provided with a better standard of living than any man of color could provide, and their children were propelled farther up the ladder of whiteness. This process of "whitening," or *blanqueamiento*, was a social practice linked to notions of racial development that sometimes went so far as to omit the mother's name from birth registration documents, a "widespread" practice, so that children could better pass for white (or whiter).[23] As many black and mixed-race women told their daughters, "Mejor amante de un blanco que esposa de un negro [Better to be the lover of a white man than the wife of a black man]." Certainly, white men of means rarely sought to marry women of color, but they frequently entered into long-term arrangements of concubinage with them, even while married to white women, since the construction of masculinity as sexually voracious made white men's adulterous, nonheteronormative relationships permissible, if still quietly so. Their adultery and engagement in miscegenation was rendered intelligible by divergent configurations of men's and women's sexuality.[24]

The mulata, however, was not granted such leeway in the sexual system of the day. Her gender and her racial status marked her as beautiful and desirable but also as lascivious, bewitching, and continuously available (or "penetrable," according to Teresa Marrero)[25] as an instrument of male pleasure. Stereotypes that branded mulatas as promiscuous were yet another means of preserving the socioeconomic order in the colony, countering her desirability with her disrespectability as a marriage partner. Yet another colonial turn of phrase speaks to the ubiquity of these ideas: "No hay tamarindo dulce, ni mulata señorita [There is no sweet tamarind fruit, nor virgin mulata girl]."[26] The complicated interplay of race, gender, and sexuality within the iconic figure of the mulata thus formed part of a repressive discourse that incited black and mixed-race women to aspire to high standards of moral fortitude while simultaneously marking them as sexually available and thus dooming them to fail.

This figure of the mulata occupies a place of prime importance in the literary and artistic worlds of nineteenth-century colonial Cuba. The novel *Cecilia Valdés*, written by Cirilo Villaverde in 1839, is said to have firmly established the mulata as the ideal of Cuban beauty.[27] The title character, a beautiful light-skinned mulata, is the daughter of a slave woman and a powerful white slave trader. She unwittingly falls in love with her white half brother, Leonardo, the legitimate son of her father. Their love, however, does not last, and Leonardo eventually leaves Cecilia and their young child to marry a white woman. Cecilia meets with her seemingly inevitable tragic demise when she is thrown in prison for her part in the murder of her erstwhile lover. This is one of countless depictions of mulatas as destined for death or disgrace by their moral degradation. More succinct are the numerous poems dedicated to portraying young Latin American and Caribbean women of mixed racial heritage as beautiful but tragic, equally desired and condemned for those characteristics that create their very desirability. The Dominican poet Francisco Muñoz del Monte's seminal poem, "La mulata," was published in Cuba in 1845 and begins with these words:

¡Mulata! ¿Será tu nombre
inuria, oprobrio o refrán?
¡No sé! Sólo sé que al hombre
tu nombre es un talismán
[...]
Tú no eres blanca, mulata,
ni es oro puro tu pelo,
ni tu garganta es de plata,
ni en tus ojos se retrata
el divino azul del cielo.

Mulata! Could your name be
injury, opprobrium or legend?
I don't know! I know only that for a man
your name is a talisman
[...]
You are not white, mulata,
nor is your hair pure gold
nor is your throat made of silver
nor do your eyes reflect
the heavenly blue of the sky.[28]

Throughout the piece, the poet describes his subject's physical form in terms that Vera Kutzinski calls "soft-pornographic," all the while driving home reminders of her nonwhite, subordinate status in an act of fetishistic "symbolic violence."[29] He paints mulatas as beguiling but dangerous temptresses who ensnare men, thereby absolving himself of responsibility for the attraction he feels and any advances he makes toward her.

Similarly, Kutzinski describes an 1881 painting by the same name, *La mulata*, by Víctor Patricio Landaluze.

> The splendid mulata, stylishly coiffured and sporting an elegant gown with a tight bodice and a lavish train, is half smiling, her head bent down ever so slightly in a coquettish greeting, a gesture of recognition not of an individual but of a particular, familiar situation. ... Her bodily syntax and facial expression indicate an internalization of the male gaze.[30]

Landaluze's mulata is accustomed to lingering looks from men she encounters in public spaces. Aware of her role in a well-rehearsed interaction, this woman performs the flirtatiousness that is expected of her. She sees herself through the eyes of male observers as a fetishized object of (white) male desire, having internalized their gaze, as Kutzinski notes. Landaluze's types represent many of the characters who made up everyday life in nineteenth-century Cuba, albeit in stylized and stereotypical forms, but as Kutzinski argues, his paintings of people of color show them always at rest, concealing the violence and grind of slave life, and the women among them are fetishized as objects of beauty and sexual allure.[31]

Perhaps most powerful are the images of the mulata seen in the lithographs that adorned cigar boxes during this period. Series of images called *marquillas* were printed on the packaging of tobacco companies such as La Charanga de Villergas, Para Usted, and La Honradez. With titles like *Historia de la mulata* (Story of the Mulata) and *Vida y muerte de la mulata* (Life and Death of the Mulata), these series portrayed a sort of life cycle in single frames: a precocious and flirtatious girl already courting the male gaze; a gorgeous young woman coquettishly entertaining the advances of admiring men; a mother with children inevitably whiter, more respectable, and more desirable than herself; and eventually, her downfall in the form of disease, destitution, institutionalization, or death.[32] Others depict the mulata as a predator who pursues and seduces white men. The mulata is shown in an urban environment, what the Cuban ethnologist Fernando Ortiz called the *"hampa afro-cubana* [Afro-Cuban underworld]" in 1916.[33] Exuding sensuality as she moved through the gritty streets of Havana, the mulata is an essential part of a bawdy world immortalized in these images. The symbolic power of printing such lithographs on boxes of cigarettes and cigars, which were already commonplace in Cuban homes, was considerable. Tobacco and sugar were not only products to which the skin of mulata women was compared—and vice versa—but also a growing signifier for cubanidad itself and for pleasure.

Over the years, this representation of the mulata as sensual, lascivious, and available has not gone away; rather, it is a resurgent and persistent theme. Strolling through the Cuban collection of the Museo Nacional de Bellas Artes, housed in a sleek, modern building in Old Havana, the image of the mulata appears in art from every era in Cuban history. The most obvious is a painting by Víctor Manuel García, *Gitana tropical* (1929), which depicts a serene and beautiful young woman with caramel-colored

Figure 3. La mulata, 1881, lithograph by Víctor Patricio
Landaluze from the series *Tipos y costumbres de la isla de Cuba.*

Figure 4. El palomo y la gabilana (male dove and female hawk), n.d., cigarette box *marquilla* lithograph for the cigar company Para Usted.

skin in an obvious ode to the Mona Lisa, setting up this mulata as an archetype of Cuban beauty and womanhood. Likewise, Jorge Rigol's engraving *Venus campesina* (1953) shows a nude woman who towers over her surroundings and whose race is indeterminate, this indeterminacy itself being readily interpreted as mixed heritage. In the contemporary art collection, on the other hand, Osneldo García's *Corset desnudo* (1968) is an iron sculpture of an Afro-Cuban woman's naked torso, complete with spikes protruding from its genitals, evoking the dangerous and bewitching nature ascribed to Cuban women of color.

Most strikingly, though, a 1938 painting titled *El rapto de las mulatas* by Carlos Enríquez depicts "a myth consecrated by the pictorial tradition" in Cuba, to use the words of the museum's own guidebook:[34] the abduction and likely rape of two mulatas by white men who could as easily be Cuban *mambises*, an archetype to which I return later, as Spanish colonialists. The men wear wide-brimmed hats and belts of ammunition for the rifles strapped to their backs, while the women appear to be naked, and, despite the painting's title, sport sly and even mischievous expressions. The sensualization of the mulata and her ever ready sexuality is clear here.

Figure 5. El rapto de las mulatas, 1938, oil on canvas, by Carlos Enríquez. Source: Museo Nacional de Bellas Artes in Havana. Printed with permission.

Throughout the early twentieth century, the alluring mystique of the mulata can also be seen in songs and poetry, especially a new school dubbed *poesía mulata*. Felipe Pichardo Moya's "Filosofía del bronce," written in 1925, is an excellent example of this style.

¡O el abuelo noble y español,
cedió al impulso que le daba
en una siesta ebria de sol,
la carne negra de la esclava!
Idilio monstruo entre las cortes de las cañas,
concepción contra las leyes . . .
[. . .]
¡Y en una copia de los horrors del infierno
que nunca tendrá igual,
sintió sobre el torso maternal
los latigazos quizás, tu germen paternal!
¡Y así llegaste hasta nosotros,
hermana nuestra y de los otros,
suprema flor de la injusticia,
que conviertes en bravos potros
las palomas de la caricia
en un anhelo vengativo
que tu grupa conserva vivo
porque tu impulse pasional
eleva, sobre los abrazos
el furor de latigazos
del inclement mayoral!

Oh, the noble Spanish grandfather,
yielded to the impulse stirred in him
by the black flesh of the slave
one siesta drunk with the sun!
Monstrous idyll amongst the cane cuttings,
illicit conception
[. . .]
And in a copy of the horrors of hell
forever without equal,
perhaps the seed of your father
felt the lashes on the torso of your mother!
And so you came to us,
their sister and our sister,

supreme flower of injustice,
who converts into wild stallions
the doves of a caress
in vengeful desire
kept alive in your haunches,
because your passionate impulse
elevates, above the embrace,
the fury of the lashes
of the merciless overseer![35]

The recurring themes of irresistible black bodies and desire are evident here, as well as the romanticization of the violence of slavery and the very real possibility of rape. The poem evokes the echoes of slavery in its almost wistful reflection on what one can do to a black female body, what it can endure, and even—perversely—what it can enjoy. The mulata, and women of color in general, continue to embody for white men the turbulent and passionate meeting of races, a fetishized and penetrable body through which this tumult can be experienced. Artistic representations such as these do not just illustrate the social mores of the time; they further entrench ideas about the sexual proclivities and morality of women of color. They give us a clearer understanding of how these ideas circulated in colonial society and legitimate certain identities and relations of power that persist to this day.

Black and mixed-race men, it bears mentioning, are all but excluded from this sexual system. They are not suitable partners for white women, toward whom they are frequently depicted as animalistic and violent, and their own female counterparts are rendered to white men as objects of lust. Thus men of color are relegated to incidental roles, if any at all, in this imagery of the mulata.[36] This is not to suggest that Afro-Cuban men are without their own symbolic burden. The imagined sexual subjectivity of black and mixed-race Cuban men tends to center on images of animalism and violence, but again, this persona is seen to be directed at white people, and in this case, white women. Black men are understood as a threat to the purity and safety of "good" women, but the script of the mulata does not render her to men of her own race but rather positions her as the object of *white* male lust.

The construction of mulatas as the willing objects of (white) masculine desire, and the counterpoint to proper (white) feminine virtue, helped to configure the lascivious mulata as the paradigmatic Cuban woman of color, a construction that endures in the jinetera. It also worked to preserve the colonial social order by excluding black and mixed-race women as potential marriage partners for the upper-class white men who sought them out as sexual partners, all the while absolving white men of responsibility for their desires and even for their (often violent) actions. The figure of the mulata strengthens cultural and legal injunctions against interracial marriage, if not interracial copulation, thereby simultaneously protecting white bloodlines and inheritance while also perpetuating Afro-Cubans' status as, at best, second-class citizens. It also laid the groundwork for what would come later: that is, more overt pathologization and criminalization of female sexual permissiveness.

FORGING A (MASCULINE) NATION

As Cuba moved into the nineteenth century, anti-imperialist and antislavery plots had begun to surface, with the first armed uprising taking place in 1836. The unequal distribution of wealth, even amongst white residents, coupled with a lack of civil liberties under Spanish rule had set the stage at long last for a major conflict. The Cuban struggle for independence began in earnest with the start of the Guerra de los Diez Años on 10 October 1868, now a national holiday, when Carlos Manuel de Céspedes issued the *Grito de Yara* that freed his own slaves and declared war on colonial authorities. The rebels were led by Céspedes and his generals, Ignacio Agramonte and Máximo Gómez. Ultimately their movement was doomed by the death of Agramonte, the destitution of Céspedes, and the end of Spain's own civil war in 1876, which freed up additional troops to subdue Cuba.

The cause of Cuban independence seemed lost at that juncture, but this first war had one key outcome: it gave rise to a new archetype of national heroism, the *mambí*. Originally a pejorative that the Spanish applied to rebels in the Dominican Republic in the 1840s, the name was imported to Cuba alongside veterans of the Dominican war, including Gómez, and adopted with pride. This new word denoted the revolutionary fighters, hypermasculine warriors on horseback with wide-brimmed hats and machetes hanging at their sides, the very picture of strength and authority, commanding respect: what Sierra Madero calls the "*héroe-hombre-heterosexual* [hero-man-heterosexual]."[37] Roberto Fernández Retamar describes the reverence for the mambí in Cuban culture.

> The most venerated word in Cuba—*mambí*—was disparagingly imposed on us by our enemies at the time of the war for independence, and we still have not totally deciphered its meaning. It seems to have an African root, and in the mouth of the Spanish colonists implied the idea that all *independentistas* were so many black slaves—emancipated by the very war for independence—who of course constituted the bulk of the liberation army. The *independentistas*, white and black, adopted with honor something that colonialism meant as an insult. This is the dialectic of Caliban.[38]

Perhaps surprisingly, there seemed to be at least some space within the mambí ideal for nonwhiteness. This must certainly have been due in part to Antonio Maceo, a man of mixed racial heritage who rose to the rank of major general during the war and became known in Cuba as el Titán de Bronce. A new Cuban nationalism had begun to take shape during the war, with the mambí as a central image in its nascent mythology.

The uncomfortable period between the wars saw considerable social and economic upheaval, even as a new, hybrid sense of *cubanidad* developed. Slavery was finally abolished in October 1886, and newly freed Afro-Cubans became tenant farmers or joined the urban workforce, while many plantations closed and their owners joined the growing middle class in the cities. U.S. foreign investment began to pour into the country in earnest, greatly altering the direction of Cuba's dependencies and also rekindling American interest in annexation. Meanwhile, the exiled Cuban poet José Martí was drumming up support among expatriates in the United States for a renewed Cuban independence movement. Martí's 1891 essay, "Nuestra América," is considered one of the founding texts of a new political notion of *mestizaje*, or racial mixing.

Martí's use of the term was implicitly cultural rather than racial, skirting some of the thornier issues underlying white fears of miscegenation. "There can be no racial animosity," argued Martí, "because there are no races."[39] As a member of the Cuban Revolutionary Party, Martí "[wrote] from within—and against—a Cuban independence movement that was markedly conservative on the racial issue."[40] He intended mestizaje to become a rallying point for Cubans in a new nation that would "rescue the Indian" and "make a place for the competent Negro," which was at the time considered a racially inclusive position, even as it nonetheless envisioned the eventual absorption—and thus obliteration—of black Cubans into the mass.[41] The idea of cultural, if not racial, integration and hybridity was meant to mark Cuba as distinct and separate from Spain, to unite Cubans and form the foundation for renewed independence claims.

Cuba's second major war against Spanish imperialism, the Guerra de Independencia, began on 24 February 1895 with uprisings across the eastern end of the island. Martí died in battle almost immediately upon arrival in Cuba, cementing forever his reputation as the martyred national hero, but Maceo and Gómez carried on. Spain responded with *reconcentración*, a program of forced resettlement of hundreds of thousands of rural people into fortified towns; this brutal strategy, which continued until 1898, caused the deaths of an estimated one-third of the rural population from violence and starvation.[42] The rebels seemed poised to take control of their country, but everything suddenly changed when the American battleship USS *Maine* blew up in the harbor of Havana, killing hundreds in February 1898 and precipitating American intervention. American forces captured Santiago with the participation of the mambises, but in the aftermath Cuban forces were excluded from the peace talks. Control of Cuba was handed indefinitely to the United States. The loss of a sovereignty not yet possessed cemented Cuba's long-simmering anti-imperialism, which would also color the 1959 Revolution.

The independence wars had been crucibles in which Cuban nationalism was forged—with mestizaje, the mambí, and Martí at its center—and they also served to elaborate the heterosexual order of the new nation, with raced sexuality as its index of citizenship and belonging. The new cubanidad posited a novel society forged from the meeting of worlds, all the while shrouding its history of slavery and assimilation in mysticism, a "subsumption of race under the national question [that] is a much-noted feature of Cuban nationalist discourse," according to Shalini Puri.[43] Cuban mestizaje claimed to be a unifying banner for all Cubans, but even its most reformist proponents still sought a form of whitening, through intermarriage and immigration.[44] Its claims to racelessness were refuted by the segregation of Cuban military units for the first time in the wake of the Guerra de Independencia, not to mention the overt racism that still typified the day-to-day existences of Afro-Cubans, and which worsened during the postwar U.S. occupation.[45]

The new Cuban political identity was also implicitly heterosexual and heteronormative in its conception, formed around the masculine ideal of the mambí. Sexual and political identities were thus fused. As Alyssa García also argues, sexuality became the "central organizing index" of citizenship under the new nationalism: that is, it helped to distinguish those valiant, manly, and worthy enough to merit inclusion in the new nation from the rest.[46] This may not mark Cuba as unique among nations, but the investment of these ideas in the figure of the mambí is significant because it is still held up as a national icon in Cuba today, appearing in political murals and even a children's cartoon called *Elpidio Valdés*—a character whose name, interestingly, is taken from the earlier novel *Cecilia Valdés*. The mambí embodies mestizaje as a "highly sexualized and racialized discourse on national culture" and a "principle signifier of Cuba's national cultural identity."[47]

It would be a mistake to posit the mulata as a counterpart or even a consort to the mambí, since the elaboration of this new cubanidad only further marginalized and sexualized the mulata: in fact, groups of "mulaticas" were brought to the rebel army camps throughout both wars, their purpose being to supply sexual companionship to the mambises, much like indigenous girls were once provided to the *conquistadores*. The mambí was configured as a true hero and paragon of masculine virtue, whereas the mulata, as ever, was lusted after but only in the same breath as she was condemned for that very desirability. The mulata as archetype was a bawdy resident of the *hampa afro-cubana*, not a consort or equal to the mambí. Sujatha Fernandes argues that the process of wartime nation building not only allowed, but required, the deployment of the mulata as a sexual focal point: "Bonding between Cuba's sons takes place upon the body of mulattas, who are both central to the discourse of national unity and invisible within it."[48] The mulata was interpreted, ever more explicitly, as a site of sexuality and provider of sexual services—and, now, as the bodily site where a new nation/nationalism was forged. Thus, Sierra Madero contends, "the ethnic and racial question entangles itself with grotesque eroticism."[49]

POST-INDEPENDENCE PROSTITUTION PANIC

The period of national consolidation was accompanied by a similarly mas-culinized concern for the well-being of the thousands of women left desti-tute by the independence wars and Spanish reconcentración. Commercial sex was not new in Cuba; rather, reports of prostitution had begun to pro-liferate as Cuban cities became heavily trafficked ports of call on Caribbean shipping routes. As early as 1657, the bishop of Havana complained about slaves being used in the sex trade by their owners.[50] A heavy turnover of ships meant large numbers of sailors coming ashore in search of food, rum, gambling, female companionship, and sex, according to complaints from religious orders.[51] Through the years, Havana gained a reputation for its seedy underworld, which only intensified incitements to keep "good" women safely tucked away. On arrival in 1762, the British navy had found the port area of Havana a raucous neighborhood full of taverns and brothels, with a "unique, easy-going, brilliant but semi-criminal, maritime and cosmopolitan character."[52] The clergy occasionally decried the sexual proclivities of certain social sectors, but by and large, this supposed under-world remained largely undisturbed and existed in much the same form by the end of the nineteenth century.

This was perhaps because, during this time, what it meant to be a pros-titute was not especially clearly delineated: as in many other places in the world, the terms *whore* and *prostitute* were more like epithets than descriptors for specific professions or identities.[53] There were brothels known as *casas de citas* where women were paid for sexual services, but by the social codes of the day, any women seen coming and going in public spaces were thought to be licentious, their poverty and race serving as further signifiers of sexual availability.[54] It could be readily assumed that any woman present in the street was open for men's propositions, espe-cially if she was not white: the mulata was already established as lustful and morally compromised in the Cuban imaginary. Such was the associa-tion of women of color with sex and moral depravity, Aline Helg notes, that men who committed rape against them could excuse themselves by claiming they had been compellingly seduced by her very being.[55] Thus, while an organized commerce in sexual services existed, particularly dur-ing the years in which Havana was a major port of call for colonial shipping routes, the *identity* of prostitute was just beginning to take shape in interaction with other sexual identities and personae.

In the wake of the independence wars, however, a sense of moral crisis over the prostitution of Cuba's women set in, one that was certainly connected to the budding of a new, upstanding masculine nation, not least in its heroic drive to intervene. More than three hundred thousand people lost their lives in the first war, and women left destitute by the deaths of husbands and fathers were seen to be vulnerable to corrupting influence in the interwar period. Authorities responded by expanding the *casas de recogidas,* a sort of respite home for incarcerating prostitutes and "at risk" women that had existed on the margins since the late 1790s. According to a report to the Cuban hygiene commission by Ramón María Alfonso y García in 1902, the Hospital Quinta de San Antonio held 461 women of various nationalities (mostly nonwhite) in December 1873.[56] By 1888, however, Dr. Benjamín de Céspedes wrote that Havana's prostitutes were so numerous and so "brazen" that decent women could not walk in the city streets.[57]

After the second war, the panic grew as half of all adult women in Cuba were said to be widows, and many thousands more had been displaced by conflict and Spain's tactics of forced relocation. Mayra Beers has found that sexual commerce constituted the fourth most common form of subsistence for women by the close of the nineteenth century.[58] Thus, at the height of the postwar crisis in 1899, the Quinta de Higiene Centro Hospitalario reported a population of 1,118 women. Contemporary accounts note several suicide attempts among women confined to the casas de recogidas, as well as one generalized uprising against deplorable conditions.[59]

The journalist Amir Valle asserts that prostitution touched a nerve at this particular moment not because it was on the rise per se but because more *white* women—whose otherwise respectable families had been destroyed by the conflicts—were feared to be engaged in it. Prostitution was therefore only a problem that attracted attention and demanded action when it affected "good" women who merited masculine protection.[60] Nevertheless, most of those who were detained and institutionalized en masse on suspicion of prostitution were young Afro-Cuban women, so the colonial authorities seemed to be both enacting and legitimizing racial and sexual prejudices: the imagined and "real" lives of women of color were becoming mutually reinforcing.

As a result of Alfonso's lengthy report to the hygiene commission, the new Cuban government enacted an even more stringent regime of moral discipline known as *reglamentación* to monitor and control suspected prostitutes. While still under U.S. occupation in the wake of the second war, the provisional government's Military Order No. 55 adopted the Reglamento General aimed at tackling prostitution. As of 27 February 1902, prostitutes could operate only out of brothels within designated *zonas de tolerancia*, paying rent to the brothel owner. The already notorious neighborhoods of San Isidro and Colón in Havana became such officially designated zones. Prostitutes were not permitted to wear ostentatious clothing or to "cause scandal," a logic that frequently functioned in reverse, labeling any woman who behaved improperly as a prostitute. Each was also required to carry a booklet called a *cartilla* with the results of mandatory medical screenings for disease. Women found to be ill during these screenings could be confined to a hospital until released by the authorities. These restrictions further infringed on women's already limited ability to appear in public space, attire themselves as they chose, or behave as they chose—and particularly, as always, young women of color. Irene Wright, an American journalist living in Havana at the time, observed, "The life of a woman is very sad here in Cuba. The only right a woman had was the right to starve to death when her support failed."[61]

In October 1913 regulations tightened. All women engaging in sexual commerce were obliged to register with local authorities, who in many cases attempted to deter them from their paths, and a special task force was created to police registration.[62] Unregistered women who behaved flirtatiously or boldly in public were frequently arrested as *fleteras*.[63] During this period, as García highlights, "the public existence of a sexualized woman of color was readily interpreted as a pathological condition."[64] The raced and gendered bodies of these women were created as objects of state power and knowledge, which inscribed them with notions of indecency and sin. Many of these same mechanisms—profiling based on style of dress or flirtatiousness, enforced medical examinations, rehabilitative incarceration—would recur multiple times through the twentieth century. In only a few years, however, this particular period of discipline came to an abrupt end, as the combined influences of maritime disasters, Prohibition in the United States, and war created a tourist boom in Cuba that for a time washed moral concerns away.

THE RISE AND FALL OF "THE PARIS OF THE ANTILLES"

A number of factors contributed to Cuba's rise as a hub in the nascent Caribbean tourist industry and, simultaneously, the "bordello of the Caribbean" in the early twentieth century.[65] On the world stage, the sinking of the *Titanic* in 1912, the rise of submarine warfare during the Great War, and the *Lusitania* disaster in 1915 gave many holiday makers pause. Where well-heeled North American travelers had once flocked to the south of France, they now shied away from transatlantic travel in favor of the Caribbean.[66] As of 1919, many Americans were also looking for a convenient escape from Prohibition at home. Only ninety miles from the coast of Florida, Cuba existed quite literally—as well as politically—in the shadow of the United States, as a mischievous alter ego to a renewed American puritanism, dependent as it was on American investment and tourism. Vibrant nightlife, plentiful alcohol, drugs, gambling, pornography, live sex shows, and ubiquitous brothels drew ever-increasing hordes of visitors each year throughout the 1920s to the Caribbean's "quintessential pleasure destination."[67] Under long-standing President Gerardo Machado y Morales, Havana became known around the world as a "naughty Paris in the Western hemisphere" where exotic and enthusiastic young women were readily available.[68] This was the fantasy of the exotic, gorgeous, passionate mulata who danced to tropical rhythms and represented the most exciting kind of escapism.

In the wake of World War II, increased air travel and postwar prosperity brought even larger numbers of vacationers to Cuba. Fulgencio Batista had become president in 1940, and though he pursued a progressive, pro-labor tack at first, with prosperity came corruption and nepotism. Cuba was increasingly becoming known as a haven for organized crime.[69] Batista moved to Florida at the end of his presidential term, only to return in 1948 as a senator. Four years later, running for another term as president and down in the polls, he executed a coup d'état three months before the 1952 elections. Cuba had considerable economic success under Batista, but his

Figure 6. "Cuba, Holiday Isle of the Tropics," 1949, poster
produced by the Cuban Tourist Commission. Source: United
States Library of Congress.

connections to organized crime, and in particular to the American mafioso
Meyer Lansky, intensified government corruption and solidified Cuba's position as a capital of vice and black market activity.[70] Commercial sex flourished largely unfettered in and around the glitzy casinos, bars, and resort
hotels of Havana and other major centers. By the 1950s men advertised the

Figure 7. "Visit Cuba: So Near and Yet So Foreign, 90 miles
from Key West," ca. 1950, postcard produced by illustrator
Conrado Walter Massaguer (1889–1965) for the Cuban
Tourist Commission, Havana. Source: Vicki Gold Levi
Collection, The Wolfsonian at Florida International
University. Photo by David Almeida.

"availability" of their sisters at ports, bars and hotels teemed with young women looking to meet tourists, and police raids on brothels became rare.[71]

Almost immediately, the Batista regime began to attract vehement resistance from university students, trade unionists, and opposition parties in Cuba, resistance that Batista answered with a vicious campaign of police brutality. Reports of arbitrary arrests and torture of dissidents became commonplace. Opposition members decried the regime's repression of civil liberties, high unemployment, and lack of moral fortitude, evidenced by repeated pandering to U.S. interests and by rampant prostitution. What was seen as the pimping of Cuba's women to provide sexual services to Americans was protested as a slight to national honor and integrity. In the lead-up to the Cuban Revolution in 1959, post-independence ideas about morality and honor reemerged and began to take on an even more protective and paternalistic tone. Prostitution was elevated past a mere social problem to a powerful symbol of Cuba's subordination to foreign powers. Railing against prostitution became a potent rhetorical tool for the anti-imperialist rebels, and its use as such would have a far-reaching impact on Cuban women.

As the Castro brothers' guerrilla movement gained strength in the Sierra Maestra through the late 1950s, Batista struggled to maintain the appearance of stability. Tourists continued to frequent the glamorous casinos and hotels of Havana even as the rebels advanced from the east. In 1958, on the eve of the triumph of the Cuban Revolution, the island accounted for 20 percent of all Caribbean tourism, mostly from the United States. The city of Havana alone was said to contain around 270 brothels, and the number of women involved in sexual commerce fell anywhere between 11,500 and 100,000.[72] Most were women of color from the lower classes of Cuban society whose charms had now achieved international notoriety, and it was this demeaning reputation for decadence and subservience to American whims that the nationalist rebels would address first.

THE ERA OF ERADICATION

Cuba's prostitutes were the earliest beneficiaries of revolutionary reform—"whether they liked it or not," García comments wryly[73]—in a new era of eradication. The revolutionary campaign to end prostitution was part of a broader humanist mission on the part of the new government to eradicate sexist and racist discrimination within Cuban society on all fronts. Legal barriers to the full participation of women and Afro-Cuban people in public life were lifted. An edifice of legal rights was created to structure the private and public spheres, while new programs of child care, education, health care, and maternity leave were established.[74] Here, though, the mission stopped for Afro-Cubans, and it became taboo to speak of racism, for fear of appearing to criticize the Revolution's handling of the issue, as Alejandro de la Fuente has shown.[75] While the Revolution opened all nightclubs and public beaches to people of all races and removed barriers to employment and education, it also shut down Afro-Cuban associations and social clubs. Public discussion of race was largely silenced and the issue considered resolved, allowing racist prejudice to persist, even amid considerable gains.

Women, however, were given the FMC, which was created in 1960 by the revolutionary guerrilla Vilma Espín to address women's issues, and foremost among its tasks was the campaign to eradicate prostitution. Its antiprostitution campaign, which began in Havana and was later expanded nationally in cooperation with the Ministerio del Interior (MININT). The first phase was dubbed "*censo, acercamiento y persuasión* [census, outreach and persuasion]" by the FMC and "*contar y captación* [count and capture]" by MININT. An army of volunteer FMC social workers performed information-gathering visits to brothels, explained the revolutionary ideals to the women there, and attempted to convince them to join a program of reeducation.[76] Meanwhile, MININT set about cracking down on pimps, closing cinemas and publishing houses featuring pornography; liquidating sex shows, strip clubs, dance halls, and casinos; and closing down *posadas*, or hotels known as destinations for commercial sex and short trysts between lovers. In 1961 MININT intensified its efforts by mounting Operación Tres P, which targeted suspected pimps, pederasts, and prostitutes in Cuba's cities.[77] Police acted to enforce heteronormative sexuality by arresting anyone associated with sexual commerce, including young women who "caused scandal" in public and suspected homosexuals, many of whom had found a measure of acceptance living and working around brothels.

Ideological, moral, and technical reeducation formed the second phase of the FMC and MININT campaign. Young women were brought to schools set up in the outskirts of the cities of Havana, Matanzas, Camagüey, and Santiago, where they were given mandatory medical examinations and classes on etiquette, hygiene, and how to dress and do their hair in ways that were not considered "over-ornate" and indicative of low morality. They wore uniforms, performed agricultural labor, and attended classes in basic education, literacy, and gender-appropriate job skills like sewing and secretarial work. The schools were said to be comfortable and clean, with medical and child care available, but the women were strictly managed and not free to leave until authorities deemed them fit to be reintegrated in society.[78] Laws against pimping and running brothels were passed in 1961, and all remaining uncooperative prostitutes were detained and sent to do agricultural labor in the countryside along with other recalcitrant social elements.[79] The FMC announced an end to prostitution in 1965—and thus to its overt disciplinary efforts for the time being.

Armando Torres, a key organizer in the rehabilitation program, gave an interview in 1970 in which he described the development of the eradication project.

> At the beginning, we didn't have any definite plans as to how to undertake this work. . . . Everything came into being spontaneously. . . . We were a trifle romantic about it. It was essentially a matter of persuasion. That is, the state let them know that their way of life wouldn't be tolerated, and that everyone would be given work. Some were afraid and said they would go for that reason.[80]

The sociologists Teresa Díaz Canals and Graciela Gonzalez Olmedo call this a process of "social rehabilitation," which they say was taken up voluntarily by most, due to the general sense of acceptance that the Revolution engendered among the population, though they also admit that fear of marginalization played a major role.[81]

The new government maintained a tight grip on the dwindling nightlife in those early years, looking to prevent a resurgence of prostitution, and the measures undertaken often betrayed an inherent distrust of women and women's sexuality. Boardinghouses were limited to renting rooms to men only, former prostitutes were carefully monitored by their local Comités de Defensa de la Revolución (CDR), single women who left cabarets with men were arrested, and artists—previously associated with the permissive underworld of Havana—were prohibited from working without membership in the Unión de Escritores y Artistas de Cuba (UNEAC).[82] Meanwhile, as casinos and cabarets were shut down in the name of moral standards, American tourism evaporated rapidly. On the other side of the Straits of Florida, a partial trade embargo was enacted in 1960 under President Dwight D. Eisenhower, and later strengthened to a near-total embargo in 1962 under John F. Kennedy. By 1968 Cuba was receiving only three thousand international tourists annually.[83]

Even private life and behavior were not free from official scrutiny during this period. Where many Cubans had previously lived in consensual unions and often shared homes with extended family, the Revolution encouraged formal marriages and nuclear family units.[84] When Cuba's popular tribunals came into being in 1966, they dealt with perceived social problems such as homosexuality, juvenile delinquency, and women's "honor." They also admitted assessments of women's honesty and virginity as evidence against them in rape cases and handed down sentences for women deemed prostitutes that have been called "vindictive."[85] These were the years in which the Revolution established itself at home and abroad, and yet it seemed to uphold the same old assumptions—that women in public spaces or who dated or had sex outside marriage were suspect.

The very notion of prostitution in Cuba was becoming no more than a footnote to a benighted past, slipping beneath the surface of public discourse for a time. In a nearly unprecedented campaign, the revolutionary government had espoused a radical new moral prerogative but one that seems oddly reminiscent of the late-nineteenth-century casas de recogidas and their Catholic morality. This new incarnation was imbued with a socialist tint of solidarity, equality, and antidiscrimination, but it maintained the paternalistic bent of reglamentación fifty years earlier. In its day, the eradication campaign was lauded for blaming prostitution on the capitalist system rather than on individual women. It was also part and parcel of the new government's aggressively anti-imperialist stance, which it linked directly to removing Cuban women from sexual commerce.

This is not to say, of course, that the exchange of sex and companion-ship for material gain ceased. In fact, far from destroying the impetus to engage in commercial sex, the Revolution for a time bolstered it: women engaged at the time in commercial sex reported a marked surge in busi-ness just before the eradication campaign came into effect.[86] What the Revolution had done in chalking up the exploitation of women to foreign influence was to avoid a deeper examination of gendered prejudice in Cuba. As it had with the issue of race, the new government tackled what it thought were the most visible injustices and then, in declaring them resolved, allowed structural oppression to continue. In its wake, Cuba's sexual economy did not wholly die out. It did, however, become consider-ably more covert and made use of a different language to conform to revo-lutionary identities and edicts.

THINGS FALL APART: FROM THE REVOLUTION TO THE SPECIAL PERIOD

During the 1960s and 1970s, the Cuban Revolution consolidated its self-image. These were times when the focus at home and abroad was on the rise of mass organizations, the Bay of Pigs, the U.S. embargo, military engagements in Angola and the Congo, new allegiances with the USSR, and the annual push for record sugar harvests as the new Cuba attempted to make a new place for itself in the world. Racial segregation in Cuban cities had begun to fade, and women's presence in the workforce and in public life had greatly expanded. The *Código de Familia* was introduced in 1975 in an attempt to alleviate women's double burden at work and at home, by inducing men to partake in household chores and child-rearing duties.[87]

Maria Auxiliadora César calls Cuba's idea of gender equality an "affir-mation of difference within equality," which did not seek to question norms of masculinity and femininity.[88] Ernesto "Ché" Guevara had intro-duced his New Man, an idealized socialist citizen driven not by material but moral rewards; like the mambí, the New Man was an inherently mas-culine and machista configuration of citizenship that effectively excluded women and gay Cubans from achieving it as an ideal. Perhaps unsurprisingly, then, the state held beauty pageants and included hairdressing services on the ration at various points while simultaneously MININT established a dress code for men and women, sometimes even arresting those with nonconformist gender presentations to induce them to adopt more "appropriate" looks.[89]

This was also the period during which queer Cuban men, because of their perceived rejection of the Revolution's norms on sexuality and masculinity, were interned in labor camps called the Unidades Militares de Ayuda a la Producción (UMAP).[90] It was believed that gay or effeminate men could not fulfill the ideal of Cuban socialist citizenship—the New Man—and must therefore be considered antirevolutionary. Fidel Castro said at that time: "We have never believed that a homosexual could personify the conditions and requirements of behavior that would permit us to consider him a real revolutionary, a real communist. This kind of deviance clashes with our concept of what a militant communist should be."[91]

According to the historian Antoni Kapcia, the camps targeted "those who simply opted out of the scarcely enjoyable regime of hard-work, mobilization and pressure to commit"—Jehovah's Witnesses and Seventh-Day Adventists who didn't want to work Saturdays, hippies and beatniks, men with long hair and women who wore miniskirts—but the UMAP camps were best known for imprisoning gay men whose perceived effeminacy countered revolutionary camaraderie.[92] The camps were indicative of a deep heteronormativity in Cuban political culture, which valued machista/masculine traits over all else, denigrating the feminine (in both men and women) as weak, inconstant, and even counterrevolutionary. The sexuality and gender presentation of queer Cubans was policed because the only acceptable sexual identities were the properly heterosexual and heteronormative couple: the New Man/mambí and his wife.

These norms carried over into social life, which my older Cuban friends recounted to me time and again while rolling their eyes, much like a woman whom César interviewed related: "The 1970s was a time of total machismo."[93] Relationships that did not conform to heteronormative expectations were frowned upon, from same-sex liaisons that were criminalized until the late 1970s to single women who simply did not maintain stable, long-term attachments to men.[94] Meanwhile, however, the Revolution began to embrace sex education and birth control and seemed only to perpetuate the idea that Cubans were sexually superior. Dr. Armando Fernández-Mouré published a study claiming that the mixing of races had created a people who "possess an ardor [*fogosidad*] and a way of having sex that is not common in other races."[95]

Amid this somewhat confused sexual culture there remained an economy of affect and sex that was used to navigate the opaque bureaucratic system and to obtain luxury items from abroad. Valle describes a practice called *convenios sexuales,* or sexual agreements, which supposedly helped many women gain access to material benefits in exchange for sexual favors granted to men in powerful positions; similarly, Coco Fusco argues that small numbers of young women who associated with embassy functionaries and diplomats were given the state's tacit approval in exchange for reporting on their liaisons.[96] In a closed economy, the exchange of sexual favors became a way of accessing scarce goods or special treatment. Rumors circulated of young women, many of them in the belief that sex was their most valuable asset, using sexual favors to get jobs or promotions, preference in the distribution of cars or travel, or access to luxury goods from abroad. Havana even saw a resurgence in posadas, rising from twelve in 1969 to more than fifty by 1987.[97]

Valle offers a virtual taxonomy of these convenios sexuales: the practice of granting jobs in the arts and culture industries to young women in exchange for sex was called *titimanía,*[98] whereas women who dated Soviet functionaries or African medical students in order to gain access to privileges accorded only to foreigners were labeled *putishas* and *afroputas,* respectively. Women who dated or had sex with foreigners who worked in embassies, or on ships in the port area, or even high-level Cuban functionaries were called any of a range of terms, from *callejera* (street woman) to *amante* (lover).[99] The crux of his argument, however, is that the integrity of any woman who chose her partner, whether for a relationship or for sex, with material or financial concerns in mind could be suspect. And it was not so much the *fact* of transactional sex but its *appearance* that was most incriminating.

In 1986 Fidel Castro loudly denounced convenios sexuales as he announced a process of *rectificación*—a tightening of the socialist ship meant to root out corruption and antisocialist behavior. Little was done to repress them, however, especially if the women could prove advantageous to the state in terms of intelligence or influence.[100] A fifty-five-year-old man named Rigoberto, whom I met in Havana, told me that he had acted as an intermediary for young women in the 1980s, helping them make contact with Soviet functionaries and other foreigners in exchange for gifts and U.S. dollars to spend on the black market. This practice, he said, was an open secret around the capital and only received police attention when those involved lacked discretion. Many in Cuba date the birth of the term *jineterismo* to this period, or even earlier, the 1970s, when it began to be used to denote practices of jockeying for advantage or using the means at one's disposal to get ahead. Rosa Miriam Elizalde, a Cuban journalist, argues that the term was originally used as a name for illegal moneychangers and only later took on its sexual connotation, but the consensus on the streets of Cuba seems to be that it always carried at least a hint of sexual undertones.[101]

The sudden disintegration of the USSR had catastrophic repercussions, forcing drastic economic and ideological compromises. Cuba was thrust headlong into the capitalist fray, all the while confronting painful shortages and austerity measures in a process of what Allen calls "re-globalization."[102] Almost overnight, the state's ability to provide the sorts of universal social welfare and full employment on which it had based its claims to egalitarianism and social justice evaporated. Between 1989 and 1993 Cuba's gross domestic product (GDP) plummeted by almost half while domestic manufacturing dropped by 83 percent and oil imports from the USSR by 85 percent. Production of milk fell by half, beef by two-thirds, poultry by 80 percent, and pigs by 70 percent. Imports of food, spare parts, and other essential consumer goods stopped entirely. By 1994 the economy was operating at only 60 percent.[103]

The state declared the start of the Special Period and enacted an austerity plan that it had prepared as a contingency for military attack: salaries were reduced, provision of food to families was slashed until the monthly ration could no longer last even two weeks, social benefits and services were scaled back, and prices for goods in stores were raised. Many workplaces reduced their hours of operation, public transit was drastically reduced, and rolling power cuts stalked Cuban cities and towns.[104] All of this was exacerbated by the ever-tightening American embargo, which was strengthened in 1992 by the Torricelli Bill and in 1996 by the Helms-Burton

Bill, allowing the United States to apply sanctions to international companies who did business with Cuba.[105] The collapse of the Cuban government in the face of such dire economic hardship began to seem like a real possibility for the first time in forty years. Cubans became thinner, and, in the constant grind of waiting and hunting for supplies, normal life became impossible. Fertility rates dropped to the lowest in the twentieth century, while rates of abortion, drug use, petty crime, and suicide increased—all indicators of how people experience their times.[106]

The daily struggle to make ends meet, which Cubans call *la lucha*, has meant a wide range of sacrifices for many people, from reverting from cars to horse-drawn carts to waiting all day in queues for food rations to mending and remending clothing to finding innovative ways to get by without shampoo, antiperspirant, plumbing equipment, school supplies, and even medications. New words emerged to express the resourceful defiance with which Cubans faced their situation: *"resolver"* (resolve), *"inventor"* (invent), *"luchar"* (struggle). The strain of coping was so great as to cause an exodus of people on makeshift rafts—known as the *balseros*—bound for the southern coast of Florida, throughout 1994, which led to many deaths at sea and further diplomatic tensions with the United States.

In desperate need of hard currency, Cuba looked abroad: a new law on foreign investment in the early 1990s allowed partial foreign ownership of large enterprises—in particular, hotels and resorts.[107] Cuba was once again opening its doors to a flood of international mass tourism. Tourism had already been quietly growing for some time after bottoming out in the early 1970s, with small numbers of Canadians, Russians, and Eastern Europeans coming in search of sunshine.[108] Now companies from Spain, Germany, and Canada arrived to build facilities and draw visitors to a reborn tourist paradise, staffed by Cubans contracted out by their socialist state employer. The state opened exclusive academies in tourism and hospitality, and soon the island was hosting more than one million tourists annually. Revenues jumped from US$243 million in 1990 to $1.8 billion in 1998, second in the Caribbean only to the Dominican Republic.[109]

Meanwhile, at the chaotic level of everyday life, the black market flourished. Underground networks reselling ration goods and illegal imports became the best bet for finding scarce goods and were open to anyone with U.S. dollars. Lucrative tourism jobs offering tips in dollars were rare and tightly controlled, and not everyone had relatives living abroad who could send cash remittances, so Cubans made an art of inventing new spaces for themselves in the dollar economy of tourism. Called upon to confront scarcity and privation with everything they had, Cubans squeezed water from stones and began letting out rooms, driving their own cars as taxis, or serving meals to foreign tourists for cash. Bed-and-breakfast-type establishments called *casas particulares,* snack stands on the street, and small restaurants known as *paladares* proved far more lucrative than most other jobs available at the time, and many Cubans abandoned professional careers to pursue these kinds of businesses.[110]

Such a lucrative shadow economy spurred what Carmelo Mesa-Lago calls "zigzagging" market-oriented reforms aimed at rerouting dollars through state coffers. In 1993 the government took the propitious step of legalizing the circulation of foreign currencies, so that Cubans could more openly use and exchange American dollars, which were far more stable and valuable than Cuban pesos.[111] Special state-owned dollar shops known as *chopines* (from the English "shopping") and currency exchange kiosks were opened in nearly every town. Next, the state legalized a limited range of private enterprises so that it could then license and tax them—the first widespread acceptance of self-employment, or *cuentapropismo,* since the Revolution. For the first time in nearly four decades, Cubans could go into business for themselves selling food, souvenirs, accommodations, and cab rides.

In 2004 Cuba created a second official currency, the *peso convertible,* or $CUC, which was freely exchangeable and replaced other currencies in the Cuban market; all foreign cash brought into Cuba was now filtered through the state. The original peso, which Cubans call *moneda nacional* ($MN), is still the currency of state salaries and can be used for basics like rice, beans, and public transit, it is nearly worthless. The new money—colloquially called *chavitos, divisas, convertibles—*is now a fixture of Cuban life and the only way to buy things like shampoo, toilet paper, school supplies, fashionable clothing, and "luxury" foods such as pasta, canned fish or vegetables, and powdered milk.

The Special Period also highlighted the ways in which gender and race still mattered, even after all these years. Many women left their jobs as the value of state-provided salaries plummeted, in order to dedicate themselves fully to the challenge of supporting their families in the crisis, "a position symbolized by lines or queues and the increasingly time-consuming 'participation' needed to secure food and the other essentials of home and families."[112] They were also more likely to lose their jobs under the assumption that a husband or male partner could provide for them, whether or not this was actually the case.

Cubans of color were also hit hard by the crisis. Afro-Cubans are far less likely to receive remittances, a source of income on which many have become dependent, because those who have fled Cuba have been those with the means to do so—and thus they are overwhelmingly white.[113]

Similarly, Afro-Cubans are less likely to have a family home spacious and comfortable enough for a casa particular or paladar. The tourist industry often hires new staff based on an elusive quality known as *buena presencia*—a combination of a congenial personality and good looks, including height, weight, teeth, and fitness, which Cabezas skeptically calls "the fashioned aesthetic of 'natives in paradise.'"[114] This is frequently interpreted in racial terms, meaning Afro-Cubans often struggle to compete for jobs, especially outside of stereotyped positions like housekeeping, teaching dance, or performing in live shows. As Cubans came into regular contact with yumas for the first time in decades, even as their own poverty increased and opportunities dwindled, some of those who were left out of the tourist boom turned to jineterismo.

INVENTAR, RESOLVER, LUCHAR

Jineterismo is a Cuban neologism derived from the Spanish word for "jockeying"—in the sense of jockeying for advantage, for the most part— but the more literal and graphic interpretation was not lost. Some people opened unlicensed casas particulares or paladares, or expanded legal businesses beyond what their licenses allowed; some trafficked in cheap rum and knockoff cigars; some began making themselves sexually available to foreigners. The rise of jineterismo as a sexual practice was colored by adversity and new patterns of desire and consumption, certainly, but also by the deep existential crisis of the Special Period: Sierra Madero describes how young people increasingly see sexual relationships as casual, fleeting, and even a leisure activity, in a world where everything has come to feel transitory.[115] The rug has been pulled out from under them before.

Young men also entered the evolving sexual-affective economy, to meet both female and male tourists, but the state's (and the world's) hand-wringing was reserved for the so-called jineteras, betraying some very traditional ideas about sexuality—and about men and women, and what they *ought* to be doing—beneath its egalitarian veneer. That these women are said to be mostly young and attractive mulatas could be as much about a raced fantasy or "tropicalist cliché"[116] as it is about the truncated range of options available to Afro-Cuban women. Kamala Kempadoo somewhat cynically calls women like these "freelancers" because they operate without brothels or traffickers, meeting foreigners casually on beaches, in bars and nightclubs, or while walking through the city streets. The reality is that little can be said for certain about these women's identities, relationships, or motivations; there are no numbers to cite, no easy causal relations or explanations to be drawn, which I explore in the next chapter.

What mattered, however, was that the word was out, both at home and abroad: jineteras were featured in major international newspapers and magazines including *Glamour,* the *New York Times, National Geographic,* and *Playboy.* They were the subjects of multiple films, including a Mexican documentary, as well as songs by Silvio Rodríguez and Willie Chirino, giants in the Cuban expat community. Aleida Guevara, the daughter of the most famous non-Cuban of the Cuban Revolution, remarked sardonically at the time, "Just a few prostitutes in a country that had none before have created quite a scandal."[117] At home, voices echoed through state institutions and media outlets, calling the existence of jineteras inexplicable in the society Cubans had now built, despite the reverberations of parallel moments in Cuba's history. Talk of a crisis of values increased as the Revolution watched its youth abandon careers that ought to have been spiritually, if not financially, fulfilling in favor of practices it saw as shallow, not respectable, and frivolous. The state railed against accusations that it was using Cuba's women to drum up tourism, responding by removing images of women from its brochures and posters, and then turned its attention to eradicating jineterismo as a sexual practice.[118]

The atmosphere of fear that surrounds jineterismo today, and that permeates the words recorded in chapters to come, has everything to do with

the state campaign to end jineterismo-as-sexual-practice that began in
the late 1990s. Whether the state was responding to the international
media spotlight, as some argue, or acting on its own existential anxieties
is not clear, but regardless of the reasons, the campaign that I described at
the beginning of this chapter became yet another example of the moralizing discipline seen in the 1890s and 1960s.[119] Today's rehabilitation
centers are notorious and strikingly reminiscent of the casas de recogidas
of the late nineteenth century and the *granjas* where recalcitrant prostitutes were sent in the 1960s, and even the UMAP camps of the 1960s.
Where the blame for prostitution was once placed on coercion, despera-
tion, and the capitalist system, the tone today is markedly different, accus-
ing individual women of moral degradation and underdeveloped personalities—a far cry from Cuba's increasingly progressive stances on sexuality
and sex education. In the years since Operativo Lacra and the U.N. report
on violence against women, there have been reports that the centers have
disappeared,[120] but these were not borne out by my own investigation or
by the young women to whom I spoke.

Cuba's struggle against jineterismo-as-sexual-practice principally affects
women. Afro-Cuban men regularly experience police harassment, but it is
not their sexual proclivities with foreigners that draw attention. What these
crackdowns do is force those who are looking to meet foreigners to be ever
more resourceful and innovative, to find new ways to avoid scrutiny, or
even to surrender a degree of control over the process to third parties—a
problematic development that merits further discussion in later chapters.
The state's discourse of jineterismo, in reducing the issue to certain wom-
en's "natural" licentiousness, erases and thereby tacitly condones this ongoing potential for violence in women's lives.

While the government claims the Special Period ended when the economy began to recover around 1996, many Cubans claim that they are still
in the thick of it. Their lives are still wracked by insecurity, and though the
economy had been slowly improving, there have been more economic
roadblocks that have only exacerbated the persistent racism and sexism.
In mid-2011 the government laid off 500,000 workers and legalized a new
list of private enterprises, leaving these people to make their own way.[121]
The government also released plans for a system of credit and small loans
for the first time in its socialist history and announced its intention to

collapse the two-currency system together, bringing the country more in line with the world financial system.[122] The worst hardships of the early 1990s are over, but the Cuban economy has yet to regain all its lost ground, and the changes and adjustments are ongoing.

Having grown up in a closed country and a closed economy where a desire for material wealth was deemed unpatriotic, young Cubans are now confronted with fashionable clothes, popular music, cosmetics and perfumes, films, and electronics—a world of luxury and leisure to which they have very limited access. Although Cubans are officially allowed to stay in the luxury hotels and shop in the dollar stores, like any foreigner can, few can even begin to afford it, and many who venture inside are asked to leave. With each liberal move comes a rollback of progress elsewhere: in 2013 the government shut down popular privately run cinemas and gaming rooms en masse.[123] This atmosphere has led to accusations of "tourist apartheid" but has not dampened young Cubans' enduring fascination with U.S. culture and materialism. Everywhere, one hears talk of iPods, Ed Hardy T-shirts, Chanel earrings, Akon, Lady Gaga, and even Big Macs, though virtually no one has ever tasted one. The contradiction of this drive to possess the trappings of consumerism in a socialist state is just one of many that characterize contemporary life in Cuba.

Meanwhile, systemic racial and gender prejudices persist. Afro-Cubans have no formal organization like the FMC, and while many people parrot the regime's claims to a raceless society, it is still common to hear racial stereotypes and ideas like blanqueamiento bandied about uncritically. In day-to-day life, Afro-Cubans are far more likely to be targeted by the police.[124] Similarly, a "distinctly Cuban machismo" still describes the pattern of interaction between many men and women, and masculine prerogatives persist in many ways. This does not mean that Cuban women are universally retiring or submissive. Contrary to the Latin American standard of *marianismo,* the veneration of feminine restraint and sexual purity based on the model of the Virgin Mary, Cuban women prefer the *hembra:* technically the female of a species but here denoting a more spirited, headstrong, and sexual femininity. Cuba is home to an intensely demonstrative sexual culture, the product of the most comprehensive sexual education in the region, which has reduced some of the stigma of premarital sex.[125] Like the rest of the Western world, Cuba experienced a liberalization of sexual values in the 1960s and 1970s, and sexuality—always a preoccupation—is now a far more openly celebrated part of daily life and Cuban identity, frequently hovering close to the surface of otherwise innocent exchanges. In Lumsden's succinct words, "Cubans show off their sex appeal everywhere."[126] Young Cubans begin having sex at a young age, relationships are often seen as transitory and sex as leisure, and infidelity and promiscuity have become even more socially normalized. Models for sexual-affective relationships are changing; they can be long-term or fleeting, serious or lighthearted, instrumental or merely ends in themselves.

Jineterismo-as-sexual-practice fits easily into this setting. Arrests and police harassment still regularly occur, and form the basis of chapters to come, but young people continue to pursue relationships with foreigners as a means of alleviating scarcity and gaining access to a perceived better life. Havana continues to host an underworld that "seems to offer an eternal prayer to the memory of the Marquis de Sade," as Valle vividly describes it, though today it is much more secretive than twenty years ago.[127] Young people and foreigners mingle every night along the Malecón, in the old city, and in the nightclubs of Vedado looking for dance partners, flirtations, and sex. In Santiago, too, one can see countless Europeans with Cuban companions under the trees of Parque Céspedes and on the terraces of bars. Even Varadero has not been entirely shut down. By the time I visited the town in spring 2010, no one would even talk about jineteras, saying they feared losing their jobs and homes; however, when I told a bartender one night that I could not find any jineteras and suspected they had disappeared from Varadero, she raised one eyebrow and slowly shook her head before quickly excusing herself.

The first thing I learned in Cuba is that the jineteras are not society's left-behinds, as the state institutions would have it. As Cabezas contends, they are "equally envied, admired, and chastised."[128] Representations of these young women as morally reprobate on the one hand or victimized on the other do not achieve currency here. For the most part, the downtrodden stigma of the prostitute is swept aside. Cuban youth culture today is full of contradictions, where old and new ideas of gender, race, and sexuality collide with consumerism and international pop culture. While many young Cubans today envision a world where the benefits of socialism—health care, education, food subsidies—can exist alongside the draw of the dollar economy, the state continues to punish those who try to merge the two worlds.

CONCLUSION: A WINDOW ON THE REVOLUTION

> Finally, the industry of the exotic has been reborn. And here
> it is likely to stay, as well as the exporting of the mythical
> Cuban paradise, where mulattas, as personifications of
> Ochún, reign in the nights of Havana and in the feverish
> imaginations of its visitors.
>
> Raquel Mendieta Costa, "Exotic Imports"

The jinetera has been a long time in the making. Her image is underwritten by the mulata and her mythic sexuality: to be a jinetera today is to "assume a mulata identity by association."[129] Both are the product of intertwining notions of race, gender, and sexual mores that go back to the very foundations of the Cuban colony and the encounter between the native of Caobana, the colonizer of Isla Juana, and the slave of the Cuba that was to follow. While the rhetoric directed at the jinetera in the past two decades is overlaid with socialist logics of productive labor and gendered egalitarianism, it is underpinned by the centuries-old threads of power, race, gender, and sex. The bodies of mulatas are inscribed as perpetually available and shamelessly promiscuous by the social codes of colonial society. The power relations intrinsic to liaisons across lines of race and gender, I would argue, meet in sexuality and in the bodies of women of color, who have been subject to moralizing discipline through systemic oppression but also in the specific sites of the plantation, the casa de recogidas, the granja, and the rehabilitation center. The grinding reality of the Special Period and the variety of ways that Cubans have found to circumvent the poverty it brought them provide a window onto the governance of bodies in Cuba today—and the continuities it reveals across eras—as the regime attempts to manage emerging dissident elements in the wake of economic meltdown, bringing its ideology into ever sharper focus.

From its inception, Cuba's revolutionary movement positioned itself as a defining moment in the history of the island by laying claim to a radical

egalitarianism fundamentally at odds with all of Cuba's previous govern-
ments. After centuries of colonial rule, puppet presidents under the thrall
of the United States and dictators like Batista, Cuba would now be free.
The "state patriarch" granted freedoms and issued guidance in the pursuit
of a society liberated from prejudice, becoming the darling of the Soviet
bloc and left-leaning movements worldwide, a status it retains in many
progressive circles today.[130] This reputation is not without concrete bases:
women, Afro-Cuban people, and eventually gay and lesbian Cubans have
all been brought under the rubric of emancipation. These freedoms have
almost without exception been *granted* by the benevolent state—rather
than *won* by the sectors in question—and only on the Revolution's terms,
such that each individual raced, gendered, and sexed subject might best
fulfill the ideal of citizenship set out for them. Frantz Fanon argues that
only when there is a genuine struggle by the marginalized against their
oppression do we see a "genuine eradication of the superstructure" put in
place by previous authorities.[131] So by denying Cubans of color the possibility to meet and organize *as* Cubans of color and by creating the FMC as
an organization that pursues women's issues only as they serve the
Revolution, and which rejects feminism as a bourgeois incursion, the
Cuban government frames challenges to raced and gendered prejudice as
nationally divisive, stalls further efforts to challenge discrimination, and
denies broad sectors of the population the catharsis of confronting their
experiences *as* people of color, *as* women, and especially *as* women of
color.

As the embodied and sexualized intersection of raced and gendered
prejudice, the figure of the jinetera/mulata in the Cuban national and
sexual imagination provides an outlet for thinly veiled raced and gendered
prejudices to find a socially acceptable expression, but this figure also
reveals the uncomfortable ambiguity of the socialist state's place in the
networks of tourism, international capitalism, and the sexual-affective
economy. By staking its future on the international tourist market, I argue,
the state also engages in a kind of jineterismo, stepping outside the ideals
of a socialist utopia and jockeying with foreigners for a better, more comfortable life. Cuba gave itself the leeway to step back from socialist goals
and to pursue foreign capital, but it has not allowed women the same
space—as to do so would be to make its own compromises more visible.

Fusco attributes the crackdowns against perceived jineteras to international criticism, saying that "saving face means more [to the government] than protecting the women involved."[132] I would like to posit that the issue runs much deeper. The state positions itself as fundamentally masculine, in the image of the New Man/mambí, and thus it views relationships between its women and foreign men as a loss of prestige, or even a sort of feminization—much as Fanon once described black men's perspectives on "their" women marrying white men.[133] The window onto the Revolution that this phenomenon provides shows a clear conviction that the rightful place of Cuban women is with Cuban men. The jinetera thus poses a challenge not just to the ideals of the Cuban state but also to Cuban masculinity, which are in many ways linked. Thus the humanist and egalitarian ethos of the revolutionary government is willing to permit, even to encourage, women's sexual liberation, providing sex education and access to contraceptive methods to that end, so long as this sexuality is expressed toward Cuban men—and not toward yuma imperialists.

This is why institutions like the FMC eschew economic and structural explanations for jineterismo in favor of individual and moral ones. Through the lens of this controversy, we can see a state preoccupied with managing not just those subjects who actively oppose it but also those who reject its ideals for the good life. Prostitution has become an *image of thought* in the Cuban imaginary that travels to the sites of state anxiety, locating weakness and laxity in the bodies of young women and creating them as a problem to be solved. The jineteras represent the trials of the Special Period and the return of capitalism, just as the mulata symbolized fears of miscegenation and the prostitute stood for Spanish colonialism, American imperialism, and capitalist depravity. The ideal of womanhood put forth by Cuba's state institutions since the Revolution is a fiction that is always riddled with exceptions and contradictions, and that has never been fully open to nonwhite women, haunted as they are by this image of thought.

In state discourse, Cuban women have one rightful place in the Revolution, and that is by the side of Cuban men as productive workers and upstanding citizens. Women constitute part of the patrimony that is the nationalist state of Cuba, and their association (or perceived association) with foreign men constitutes a defilement of the Revolution's fierce program of socialist nationalism and independence, in spite of its commitment to producing sexually liberated women. More than fifteen years since the crackdowns on jineterismo began, the stories of young people engaged in sexual-affective economies of international tourism in Cuba help to illuminate what jineterismo is, what it means, and what it does as a discourse of sexual ethics.

2 Love, Sex, Money, and Meaning

INTERROGATING JINETERISMO ON THE GROUND

Listening to them, I felt I was watching the saddest part of
Cuban socialism's last chapter—living proof of the island's
own nihilistic version of a Generation X without any
dreams of a future beyond the next purchase.

Coco Fusco, "Hustling for Dollars"

The very idea of the jinetera in Cuba today is overlaid with knowledges
about race, gender, class, and sexuality, about moral and social values, ethics, and lifestyles that date back centuries. While I set out to understand
jineterismo as a sexual practice in the rapidly changing world of post-
Soviet Cuba, it is impossible to come to grips with contemporary sexuality—the meanings attached, the expectations, the parts to be played—
without engaging with the interlocking histories of colonial subjugation,
slavery, and machismo, alongside a profoundly masculinist process of
nation building through war and revolution. The way that young people
pursue and interpret sex, and especially with foreigners, is heavily laden
with entrenched ideas that frame the sexuality of women of color as insatiable and deviant and sex between Cuban women and foreigners as a
form of imperialism. Here, I investigate this notion of the jinetera, bolstered and reinforced by this history, and how it is—or rather, is not—
borne out by the lived experiences of young people in contemporary Cuba.

The word *jinetera* is bandied about fairly readily in Cuba today. Many
people were willing to tell me where to find jineteras, what they looked
like and how they behaved, and how to pick them out in a crowd—usually
women they had never met. Sometimes the word was used as a piropo,

called out to women in the street or used casually by men talking to their female friends or even coworkers in jest, the implication being that jineteras are beautiful or sexy. This kind of flippant, day-to-day usage belies a far more complex and often contradictory set of actors and activities. Unpacking the discourse that surrounds today's jinetera is central to a better understanding of the way in which this label serves to discipline gendered and raced bodies, as well as to highlight how it conditions the lives and lifestyles of the individual young people who fall under its remit. Though some wear the name jinetera with pride, labels such as these are most frequently applied from the outside, becoming ever more entangled with notions of race, gender, sexuality, and class.[1]

This is not a process by which the jinetera is objectively described but rather one by which the idea of the jinetera is continually produced and reproduced over time, actively creating a supposedly already existing social group. It is a process by which some women's sexual selves become a matter of public record and inquiry: those who dress or behave in certain ways, are present in certain spaces, or are black or mixed race. This is yet another moment in Cuba's history when women of color and white women are treated and thought differently, in line with the knowledges produced about their sexualities and personalities. In practice, such a broad range of relationships, from brief encounters to long-term committed partnerships, have come to be swept under the umbrella of jineterismo as a set of sexual-affective practices that trying to find a clear definition of who is in and who is out is useless, as has been suggested most notably by Amalia Cabezas.[2] What matters is the *idea* that certain truths can be known about someone's sexuality and morality just by looking at them, if that person is a young and attractive mulata woman.

This is a discourse that has proven disciplinary and even repressive to a broad sector of the Cuban population in recent years. The stories of several of the young Cubans whom I interviewed challenge simplistic understandings of jineterismo and destabilize its power as a category that seeks to discipline Cuban youth, and particularly young women of color. The testimonies of these young Cubans give a nuanced picture of how they view their relationships with foreigners, their place in Cuban society, and their experience of the political and ideological scene in which they live their lives. These interviews explore what or who the jinetera is, what jineterismo means as a practice, and what these ideas do in terms of challenging prescriptive assessments of who these people are and what their activities, as well as their identities, mean for Cuba.

BEHOLDEN TO NO ONE

Early on during my time in Cuba, I began frequenting the terrace of the Hotel St. John as a place to take stock after a day of research and commit the interceding events to paper in my field journal. There were a number of regulars there, mostly foreigners like me, but a pair of them caught my eye in particular: a young woman and her older companion, easily thirty years her senior and clearly foreign, even to my untrained eye. A friend of mine, over coffee at the St. John, had once glanced pointedly in their direction and then back at me with one eyebrow raised, saying wryly, "Fieldwork." I waited for an opening to speak to them, until one day they chose the table next to mine and we fell into easy conversation.

Yakelín comes to the Hotel St. John nearly every day around two o'clock in the afternoon. Most days, Jean-Claude is already there, ensconced on the terrace with a glass of dark rum, chatting amiably with the staff or pensively smoking a cigar as he waits. When she arrives, she kisses him discreetly before settling down for a drink. The hotel is rather unassuming, but it sits just steps from the busy east end of Calle 23, known as La Rampa, and blocks from the historic University of Havana, and as such it has become a haven for tourists and foreign students who come here for strong coffee and cold beer. After an hour or so, Yakelín and Jean-Claude walk away together, hand in hand.

This same routine has been going on for more than two years now, since the day Yakelín first met Jean-Claude, walking along Calle 23 with a friend. She was twenty-one years old, living in a small flat with her mother, father, brother, two sisters, aunt, uncle, two cousins, and grandmother. After spending her teenage years at a boarding school in the countryside, she had elected not to continue to university and was back in Havana with her family. Like so many others, her family worked hard to make ends meet, and Yakelín was looking for ways to lighten the burden. Not long after they met, Jean-Claude made her a proposition.

"He suggested," she told me, "that since I was struggling to get by [*en la lucha*], you know, he suggested that I no longer be in the streets [looking for leads on work, food, clothes] and that he was going to help me solve my problems [*resolver mis problemas*]. And since then, he's my boyfriend."

Jean-Claude is married, but Yakelín says that in spite of that they have a "formal relationship." She lives in a comfortable casa particular, for which he pays, and they spend every afternoon together. As a retiree, Jean-Claude lives more or less permanently in Cuba, leaving only to attend to his affairs in France and returning laden with gifts including clothing, jewelry, and even a television. He provides her with spending money and helps to support her family as well. She says she loves the independence he has given her, even though she readily acknowledges the implied contradiction: she has found her freedom in total dependence on him. Yakelín has no official work at present, because she feels that the meager salary is simply not worth the trouble.

They make a striking couple. Jean-Claude is a heavy-set Frenchman with thinning white hair, the quintessential European tourist with a gold chain showing through the loosened collar of his *guayabera* shirt, an ever present cigar, and a burgeoning self-assurance that suggests affluence and social status. Yakelín, on the other hand, is a slender, arrestingly beautiful young woman with espresso skin and hair that falls to her waist. She wears tight-fitting, stylish clothing and obscures her eyes with immense sunglasses, her many gold bangles jingling with each languid movement—the quintessential *cubanita*. It comes as no surprise, then, that they attract attention as a pair; indeed, she is frequently stopped by the police and asked for her identification when they are together, at which point Jean-Claude assures the officers that she is his girlfriend, not a jinetera, and need not concern them. Usually, they say, that works.

Jean-Claude, for his part, speaks often about the difficulties involved in pursuing a relationship with a Cuban woman as a foreigner—the bureaucratic and administrative hurdles that prevent Cubans and foreigners from cohabiting but also the constant attention from the police. He mentions briefly that he worries Yakelín will one day be arrested in his absence but then waves away the unwelcome thought like a bothersome fly.

"When they see us, when they see the age difference—me with a tourist—they think I'm a jinetera," she says, but that is one thing that Yakelín

Figure 8. A terrace in Havana, 13 February 2010. Photo by author.

is clear that she is not. She never went looking for a relationship with a tourist, she says, nor does she know many foreigners. While Claude's money has certainly profoundly improved her circumstances, she insists it is not central to their affective bond and that she is not seeking a way out of Cuba. She would like to see France, certainly, but she would miss Cuba far too much to leave it forever. Yakelín knows what her relationship looks like to outside observers, particularly given that she does not currently have a job, so she is very careful not to court trouble in other respects: she regularly attends her local CDR meetings and is a dues-paying member of the FMC. Beyond that, she wants nothing to do with politics. She does not see the point in even broaching the subject.

When asked about the future, Yakelín takes a moment to think, looking across the patio at Jean-Claude where he sits conversing with a friend a few tables away while we talk. "I would like to get married," she says with a wry smile. "But not to him. I love him very much, but unfortunately, he's already married. What I would like—what I would really like—is my own house. I like my independence, you know, and I want to be beholden to no one." She has no immediate plans for anything to change, though, and in the meantime she says she is happy spending her afternoons on the terrace of the Hotel St. John.

What had first drawn me to Yakelín and Jean-Claude was outside appearances: they could not have fit the stereotype of a jinetera and her foreign date better, but on closer examination they gave the impression of genuine and utter normality, despite their circumstances, which were atypical to say the least. Yakelín herself challenges commonly held ideas about who (or what) constitutes a jinetera. Her physical form is paradigmatic of the category—she is a young, attractive, very dark-skinned woman attired in designer clothes and elaborately manicured nails, which defy the income of the vast majority of Cubans—and this is brought all the more sharply into focus when she is seen alongside Jean-Claude. Outside observers regularly presuppose their relationship is purely transactional and devoid of genuine emotional attachment, basing this judgment on the assumption that money and love are antithetical, mutually repellent concepts—and that sex can occur only in the context of one (prostitution) or the other (a "real" relationship), and never the twain shall meet. Yakelín herself, however, is secure in her understanding of their relationship as genuine and affectionate. Claude supports her and pays her way in life, but she contends that he does this out of love for her and solidarity with her circumstances. Their relationship challenges the notion that any liaison between a Cuban (especially a Cuban woman of color) and a foreigner (especially a foreign white man) must necessarily be construed as jineterismo, in the sense of it being purely a financially interested relationship, or even prostitution.

To Yakelín, this relationship provides a better life and the freedom to spend her time as she wishes and with someone for whom she cares deeply. Her experience here is borne out by centuries of history wherein, for women, future financial well-being and security have been important factors, sometimes the determining factors, in choosing a partner. This certainly continues to be a salient theory in Cuba, where traditional machista understandings of gender roles persist and have been cast in ever more stark relief by the hardships of the Special Period. Though socialist ideology has long pushed for women's total inclusion in education and the workplace, with a great degree of success, it is nonetheless still quite common to hear beliefs from both men and women that in the absence of a partner who can support her a woman will quickly become destitute, not able—or, in some cases, willing—to subsist on her own earnings. Troubling as this revelation may be, it does nothing to diminish the affective bond that is both potentially and actually present in such relationships; indeed, Viviana Zelizer argues that, far from necessarily contaminating a loving relationship, financial support often plays an affirmative, reinforcing role: "money cohabits regularly with intimacy, even sustains it."[3]

The label "jinetera" is often applied from the outside, as a sort of judgment on the veracity or legitimacy of a pairing, but Yakelín does not feel it describes her experience at all. Her current relationship is stable and based on mutual affection, whereas jineteras are thought to be young women who specifically seek out yumas and who flit from one man to the next both frequently and easily.[4] Yakelín's story goes a long way toward demonstrating that there is no one type of woman who becomes romantically and sexually involved with a non-Cuban man. Her behavior and her relationship do not conform to the received knowledge on jineterismo as a sexual practice in Cuba.

None of this, of course, means that Yakelín is not regularly brought under the rubric of jineterismo by virtue of her physical appearance alone. She is regularly stopped by police officers for identification checks, and she and Jean-Claude have struggled to find permanent accommodation where they can legally reside together. When I spoke with her, Yakelín seemed confident and unafraid, even flippant, which was not something I saw in many of my interviewees, but it became clear as the conversation wore on that this came down to Jean-Claude: he was providing for her for the foreseeable future, and he was willing to own their relationship, at least thus far. Her careful observance of some important tenets of Cuban socialism, such as the CDR meetings and membership in the FMC, is also noteworthy. Being with a foreigner and not having a state-sector job both count as strikes against her, so it becomes increasingly important to tick all the other relevant boxes. While she did not lay claim to any explicit or transformational political views, even seeming to have despaired of the possibility, Yakelín is a savvy actor within the current political system and acutely aware of her precarious position. Her experience is marked in particular by her race and her gender, and by assumptions about her sexuality based on these factors, which together ensure that her relationship will never be taken at face value and will continue to place roadblocks in her path.

NEVER FOUND THAT PERSON

Nadia's experience has been markedly different from Yakelín's. She grew up in a small town in Pinar del Río province, west of Havana. At the height of the Special Period, she says, her family subsisted on nothing more than potatoes, as staples like rice, bread, meat, eggs, and beans disappeared from the shelves of shops. It was on a day such as this, with nothing to eat, that Nadia was hitchhiking to school when an Italian tourist stopped to pick her up. They chatted along the way, and eventually he asked her to go out with him in the evening, and she agreed. The two of them spent the night in a casa particular that he had rented for the occasion, and he slipped a clutch of U.S. dollars into her pocket as they said goodbye. She was fifteen.

Two years later, Nadia went to Pinar del Río city with a friend, where they met another foreign tourist, this time from Spain, and the three went to bed together. In both cases, Nadia says, she never made any request for money. "I wanted to do it, but not for money. I never asked, but they gave it to me, like a gift," she says. "And I didn't say no. Who would say no? I was desperate. I was about to start college."

The Spaniard returned the next year, while Nadia was studying in Havana, but she told him at the end of that visit that she didn't want to see him again. "He was a nice man, more or less," she says of him now. "But he used us."

She tried to turn her focus to her studies and her future career, but a student living allowance of only $100 MN per month—less than US$4 at that time—meant that financial security was never far from her mind. Delighted as she was with her studies in English language and literature, Nadia knew she couldn't survive that way, so she did what some Cuban university students do: she entertained the advances of foreign men, and in exchange she got restaurant meals and gifts of cash or clothes. Eventually, she met another Italian traveler, who became a longer-term companion, taking her with him to Varadero, Trinidad, and Cienfuegos.

"He was here for a month, and we were girlfriend and boyfriend. We were a couple. We had an arrangement. I felt more confident and . . . just *better* with him, you know? He knew how to treat me," she says.

At the end of his month in Cuba, Nadia's Italian friend asked her to come to Europe with him. She refused, she says, simply because she was afraid of taking such a giant leap. These days, she sometimes regrets that choice, but her Italian companion was married, and she wasn't sure how much she could depend on him, moving to Italy as a mistress rather than a wife.

Soon, with pressures to make ends meet mounting, Nadia began dressing up and going out in the evenings with a friend from university to places like the Malecón and Quinta Avenida, to actively seek out tourists' attentions. These were mostly brief interactions, she says, and the money they received was used to pay for the girls' food and housing while they were students.

"We were students, but we needed the money. We were together, and I wasn't scared." So the two of them continued this way for more than a year, studying during the week and going out in search of foreign men on weekends. Even in all this time, she says, she never had any trouble with the police, a lucky fact that she credits to her fair complexion, her light brown curls, and her student card, which were enough to convince officers performing random checks and sweeps that she was not "that" kind of girl.

Once she had finally completed her studies, Nadia became an English teacher, but only three months into her career of choice, she received the news that her stepfather had passed away. She found herself back in Pinar del Río, teaching at the local school and helping to support her mother. Yet another Italian man appeared in her life, and Nadia entered into a second longer-term attachment, but all the while she hid the relationship from her mother, even as his contributions helped to support her entire family.

"I told her that I had a Cuban boyfriend with money, that he had family abroad," she says. That was the last time she spent time with a foreigner.

Seven years later, as we sit in a seedy fast-food restaurant in noisy Centro Habana, Nadia fidgets, turning an empty pop can over and over in her hands as she thinks back on those years. She has long since quit teaching, having damaged her vocal chords, and has moved back to Havana to try to make things work with her Cuban partner, bringing with her their eight-month-old baby and her five-year-old daughter from another relationship. Her Cuban partners have each known a little of her past, but neither know as much as I now do; her family and friends at home in Pinar del Río, however, still know nothing, and Nadia intends to keep it that way.

"I think I need to see a shrink, to let it all go. I wonder if there was another way to make money, but I had to finish college," she says, shaking her head. "I had low self-esteem back then. It stays with me."

She tells me that she has found various ways of making money, from taking photos of tourists along the Malecón to her current job as a horse-and-buggy driver in the old city, but making ends meet is still a constant challenge. Though years have passed and she no longer goes looking for foreign men, considering herself too old at thirty, Nadia still dreams of finding someone who can remove her and her children from financial struggles.

"All that time, I just wanted to get out, but I just didn't find that person. I didn't want to leave with someone who knew me like that. I wanted a real boyfriend, but I needed the money too badly to look for that. But it's so hard here. For everything. I want to go to church and pray to find someone, or to accept this life. I don't understand why people smoke and drink here, when there's no money for food, but then I do understand because it's an escape."

She sits silently thinking, and I'm loath to interrupt her thoughts. The conversation hasn't been an easy one. Her memories seem to trouble her, but the present seems no more comforting. She looks up finally, and, with a sadness that belies the determination of her words, she says, "I'm not willing to live and die here."

As I walked away from that interview, having left Nadia with her partner and their daughter, I reflected on those final words. They spoke both to her personal experiences and to the way so many young Cubans felt about their lives and the intense pressure they felt to either resign

Figure 9. Avenida Zanja, Havana, near where I met Nadia, 29 July 2010. Photo by author.

themselves to austerity and accept the life laid out for them, or to resist and carve out something new, as yet incomplete and unknown. Forming relationships and making connections were ways to access opportunities, not just for financial security, but for a different kind of life—and this was true whether or not those connections were sexual. Like Yakelín, many of Nadia's relationships defy the neat opposition between love and money that Zelizer and Cabezas discuss. In fact, Cabezas argues that even deliberately short-term relationships operating with implicit financial goals cannot be reduced to simplistic, transactional affairs in Cuba.[5] Derrick Hodge also takes up this point, arguing that "there is no clear boundary between sex work and recreational sex" in Cuba, or in many comparable locales for sex tourism.[6] The emotional/affective facet of even the most fleeting sexual encounters between Cubans and foreigners is not so much feigned as it is a means of maintaining the open-endedness of the interaction and the possibility for it to lead to a more serious relationship. Nadia, like many other young women, knew she was seeking out these men in order to alleviate her immediate economic struggles, but she kept an open mind to possibility, much like any dating scenario.

Nadia's story stands in stark opposition to Yakelín's in one regard: she was more than willing to call what she did *jineteando,* and yet she was never treated as a jinetera. She managed to maneuver through the world of dating and hooking up with yumas for many years without ever finding herself in serious trouble with the police. Nadia says that she was rarely subjected to random checks or asked to produce identification, and when she was, her status as a student and a white woman established her as a morally irreproachable "good girl." Her whiteness, along with the social capital attached to university study, served to absolve her of suspicion and to recast her attachments to tourists as innocent rather than degenerate.

In Havana, where the large university borders on some of the most heavily touristed zones in the country, thousands of Cuban students come into proximity with foreigners every day. Observed in public with foreigners—that is, with white men—young white women are assumed to be in dating relationships, while young women of color are deemed to be engaging in jineterismo. Where whiteness stands as a marker for purity of morals and intentions and even sexual passivity, black and mulata women are inscribed with greed and promiscuity. "Put another way," notes Cabezas, "desire and affection are defined as 'lighter' and prostitution as 'darker,' effectively racialising the entire process."[7] Thus Nadia was able to carry on longer as a self-proclaimed jinetera, unmolested by police scrutiny, than many young women of color who claim no such title.

Nadia's reasons for seeking out foreign men are clear, as are her feelings about it. Grinding poverty, her own and her family's, was the catalyst for becoming what she calls a jinetera. The relationships she had, ranging from one night to several months in duration, meant momentary escape from adversity through the gifts of cash and goods she received. On top of that, they gave her the ability to continue pursuing what she still considers her calling: languages and teaching. Today, she would no longer call herself a jinetera, but her desire to meet a foreign man who could make her life easier has only increased. In Nadia's eyes, spending time with foreign visitors to the island meant freedom, an escape both from real adversity in her life and from the stress of confronting that adversity. Nadia did not have much to say about politics, but she repeatedly articulated a deep dissatisfaction with the current state of affairs in Cuba, a dissatisfaction that resonates across the island and bears deep political implications. Whether or not she would have found the happiness she sought in leaving Cuba as a foreigner's wife cannot be known, but this desire alone speaks volumes about her experiences.

LA TIERRA DE LOS MANGOS BAJITOS

Lili has always had one goal: to leave Cuba. When I first met her, however, this wasn't so readily apparent. She was flirting with my Australian friend, Danny, and we were among friends, having drinks at a bar on Plaza de Dolores in Santiago, laughing and chatting. Several of the other tourists with us that night marveled at how sweet and guileless she seemed, totally without ulterior motive, a stark contrast to the girls who regularly approached them. She's the real deal, they said.

The following day, at the beach, I saw a flash of that resolve when I told Lili about my research. She propped herself up on one elbow in order to look at me directly and said, "We all want to leave Cuba. These girls just want their papers. The men—it's like they're buying your freedom, like they're buying you. Or at least, that's how I see it." Then that determined look disappeared again, replaced by gaiety, as our friends returned from the water.

Today, it's just Lili and me, facing each other across a wobbly table on the patio of El Piropo. Her beautiful spiral curls are pulled back tightly from her face, and that intensity has returned. As she begins to tell me about her life and her world, a very confident and well-spoken persona emerges. Lili is twenty-five. She was born in Santiago de Cuba and has lived there her entire life, with her mother, two brothers, uncle, and grandmother together under one roof. She did preuniversity study but wound up enrolling in social work at a local college instead, as it would land her a comparatively good salary of $475 MN—around US$19—per month within a year's time. What is more, she is able to travel around Cuba to attend conventions and training sessions. Still, Lili is cynical about her work.

"I really don't like it anymore," she says. "I work with people who have a lot of problems, but I don't have the power to resolve anything. It's out of my hands."

She started studying English two years ago so that she could eventually get a job in a restaurant, where the pay—and the tips—are much better. Waitressing, though, is not Lili's long-term plan. She cuts straight to the chase without my asking.

"I don't know too many people who've had relationships with foreign men, because when I go out, I go out alone. Me, yes, I've dated foreigners. Not many, but a few. It's normal here, because of our situation [*por la necesidad que hay*] and because there are no other options. If you turn to *jineteando*—or to stealing or what have you—it's because of the desperate situation we're in [*la necesidad que hay*]. Young people, they want to have clothes, you know? They want to go out, to eat, everything. And here there's nothing.

"In my case, yes, I'm looking for a foreign man because I want to leave this country. That's my case. I'm not looking for someone who comes for a vacation, has some fun with me, gives me money, and then leaves. No, no, no—nothing like that. I want something serious, I want him to fall in love with me—you know what I mean? I want him to take me back with him." She taps the table with each word.

What about love? Is that important for her as well?

She laughs cynically. "Look, I would really, really like to wind up falling in love with him, too. I would really like that. I don't want him to buy me clothes or a cell phone, or to fix up my house. I want to leave Cuba—that's all I want. That's my objective. When I meet a foreign man, if there isn't anything that attracts me personally to him, then I can't. I won't even consider it."

Now for the big surprise: she's already engaged. All of this time we had been speaking in hypotheticals, when her plans to move out of Cuba were already well under way. My thoughts turn to Danny, with whom she had spent the night the weekend before, but I don't want her to clam up. I bite my lip and let her continue. Her fiancé is a thirty-two-year-old Canadian who comes to visit every month and calls every day. Lili lights up, that bubbly persona returning as she describes him: he's tall, a bit heavy-set, but attractive and attentive. Cuban men, she pauses to point out, are not generally to her liking; they're unfaithful, aggressive, even violent, and only interested in money, she says. Foreign men are different, in her view; they hold the door and let you pass through first. She quickly steers the conversation back to her fiancé.

"He's the best," she says. "I know that when I move to Canada, what I want to do is build my life with him. I don't want to move to Canada and then leave him, you know? I'm serious about this. I want peace and security, and he can give me those, so I'll stay with him. I want to get married and to work and to have a simple life. He worries that I'll leave him, but when we get married, it will be serious business." With a twinkle in her eye, she adds sardonically, "I fully intend to die there.

"I'm a little afraid to move to Canada, because I'm not going to see all the people I love here. The most important thing for me is to leave this country and to help my family. It hurts me to know that they have no way of getting ahead in life. It hurts me when there's nothing to eat in my house. Every day, I ask God to help me leave this country so I can help my family. I don't have a husband here, not a boyfriend, nothing. My one purpose is to leave Cuba and, bit by bit, to get my family out if I can.

"But I never approached men on my own. I met my fiancé when we were introduced. There are different types of women out there, working to get by and to support their families. I see the same ones every day in the same places, one day with one guy, the next day with another. I don't know anyone who does that, because my friends are all social workers and university students, and they're mostly married with kids. But then again, some of those girls are made to do it by their Cuban men."

She has been speaking rapidly, punctuating her thoughts with jabs on the table's surface and in the air. I've barely spoken a word, but at this point I decide to press her. I ask about her experiences with the police. Has she ever been targeted for identification checks or called a jinetera?

"No, never, but that is because I have always been very careful, you know? My fiancé and I don't go out often, and when we do—well, how do I put this?—he's the same color as me. Mixed race [*mezclado*]. He looks Cuban. As long as he doesn't speak, they think he's Cuban. That was important to me."

I feel suddenly and ridiculously sheltered, for the simple fact of never having had to consider such obstacles to a relationship. Lili is well aware of the risk she runs in being seen with foreigners, and she has taken calculated steps and conditioned her behavior to mediate that risk. She mentions the registry books, which every casa particular is required to keep and in which every guest is required to be registered, and how these are frequently used to track young women's activities. If a woman's name appears on the books of any casa particular alongside different men, Lili tells me, she could very easily be sent to prison for prostitution. She shakes her head in disbelief.

"What bothers me most in this country is that men—old, really old men—come here looking for young girls, wanting to pay them $5 CUC, even $3 CUC. They know how desperate people are here. They know they can't do that in their own countries. Everyone does what they have to do, and if someone wants to sleep with a foreigner for $10 CUC, fine. No man will ever buy me like that, not even if I were dying of hunger. They don't have enough money, frankly. I'm worth way more than $20, $50, $100 CUC. But, like Los Aldeanos say, this is the land of low-hanging fruit [*esto es la tierra de los mangos bajitos*].[8] Our situation is bad, and people are desperate. Everything here is a lie."

I barely said a word while I sat at that table with Lili. She had so much to say that I didn't really need to say anything at all. She was very explicit in her political views. She felt the Cuban system had rotted away in its fundamental values, that those principles exist today only as a smoke screen to conceal the self-interest of leaders. On the state measures to control jineterismo, Lili's thoughts were patently unambiguous: young women are punished for taking those limited options that are available to them. This, she felt, is both unfair and counterproductive, since it does nothing to address the roots of the issue or to give these women other means of addressing their pressing financial need.

The knowledge that her race renders her suspect has conditioned Lili's choices, precluding her from spending time in certain parts of her city, even causing her to keep to the relative safety of her own home. She has gone so far as to consider racial markers in choosing her partner, whose skin tone does not immediately identify him as a foreigner in the eyes of most Cubans. Lili's experience is far from unique in this regard. On the street in Cuba, a woman of color seen with a white man is assumed to be a jinetera. It is also a broadly held conviction by many Cubans that women of color are less appropriate choices as marriage partners and thus that white men seen with women of color must be foreign and with them only for sex. One can do this with female bodies of color, this logic implies, whereas white women require more commitment. Race thus plays a pivotal role for many who seek to identify Cuban-foreign pairings.

Clearly, for Lili, a relationship with a foreign man means freedom she could not otherwise have: the freedom to leave Cuba's borders, to work at a more fulfilling job, to travel, and to provide for her family in the way she has so obviously always wanted to do. It means a better chance at financial security and peace of mind. She challenges the stereotypes about young women who pursue relationships with foreigners in many ways: she is educated, she holds down a regular job, and she does not angle for gifts or cash from the men she has met. Her expectations for an as yet unknown life in Canada are modest. Lili is intelligent and articulate, and although she actively and specifically sought out foreign boyfriends, she entered into those relationships, she says, as she would into any other—as equals. She felt her freedom had to be bought, but she was willing to enter into that type of bargain only with someone she considered to be as worthy as she was.

The picture that Yakelín, Nadia, and Lili paint of this phenomenon of sexual jineterismo is varied, uncertain, and nebulous at best. The jinetera clearly does not exist. There is no essential category of individuals with any demonstrable similarities or common characteristics that explain their behavior and their ideological impertinence. What is more, the meanings attached by young Cubans to their relationships with foreigners cannot be accurately assumed or determined from the outside. Freedom of movement, and even emigration, are important goals, but they are not universal. Financial well-being plays a prominent role, certainly, but not for everyone. There are those who believe, for whatever reason, that European and North American men make better partners, those who see an opportunity to learn about the outside world and practice their language skills, and those who simply made an unplanned and unpresumptuous connection across cultural divides. Zelizer argues that certain processes occur in the formation of relationships across the board:

> First, we construct the most coherent set of social worlds we can by negotiating and adopting meaningful ties to other people, but differentiating

sharply among the rights, obligations, transactions, and meanings that belong to different ties. Second, we mark the differences between ties with distinctive names, symbols, practices, and media of exchange.[9]

Yakelín, Nadia, and Lili all spoke of the active, delicate process involved in differentiating their relationships from other, less acceptable forms, the heavy burden of assumptions and stigma always at their backs. This process of differentiation has itself become a site of contestation, when it comes to race, as these three women's stories show, but also when it comes to gender.

WHAT'S YOUR SECRET?

To understand the way gender plays into the image of the jinetera, there seemed only one logical way to proceed: talk to a jinetero. As I mentioned above, the word *jinetero* can denote a range of roles in the tourist-oriented shadow economy, from acting as a tout for casa particulares and paladares to selling black-market rum to acting as a companion to bewildered foreigners. For this, however, I wanted to speak to someone who was also involved in the sexual-affective economy, the way jineteras are understood to be. Through a string of contacts, one leading to the next, I met Ricky.

Ricky never stands still, not even for a minute. He also displays one characteristic that I found rare among my interviewees: he's fastidiously punctual each and every time we meet. As I walk down Calzada de Infanta toward Café Bim Bom, I can see him outside, on his own, salsa dancing in a solitary reverie while he waits.

As we begin, I tell Ricky that I will be changing his name in my book as a safety precaution. He laughs, grabbing my voice recorder, and clearly enunciates his full real name into the microphone. Setting the recorder back on the table, he smiles evenly and motions for me to go ahead. Ricky has nothing to fear. Now the stories and opinions start to flow from him like water. At twenty-nine, Ricky is on his second marriage. He has lived in Vedado his entire life, but that has not kept him from building a network of friends and acquaintances that stretches around the globe. I met him through his wife, who is English, who said herself that he had a story to tell.

Figure 10. The Malecón, near Café Bim Bom where I
interviewed Ricky, 20 March 2010. Photo by author.

"I was working with the government two years as *electricista*—electri-
cian. After, I find the money isn't worth it, so I find my own life in the
black market, you know, selling cigars, doing little things. I was a jinetero
too, yeah? I was with a few—or plenty—of foreigners before. At the beginning, I was working in the market near to Hotel Cohiba, and there it
wasn't necessary to go out [to meet foreign women]. I was good there,
yeah?" He laughs heartily. "But after that, I was going myself out to find
them. Different places—most of the time it was in Vedado because, like I
said before, I live in Vedado, but yeah, sometimes it was in Habana Vieja.
All the places where you can go to try to pick up foreigners—Casa de la

Música, the beach, other places. When I was twenty-three years old, I got into a relationship with a Cuban girl, but at the same time I was still doing my thing, you know, with foreigners—selling cigars, being with girls for money."

He seems to be enjoying himself supremely, bobbing his head and grinning while he talks.

"At the beginning, I was pretending to be in love, you know, and taking a piece, you know? That's what's said. I never robbed no one—that's for sure, I'll tell you. Most of the time, I was trying to find girls from Europe—Spain, Italy. Scandinavian girls too, like Norway and Finland. It was sex and money, and I really did like the girls. At that time, I was doing whoever. Some of them just wanted to go to bed, but others, it was like, 'I want to fall in love, I want to have something.'"

Some of those women kept in touch, and some visited time and time again, bringing Ricky gifts from abroad. He paints a fairly rosy picture, so I can't help but ask if it really came so easily, and in reply he laughs merrily.

"Was it easy? As everything, it was easy once I had the tools. When I say tools, I mean clothes, a bit of money to go to nice places. In this society, the way you look—that's how you're going to find things. If you're a jinetero and you look like crap, you're going to find crap," he says frankly. Then, with a smile, he adds, "But if you look cool, then you're going to find something cool!"

Back then, he says, it was all about leaving Cuba. "At the beginning—because now I have retired," he grins. "Yes, at the beginning, I was trying anything. At that time, I would leave with anybody. Not anymore, though—now, it would have to be with the right girl."

Today, Ricky is waiting to find out if he can get the necessary visas to make the move to the United Kingdom with his wife, Sarah, a thirty-two-year-old U.K. citizen. They met at Club 1830 in Vedado, a popular spot where tourists and locals alike go to dance salsa, a passion of Ricky's, and to mingle. Ricky was already married at that time—to another English woman, this one nineteen years his senior, in fact—and thus already "retired" from jineterismo, as he puts it. But with his then-wife out of the country, he pursued Sarah, and the two began a relationship.

"So, yes, I was cheating on my wife, that's obvious. What can I say? I was lying to Sarah too, when she asked if I had a wife. I would say no—

typical Cuban! It was a secret for a while, but when Sarah found out, she forgave me after maybe four months."

A protracted and unhappy breakup with Ricky's first wife ensued, but with all of that in the past, Ricky is optimistic about his future with Sarah. "I move in September," he says, beaming impishly. "If I don't find another girl first and decide to get married again! I'm married, but I'm not dead—that's a typical Cuban sentence. If we're with just one girl, it doesn't work. I think we have that in the blood."

I feel like I have to ask if he expects the same from Sarah, and Ricky's response is unsurprising and yet at the same time reflective in its own way: "It's quite complicated to explain, because we are *machista* here. We want to be with so many girls, but we want to have one girl of our own, and she's not allowed to have anybody else. I know that I'm cheating on her many times, but if I find out that she cheats on me once, I go mad." He says he thinks women only cheat as retribution for their partners' adultery. "Cuban men can't—I'm sorry for be rude, but—Cuban men can't be keeping it in their pants for very long."

From where he sits now, as a retired jinetero, Ricky says he's happy with his past, but he's come a long way. "At the beginning, I was comfortable with everything, because it was fun, because I met so many people that was interesting at the time, people who has been every single places I couldn't go as a Cuban, you know, with a Cuban salary. It was a bit greedy—only about money, to make money for myself and for my family. And after, when I was retired, I realized that all this was, like, bullshit. All this about money . . . I mean, you can have everything and not be content. That's what I think. But of course, I realized this after going all the places I want to go and staying in all the hotels I wanted. I feel alright about it—I feel fine! Sure, I was in some situations where I lied, because to do all these things, you have to lie. I feel bad now for that, not at the time. And plenty women knew exactly the story, you know? I think, looking back, it was a part of my life, and I don't like people to just tell me things. I like to experience things for myself and after decide if it was good or not."

I ask him about his family and friends. Did his being a jinetero affect his place in their lives at all?

"At the beginning, when I worked in the market, and it was girls and girls and girls, my mother noticed it and she say to me, 'Stop it,' but I said to her,

'It's my life.' When I got married the first time, she didn't like the idea because my ex was older than me—it's true, she was nineteen years older, but she looked good." Here, he pauses to show me a photo of her that he still keeps on his cellphone, bobbing his eyebrows suggestively and watching for my reaction. "I like women older than me. I don't like young girls. I dated women mostly three, four, five years older than me. Not old, though. Never any, you know, hippopotamus—no, no, no. But my mother say to me, 'You going to marry this girl, and yeah, she's pretty, but what about your future?' She thought we couldn't have kids. But she likes my new wife a lot.

"And my friends? I'm not the kind of person with a lot of friends. I'll be out all the time on my own. I do what I want. I never care what people think. I don't care what people say. It's like, some people look at you, if you're a Cuban and you're speaking English, and your friends, they'll be just like, 'Oh, he try to be better than us—he has plenty of foreign women, plenty of friends.' That's what I think. I don't want to make myself sound big, but I think it's jealousy. I didn't do nothing to them, but you can get, like, dirty looks—you know what I mean? From girls, from guys. And the girls, they don't like it at all. For them, it's like, women—foreigners—steal the men. They don't like at all, Cuban guys with foreigners."

He shrugs. I scan my notes. Ricky is so confident, so flippant about everything, that I'm sure I can start asking him more pointed questions. The logical place to begin seems to be by asking about his interactions with the police, so I press him on his experiences with the random stops and identification checks that seem to play such a prominent role in the lives of young Cubans of color. Ricky has very European-looking features but tightly curled, close-cropped hair and dark skin, so I'm willing to venture a guess that he's had more than his share of unsolicited police attention. He smiles like he knows what I'm thinking, daring me to ask, so I do.

"Yes, of course, plenty of times. But I tell you now, they don't stop me anymore! I think they know I'm quite verbal, and they know I'm married now. It's not like I'm famous, but around here and in Habana Vieja, they know me. Before, though, yes. They ask for ID, say, 'What you doing with foreigner?' That kind of thing. The thing with them is, it's not a problem— it's not a problem at all!—if you're a Cuban and you're walking with a foreigner. You just have to say to them, 'She's my girlfriend' or 'She's a friend to my wife' or 'I have a wife already' or something. If you have a

document, like me—I'm married to a foreigner—it's not a problem at all."
He pulls out the battered photocopy of his marriage certificate that he carries with him at all times. "If you don't have this, they can take you to the
police station. They can put you under arrest. Even if she's your friend,
yeah? They can do that."

So having a sexual relationship with a foreigner makes it all okay?

"Exactly."

But why does it matter to them if you're walking down the street with a
foreigner who's just a friend?

"They're afraid about what the Cuban going to say, because at the end
of the day, foreigners and Cubans, they're going to end up in political conversation—this kind of stuff. At the same time, they think they protect the
foreigners, but they don't. They just harass the Cubans."

Is it different when it's a Cuban girl and a foreign man? How do people
feel about jineteras? Ricky pauses to think for a moment before replying.

"That's a really good question. Here's the thing. Women, sometimes, or
most of the time, they have kids. They want to improve their lives. I think
women, really, they have to do more. It's a harder situation. Women have
to do whatever the [foreign] men want. If you're a beginner, if you're just
starting out, you have to take whatever. The beginners is going to the sort
of places they can afford themselves, like Casa de la Música. The professionals, though, have some money in their pockets so they can dress a little
better, they can go to a bit more expensive places, and they can choose
their men. And there are more beginner jineteras than jineteros. You
know why I think so? Because most of them, they come from the countryside, yeah? People from Havana too, of course, they do the same thing, but
most of them come from the countryside. So I mean, the guys from the
countryside—they came to be policemen. They have that choice but not
the girls. The girls come to Havana and sometimes they're with foreigners
right away, but sometimes they're with Cuban men just for a place to stay.
They have more need.

"Me, I never had need. It was a way to get money. I was wearing nice
clothes all the time. I wanted to go to nice places. I was looking for fun. I
used the money for my family, but I had all the time food at my home, you
know, and my mother was supporting me. I did it for greed—that's a better word than 'need.'"

What about with the police? Are the jineteras treated differently than the jineteros? Again, Ricky considers the question carefully. Eventually, he tells me that young men who are arrested in tourist areas will usually be accused of harassing tourists; women, on the other hand, could face the same charges, but particularly if it's not the first time, they could be detained for prostitution based on suspicion alone.

What is jineterismo, then? Is it a crime?

"No, I don't think so. I think, like, everyone can do with their bodies what they decide when they don't do anything bad to the whole people. When you're not hurting anyone, and I mean not just physically, but yeah. I'm not a political activist. I just tell the truth. If I see something's green and I know it's green, why do I have to say it's orange just because they say me to?"

Ricky tells me that he believes the Revolution changed Cuba in important ways, that it was a response to genuine grievances and profound injustices—he lists lack of health care, illiteracy, and racial inequality on his fingers—but he feels that now many of the Revolution's gains are rapidly eroding while others never materialized at all.

"I can make you a good example. I have a friend now who is in Hospital Cira García, which is the foreign hospital. It's all clean, and you have to pay. If you're a Cuban, you're not allowed to go there—you go to Calixto García. For god's sake, it's like . . . fucking *cucarachas* [cockroaches], everything dirty. Everyone says, yes, you are really equal. You are free to go anywhere, but you go to 23 and Malecón, and you're going to see, we're not equal. And if you come to Varadero? Aye aye aye aye aye! They say, 'What are you doing here? No, no, no!'" He snaps his fingers in the air. "So you leave. It's like, 'We're not racist.' Oh, right, yeah. And the people know, and they don't do anything about it. Like me—I talk and talk and talk with people like you, but I don't do anything either."

Ricky's smile has faded, and he raps his knuckles against the table in what appears to be frustration. "In any country, no one's perfect, any system isn't perfect. All of them are after the money, and after that, the people. Politicians—they're all the same. You know the CDRs? I don't participate in any CDRs at all. They come and they say, 'Come,' and I say no. They say, 'Oh, but maybe in the future,' and I say no. I don't care."

And when he gets out of Cuba? What will he do then?

"I think I'll just be making my life. I want to study and work. I'm going to move on with my life. I want to be a plumber. I want a car. I want to have kids in two years' time. I'm quite happy to live in my wife's town. That's my dream—quite simple."

I ask if he has any predictions for Cuba once he's gone, but he seems cynical about change. "I hear that story from nine years old. It's going to change, going to change, going to change. I think it's going to change, but it's going to be at least ten years. I won't say five—I give it ten."

As we finish the interview, I feel badly that it had to end on such a cynical note, having begun so cheerily, but Ricky seems unfazed, jiving to the music as we step out into the beating sun. We haven't walked ten steps from the café, though, when a man in the now-familiar gray and navy police uniform steps out and blocks our path. He gestures wordlessly to Ricky, with no need to explain what he wants, and Ricky blithely produces his *carné de identidad* along with the copy of his marriage certificate but making sure to note aloud that I am not his wife. The officer scrutinizes both carefully, then glances up to assess me with equal interest, clearly assuming I'm Ricky's girlfriend. Then, shaking his head as he hands Ricky back his documents, he says, "What's your secret, man?"

If I hadn't heard it so clearly, I might not have believed it. Ricky tells me it happens all the time. We walk on in silence for a few blocks up Calle 23 before parting ways. For days afterward, I find myself returning to that moment with Ricky and the cop. His marriage to a foreigner, any foreigner, seemed to validate interactions with any other non-Cuban in the eyes of the officer, and what is more, this particular officer envied Ricky's perceived good fortune. The officer also clearly assumed (without evidence) that there must have been a sexual relationship between Ricky and me—why else would a woman (especially a white foreign one) walk out of a café with a man (especially a black Cuban one)?—which was ironic, because Ricky became a good friend and was the only one of my male contacts who never once propositioned me. He was an easygoing and amiable person who respected not just my boundaries, but those of everyone else around him. To this police officer, however, we were both easily identifiable types, and he knew who and what we were at a glance: a tourist and her beach boy.

This experience with Ricky was borne out by many similar instances with male Cuban friends and contacts: by telling an officer we were in a romantic relationship, or even holding hands as a ruse, we were able to carry on unmolested. Some police officers even seemed embarrassed about having bothered us. This is not to say that the relationship between the police and young male Afro-Cubans is a harmonious one; in fact, the reverse is generally true. Young men are stopped constantly for "random" identification checks and general harassment, their race serving as a marker for criminality and ill intent. Some of the male Cubans I met refused to pass through the heavily touristed neighborhoods of Havana and Santiago, where the police were always stationed at nearly every corner, because of the danger of arbitrary arrest for loitering or some other unfounded allegation. Most would not even attempt to enter the large hotels around La Rampa, knowing that they would be turned away by the security guards for the mere fact of their appearance. Claiming a sexual relationship with me, or any other foreign friend, acted as a shield against that kind of discrimination and harassment; however, the marked difference between judgments of men's and women's sexual liaisons with foreigners is striking. For women, sexuality is the problem, whereas for men, sexuality is the solution to the problem.

This difference was also evident in the confidence that young men like Ricky showed in speaking to me. He and others like him talked openly, proudly, almost gleefully of sex and money, and in that way young heterosexual men's engagement in the sexual-affective economy brings to mind Robin Kelley's notion of "play-labor."[10] Virtually none of the men demonstrated any fear that talking to me could put them at any risk. By contrast, getting interviews with young women was often very difficult, and many were anxious about speaking to me or being seen with me. Sexuality for young male Cubans is celebrated in a way that it simply is not for their female counterparts; its presence absolves men of suspicion of selling counterfeit cigars or cheap rum, touting paladares, even pickpocketing or other illegal activities that are seen to be men's purview in the shadow economy.

The jinetero, as a young Afro-Cuban man who dates foreigners for material gain, is a known entity in the tourist zones of Cuba, but his activities are not met with the same censure as those of the jineteras. This, as Kemala Kempadoo notes, may be because young men who pursue foreign (white) women are working to affirm and vindicate black masculinity. In

having promiscuous sex and seeking out liaisons with women, and especially white women, the so-called jineteros are doing what men *ought* to
do, whereas the jineteras are betraying their properly passive, demure role
in the sexual system.[11] As Ricky said, men are expected and even incited to
be unfaithful, licentious, and sexually aggressive; their inability to "keep it
in their pants" is accepted and normalized. Women's infidelity, when it
does happen, is read as reprisal against their partners rather than their
own expression of sexual desire and agency.

Ricky's experience of jineterismo, as well as his thoughts on women, say
something in turn about women's place in the world. He remarked that he
felt young women had less choice when it came to finding a livelihood
outside state-sector employment; men could migrate from the countryside to hustle in some other capacity, or even become police officers, but
women's only valuable asset was their sexuality. This attitude reflects what
Ian Lumsden argues: that is, despite rhetoric and real progress to the contrary, many (women and men) still believe that a woman's true value lies
in her body—her beauty, her sexuality, even her fertility.[12]

My friend Natalia echoed this sentiment when she told me one day that
Cuban men have it easier once they move abroad with their foreign para-
mours. "They can leave their yuma once they get there, if they want, and
go make a new life for themselves. But the girls—what are they going to
do?" Natalia saw men as agents in their own lives who can walk away from
a relationship, or at least feel able to do so; women, on the other hand,
need a relationship and would be destitute without one in the very same
situation. By this logic, relationships are a woman's way in the world. This
could, of course, be for a number of reasons, but the effect is the same.
Whether it is because women genuinely cannot (or believe they cannot)
make their own way in the world or whether other people simply think
that is the case, the effect is a circular process by which women's value is
located in their sexualized bodies, but they are blamed for embracing that
belief to their own advantage.

It bears noting that this imagining of women and of jineteras differs
from the lived experience. While Natalia worried about the fate of women
who go abroad, many of the women I interviewed said their liaisons with
foreigners constituted a deliberate choice to have better lives and relationships. Indeed, Lili mentioned that she considered foreigners "gentlemen"

who opened doors for her and treated her well. Valle writes about a woman named Paddy who acted as a jinetera along with three of her friends and told him, "We were doing it as a kind of revenge against men. The other three had also been screwed over [*cuerneadas*] by their husbands and one of them had a little boy, just like me."[13] Paddy says she dates foreigners for the freedom it gives her, because none of them oblige her to do anything she does not want to do.[14] Ana, one of my own interviewees who will appear again later, had a bleaker way of expressing her preference for foreign men, one that speaks to her own experience of sexism in Cuba: "Foreign men don't hit." These instances show how pursuing sexual-affective relationships within a machista society, where some women feel their possibilities for a better life are restricted, can be a form of resistance to patriarchy and to the gendered strictures of a machista society.

The image of the jinetera as the bearer of deviant sexuality and the seducer of men excludes (and thus, to an extent, protects) men—from the stigma of prostitution or promiscuity, from police scrutiny or other disciplinary measures aimed at correcting sexual deviance. Young women are sometimes arrested when their names have appeared in casa particular registries twice in six months, and the FMC claims to receive reports from medical professionals when they suspect a patient of theirs has had sex with multiple men, when in neither instance is it possible to ascertain if money indeed changed hands, or under what circumstances. Young women who dress provocatively or behave in a sexually assertive manner are routinely scrutinized by the police, but frequently even a young woman's presence in a tourist zone and her race are enough to bring her under the surveillance of ubiquitous patrol officers. Cabezas highlights this, arguing that "female sexuality is worthy of representation and protection when it is embedded in the depiction of an injured and violate female sexuality, a depiction dependent on representations of passive female sexuality that conforms to heterosexual norms."[15] Because they have (or are presumed to have) stepped outside the bounds of heteronormative female sexuality—a chaste, monogamous passivity that most Cubans claim to have long since left behind—and, crucially, with *foreign* men in particular, these women have been pathologized and made available for intervention and coercion.

By contrast, Ricky found the idea of prosecuting men for prostitution or jineterismo a bit absurd, and said any arrests were usually a misunderstanding or for something else. The police thought a young man was trying to sell black-market goods to a tourist, for example, when in reality he was sleeping with her. I heard nothing about the registry books when it came to male Cubans staying with foreigners in their casas particulares, or about medical staff reporting them. Men appeared to be carrying out a role that was seen as normal, healthy, and even admirable in their relations with foreign women.

Young Cuban men who seek out foreigners for same-sex encounters seem to be understood in more or less the same way by the people I asked about it. Gisela Fosado's work supports this: they are asserting Cuban (black) masculinity by—presumably—sexually dominating foreigners.[16] The image of the jinetera seems to be one that is inherently female and meant for the eyes of foreign men only. Young, attractive Cuban women of color *are* the corpus delecti—the desired body.[17] Cuban men such as Ricky, on the other hand, are fulfilling their roles as desiring bodies.

LANGUAGE AND THE STRUGGLE FOR MEANING

If *jineterismo, jinetero,* and *jinetera* are in fact empty signifiers, then what purpose do they serve? Relations of sexual intimacy, as Zelizer so aptly demonstrates, are frequently accompanied by transfers of economic resources, often as a means of exhibiting care and attachment; furthermore, the parties to these kinds of interactions, particularly in sensitive scenarios such as these where the stakes are high and confusion is likely, are usually vigilant about clarifying "whether the relationship is a marriage, courtship, prostitution, or some other different sort of social tie" through what Zelizer calls *relational work,* or what Denise Brennan calls *love work.*[18] One of the ways in which they do this is by marking relationships with names and labels that speak to their intended perceptions, be they long or short term, permanent or fleeting, serious or lighthearted. However, outside actors are equally likely to assign meaning to what they see. In Cuba, this has led to a discursive tug-of-war, heavily laden with normative assumptions about women's sexuality, promiscuity, and moral integrity. As a function of this, a new terminology has sprung up around jineterismo and the people who populate it as a field of relations.

There are many different terms used to describe people engaged in sex-ual-affective economies, in Cuba and elsewhere, the meanings of which are neither absolute nor static. Far from simple semantics, defining and nam-ing allows various actors in the field of relations—government, police, journalists, mass organizations, individuals, and society at large—to situ-ate young Cubans on either side of various binaries, including good/bad, right/wrong, virtue/vice. Each of the terms speaks to raced and gendered histories in different ways, giving us an idea as to why the jinetera is imag-ined the way she is—as a young, attractive, well-dressed woman of color whose good fortune must belie depravity of some kind. The point here is not to contest the application of the labels but the labels themselves, focus-ing not on *categories* but rather on *practices of categorization*—the essence of feminist, queer, and antiracist inquiry.[19] Linguistic practices that chal-lenge and subvert categorization have become important weapons in a battle for self-definition, observed in action in Cuba. The labels in play merit further elaboration, as they cover a range from crass to enigmatic, tending to ebb and flow over time in popular parlance, each loaded with different raced and gendered implications and political commitments.[20]

Certainly, words like *prostituta* and *puta* (whore) exist in Cuba, along-side a range of other slurs—*atrevida* (brazen) and *descarada* (shameless), for example—that are used, like they are around the world, to shame and silence women for any number of behaviors deemed not properly femi-nine. The standard jinetera (and its masculine variant, the jinetero, which carries a different set of connotations) remains far more popular for describing sexual commerce, however, at least in part because of its inher-ent fluidity as it continues to represent a broader notion of what these relationships mean. Without question, it carries less stigma than prosti-tuta, which seems to be used almost exclusively by state organs.

As I noted above, the word *jinetera* has evolved over time as a uniquely Cuban neologism; it is not used in any other Spanish-speaking country. Lumsden contends that—in the years before the Special Period but after the closure of the UMAP camps where many gay Cubans were imprisoned—*jinetero* was sometimes taken to refer to men who had sex with *entendidos,* or men whose homosexuality was something of an open secret.[21] Elizalde, on the other hand, locates the etymology of jineterismo in illegal money changing in the 1980s, which was essential to the functioning of the black market. Amir Valle disagrees, maintaining that *jinetera* has always carried a sexual connotation.[22] Díaz and González, on the other hand, say that its roots lie in Mexican slang, meaning someone who lived off "ill-gotten gains [*ganancias en forma indebida*]."[23]

However it came to be, by the 1970s, the term *jineterismo* was already in use to denote the exchange of sexual favors (usually by women) for access to scarce goods (usually from men) in a closed economy. Through the late 1980s and very prominently in the 1990s, it came to signify the phenomenon of Cubans interacting with foreigners in various ways as a means to alleviate hardship; when it came to sexual liaisons with said foreigners, the Cubans in question were (and continue to be) presumed to be women of color—and vice versa. Noelle Stout argues that far from being a "misnomer for prostitution," the term *jineterismo* is indicative of a more emancipatory paradigm that challenges "traditional notions of the victimized prostitute" and recasts them with greater agency and power.[24] Or, as Teresa Marrero somewhat more colorfully puts it, "the word prompts the nature of the exchange; *jineteras*, like *jinetes*, mount and control the animal being ridden. This worldview suggests a rearranging of standard notions of the nature of (sexual) consumerism. While contemporary marketing notions hold that the buyer of goods and services reigns supreme, here Cuba's *jineterismo* suggests that the provider of services can play and manipulate to its advantage the relation between consumer and provider."[25]

There are those who argue that jineterismo is nothing more than prostitution, but its use in Cuba suggests something more fluid, indeterminate, and contingent than such a simple comparison implies. In the early days of the Special Period, *jinetera* was a term that served to distance young women from the perceived criminality and low morality associated with prostitution. Fusco describes how jineteras have become folkloric figures in post-Soviet Cuba, appearing in brightly coloured *naïf* paintings for sale in the tourist markets and coming to embody the deeply engrained fantasy of Cuban mulata sensuality. Says Fusco of her visit to Cuba in the mid-1990s, "I got the sense that on the street these women are perceived as heroic providers whose mythical sexual power is showing up the failures of an ailing macho regime."[26]

Over time, however, *jinetera* has begun to take on a crassness that has led many of the young people with whom I spoke to eschew it in favor of other terms or, perhaps most important, no terminology at all. *Jinetera* is also now understood across Cuba to have a specifically racial connotation, another source of stigma for some, as it has become inextricably linked to the lascivious image of the mulata—yet another example of the imagining of the jinetera. Thus while *jinetera* is unarguably still the standard terminology in play, other terms have appeared to challenge its supremacy and avoid creeping stigma. Some of these, used self-referentially by two of my interviewees in particular like banners for new identities, go even further toward expressing how young people in Cuba feel about their situations and the meaning of their actions.

The first new label came from Andre, a twenty-five-year-old living in Centro Habana whose story features later in more detail. He told me that the government of Cuba is afraid of the *jinete,* but the way he sees it everyone is engaged in the practice in some way or another, whether it's renting out rooms to foreigners, running a paladar, buying and selling on the black market, or becoming intimately involved with tourists. Andre spoke of the tendency in Cuba to refer to tourism and tourists as *el fuego* (the fire)—they ask one another, *¿Estás en el fuego?* (Are you in the fire?), or say, *Me voy al fuego* (I'm going to the fire), when they are going out to meet foreigners. They use this term for multiple reasons—the fact that it is seen to be engulfing the country, the likelihood of getting burned, and, in Andre's eyes, its irresistibility. Andre finds the word *jinetero* somewhat vulgar; to that end, he calls himself a *candelero,* or candle bearer.

Ana, on the other hand, prefers a different handle. I spoke to her and three other girls, Taimí, Sara, and Yoaní, all from Batabanó and ranging in age from eighteen to twenty-eight. They were telling me about the tourist men who approached them in the nightclubs of Havana. The entire conversation had been tense and stilted, no matter how hard I tried to put them at ease. I had found one area of relative success: we were talking about labels, with me listing a few different ones and them telling me what each word evoked for them. They spoke with a sullen air of resignation, even shame, and said they did not see themselves reflected in any of the terms. The last label I posed to them was one that I had only recently encountered: *luchadora.* Ana, seated directly to my left, smiled for the first time, her face lighting up. She said that she liked that one, that it seemed strong and beautiful. The mood in the room lightened considerably from that point. All four girls appeared as if a weight was lifted from their shoulders, and we continued the interview on a far better footing.

These two examples illustrate that labeling is far more than a semantic issue; labels do work, they support and reject, they build up and break down. For the so-called jineteros and jineteras of Cuba, simply using a different word can radically change the game on multiple fronts. It can allow young people to subvert some of the stigma of being branded as criminals or whores. *Prostitute* may not be an identity that many are proud to espouse, but as the majority of my interviewees confirmed over and over again, these young people do not consider themselves prostitutes, and neither does Cuban society. As García notes—and as I easily observed in Cuba—being a so-called jinetera in the eyes of the public indicated "a sacrifice of revolutionary values, but one that is not deemed shameful because it is done to help others."[27] Their involvement with foreigners is not understood as a slight to their moral integrity, or as necessarily transactional or artificial. Such a framework for understanding their lives and relationships holds no value to these young people and even serves to repress them, whether they deploy it themselves or not. Thus reinterpreting sexual-affective relationships with foreigners in this way helps to build a counterdiscourse against that of prostitution.

Second, rejecting the identities of prostitute and jinetera leaves open the possibility that relationships with foreigners can evolve and take any number of forms in the future by denying a client/prostitute relationship with the foreign partners. Yakelín and Lili, and many others like them, were concerned that their relationships be seen as genuine and their intentions as honest. They want their foreign connections to see them as viable long-term partners and the world to see their relationships as valid and real. Avoiding terms like *prostitute*, and even the increasingly restrictive *jinetera*, underlines the incompleteness, open-endedness, uncertainty, and mutability of lived experience.

Their foreign dates and partners, for their part, seem also to value this fluidity: some are concerned with avoiding the sordidness of prostitution, but others are simply pleased that their relationships with locals can be as casual or serious as they want, no matter the circumstances under which they met. This indeterminacy, while it does not necessarily set Cuba apart from other locales, does prevent the "congeal[ing of] identities" and "provides more spaces of liminality and control" than are available in places like the Dominican Republic.[28] Young women who take part in opportunist, spontaneous relations with foreign men—once or many times—need not feel confined to a prostitute identity.

Finally, and perhaps most crucially, young people's refusal of a prostitute identity matters because it allows individual subjects not only to say what they are not—that is, sluts and criminals—but also to effectively articulate what they *are* and to create new identities. These young people are creating new lives of their own design that are completely different from what is desired for them by Cuban socialism, which once staged arguably one of the most calculated overhauls of political subjectivity in history: Guevara's New Man. By taking on a label such as *candelero*, Andre is creating an identity that paints himself and others like him as enigmatic, even brave figures. He becomes a romantic figure casting light in the darkness, one who shows the way for those around him. A conceited image, perhaps, but not one without basis: Andre has managed to boost his family's standard of living considerably in the last few years.

Ana, on the other hand, uses *luchadora* to situate herself within la lucha, or the daily struggle to make ends meet, a highly evocative and relatable concept in Cuba. A luchadora is a person of great resourcefulness and integrity, one who relies on no one but herself to get by. By placing herself and her relationships under the umbrella of la lucha, Ana shows herself to be no different from any other Cuban who is engaged in the daily struggle to make do and to provide, as worthy of the storied Cuban socialist solidarity as any other. She also draws on the idea of *hembrismo* as a new and developing kind of Cuban womanhood, in contrast to the passive, demure femininity of marianismo. The *hembra*, like the luchadora, is strong and resilient, drawing on post-revolutionary rhetoric of emancipation, the idea of la lucha, and even santería. Cabezas writes that santería does not subscribe to the same binaries as Catholicism, which can help women break away from Madonna/whore-type zero-sum categories.[29] As she notes, this way of thinking fits well with the notion of the hembra and the luchadora. Indeed, some of the women Cabezas interviewed believe their foreign partners were sent to them by Yemayá, the female oricha who protects women and presides over the sea. An hembra or luchadora is resourceful and makes use of what the world offers her to carry on her own lucha, for herself and her family.

This is no simple issue of rebranding; on the contrary, labels are one of the major weapons employed by certain young Cubans in a discursive struggle to define what sexuality and relationships mean in Cuba today, to deny the state-dominated discourse that would brand certain women as whores, criminals, and deficient citizens, and to begin to create new and different lives in their own images. The use of an umbrella term like *prostitution* to denote such a range of activities, relationships, and identities enacts what Shalini Puri calls a "dehistoricizing conflation": the specificities, histories, and circumstances of individual lives are denied in favor of a monolithic, decontextualized generalization.[30] The discourse of prostitution, in which certain women are classed as good and others as degenerate, dangerous, pathological, or immoral, forms part of a binary that seeks to control, regulating the behavior not only of the ever-increasing sector of the population that it has rendered suspect but also of young women in general in Cuba today. To quote Stuart Hall and his colleagues, "The use of labelling and criminalisation as part and parcel of the process of legitimating social control is clearly not confined to the past."[31]

The uncritical use (by state institutions and other actors) of words like *prostituta* serves to depoliticize the process by which certain women are deemed to be good while others are judged to be in need of—and available for—state intervention. While few terms imply such fluidity, being both progressive and regressive at once, words like *jinetera*, as empty signifiers, have been increasingly drawn under the rubric of prostituta. The use of terms that go beyond this binary relation, whether luchadora or candelero, or—perhaps most important—the act of denying any terminology at all, of disidentification, destabilizes the simple opposition good woman/prostitute, opening up possibilities for new relationships, identities, and subjectivities. On a small scale, this reverses the operation that Foucault exposes in his *History of Sexuality*, whereby activities congeal into identities—the sodomite becomes *the homosexual*, most notably, but the seller of sex also becomes *the prostitute*, no longer a "temporary aberration" but a "species."[32] Jonathan Goldberg, carrying on from Foucault's discussion of sodomy and homosexuality, shares insights that have resonance for prostitution as well: "[It] identifies neither persons nor acts with any coherence or specificity. This is one reason why the term can be mobilized—precisely because it is incapable of exact definition; but this is also how the bankruptcy of the term, and what has been done in its name, can be uncovered."[33]

Goldberg argues that bodies cast into such categories are produced as "the body that needs to be effaced."[34] In denying, refusing, and revealing the bankruptcy of the term *jinetera*—either by rejecting it or by refusing to be precisely what it purports to describe—young Cubans work toward a denial of the power of the discourse of prostitution.

CONCLUSION: CREATING LIMINAL IDENTITIES AND DEFYING MARGINALITY

> As if the wish of Ochún had been to bless her black half and curse her white half, the mulatta was split in two. As no other Cuban woman, she became the bearer of goddess-like attributes: passion, sensuality, eroticism, the desire for the forbidden or the exotic. As no other Cuban woman, she has been abused and vilified; she also became the symbol of opportunism, the huntress of white men, the source of discord, the prostitute.
>
> Raquel Mendieta Costa, "Exotic Exports"

The exchange of sexual intimacy for material and social benefits is a complex, contested, ambiguous, mutating set of relationships, activities, and identities whose meaning(s) cannot be specified in advance or accurately determined from the outside. Affective relationships between people of disparate cultural, racial, national, and socioeconomic backgrounds always exist within a framework of gendered and raced understandings of sexuality and morality, and of legitimate and illegitimate sexual interaction. In Cuba, the idea that there is a class of promiscuous and economically motivated people known as jineteras, who many argue amount to little more than prostitutes, works to shame and discipline young women's sexual activities and identities, casting an ever wider net based on age, gender, race, and style of dress.

Speaking to young people, and in particular young women of color, who have had relationships with foreign visitors to Cuba—and thus fall under the scrutiny of the disciplinary mechanisms of the state—it became clear that the jinetera, as a marker for a group of people engaging in certain definable activities and bearing identifiable characteristics ranging from low self-esteem to a preference for designer perfumes, does not exist. Even at the most basic level, much of the knowledge produced about the jinetera can be easily seen to be false. There are no real trends when it comes to their perceived racial background, education, work lives, and career paths, whether or not they have children, or even their marital status.[35] Given that these are the traits by which more fundamental judgments on their moral standards, self-esteem, criminal tendencies, ideological fortitude, and even their worth as citizens are frequently evaluated, a growing number of young women appear to be swept into the category "jinetera" without any kind of evidentiary grounding.

Differences of race and gender frequently characterize relationships between Cubans and foreigners, not to mention significant economic disparities, but it is nonetheless inaccurate and regressive to portray the interactions as necessarily either economic or romantic, as racially motivated or more "pure," or even as a matter of exploiters and exploited, as is frequently done in literature on sex tourism and transcultural relationships.[36] John Urry contends that the encounter of tourists with the local other is organized by what he calls the "tourist gaze"—an exoticizing gaze that is overwhelmingly masculine, heterosexual, and white, and which is also frequently sexual, taking the very bodies of local people as its object and the embodiment of difference, with all the raced and gendered implications that suggests. "The male look through a kind of 'porno-tropics,'" argues Urry, "is endlessly voyeuristic."[37]

Thus privileged desire clearly has a stake in figuring the possibilities available to disadvantaged people in tourist destination countries like Cuba—Nancy Wonders and Raymond Michaelowski also highlight this[38]—but such a reductionism obscures the actual experiences of the people concerned, most of whom are already marginalized by raced and gendered prejudices. Laura María Agustín clearly shows that depicting women involved in sexual economies as manipulated or helpless victims serves only to further silence and erase those very women who, though faced with a limited range of options, are nonetheless speaking subjects acting in their own right.[39] So it is in Cuba, where young women's relationships are sharply divided between the commercial, which is understood to be emotionally empty and sexually fetishistic, and supposedly normative relationships. The state-led discourse of prostitution, which informs my fourth chapter, has taken a strong hand in determining which relationships are genuine and which are false. It works first to engineer a need for such classification and second to fabricate both the right and the authority to classify.

The stories of Yakelín, Nadia, and Lili, as well as Ana and Andre—not to mention the many others I interviewed for this project—paint a far more conflicted and ambiguous picture of how contemporary youth in Cuba view their role in society, their futures, their relationships, and their political system. Stout asserts that young Cubans today espouse a more complex world in which socialized health care, food subsidies, and universal education are inalienable rights that effortlessly coexist with the drive to acquire stylish shoes, clothes, and other luxuries of the dollar economy.[40]

These young Cubans contend that the socialist ideals with which they have grown up, and to which many in Cuba still subscribe, need not be seen as diametrically opposed to material well-being, or even to international pop culture and fashion. Likewise, the meanings behind relations between Cubans and foreigners are complex and cannot be determined in advance but are constantly being negotiated. By crafting new identities and subject positions that defy traditional notions of race, gender, and even class, young Cubans are mediating their own circumstances in ways previously unavailable to them.

The economic adversity experienced during the Special Period, which is still felt today, has opened up new spaces to enact new political subjectivities and new sexual identities and practices that are able to alleviate economic, social, and cultural shifts. Through the influx of foreign tourists, these Cuban women have situated themselves as both desiring and desired in a political setting that seeks to prescribe their goals and ideals for them. Young Cubans, and especially young Cubans of color, are resisting the life prescribed for them through bodily practices, sometimes at great personal risk, and thereby carving out a new space for themselves. The revered Cuban novelist José Lézama Lima referred to the capacity to find escape in artistic creation as "internal exile."[41] I want to take this idea beyond the artistic to the political—or perhaps, to posit artistic creation not just of tangible objets d'art but also of the self—to describe the ways in which young Cuban women are deploying their sexualities to fashion new lives and opportunities for themselves.

This is not to say that young people engaging in sexual interactions with foreigners have created an entirely emancipatory space without repression or retribution from state-centered institutions and sites of power; indeed, the racialized bodies of young women in Cuba have become the objects of state-led violence—physical, sexual, and symbolic—in an effort to control young women's sexuality through the discourse of jineterismo. While Afro-Cubans of all walks of life experience heightened police scrutiny and abuse, it is only when directed at young women that this form of discipline addresses itself directly to sexuality and sexual deviance. Nor have I intended to imply that the process of turning away from one life is a neat and tidy process, a clean break that results in complete freedom or a demonstrably "better" life. The image of the jinetera that has been elaborated here and in the previous chapter renders certain women visible, intelligible, and available for coercion and even violence, but the ways these same young people have found to subvert, avert, and co-opt the power relations that characterize their daily lives show marked innovation and resilience in the face of austerity, violence, and moral discipline.

3 Lessons in Subterfuge

EVERYDAY ACTS OF REPRESSION AND RESISTANCE

> We have already travelled some distance from the world of
> hard facts—'social facts as things'. We have entered the
> realm of the relation of facts to the ideological construction
> of 'reality'.
>
> Stuart Hall et al., *Policing the Crisis*

Ideas like prostitution and the jinetera are not static, with one set meaning over time; they are together reinforced and reproduced on a daily
basis through practices of categorization and labeling. The jinetera as a
figure and as a sexual identity is a fictive manifestation of raced and gendered structures of prejudice. Among those women who are deemed to be
jineteras, by themselves or by others, there seems to be little in the way of
demonstrable similarities, whether in terms of race, employment, parent-
hood, childhood experiences, or even ideological grounding. That said,
however, the jinetera is very real in the sense that this understanding of
the sexuality and morality of certain women creates individual young
women of color as knowable subjects with certain moral attributes and
sexual behaviors. Yakelín's, Nadia's, and Lili's stories show that the determination of who is and who is not a jinetera is made largely from the
outside, based on images of raced women who are produced as promiscuous and deviant. Their lives and relationships have been conditioned by
the ever present need to avoid and subvert the label "jinetera." With time,
however, I began to encounter people in Cuba whose stories of repression
and resistance revealed the true violence of the discourse of prostitution,

casting light on a clandestine world whose very existence is frequently denied in official circles.

In practice, this violence is carried out by a range of actors—many of whom, but not all, are agents of the state—acting through, around, and above the law. The stories that follow detail individual experiences of discipline and state control enacted both directly and indirectly on the bodies of young people, and especially young women, deemed to be jineteras. Speaking to Cubans who have personal experiences with the Policía Nacional Revolucionaria (PNR), the rehabilitation centers, or *chulos*—men who act as intermediaries or managers for women's sexual transactions—is a delicate operation, one that is dominated by fear of retribution, which could come in many forms. These were difficult interviews to obtain. I worked through a network of contacts to meet people who gave accounts of repression carried out through both legal and extralegal means, each of which I discuss in detail. They also, however, spoke of the subtle and dynamic means they have found of resisting disciplinary violence on a day-to-day basis. These "weapons of the weak"[1]—seemingly insignificant acts that defy and reframe the exercise of power—enable genuine, albeit small-scale, resistance to oppression in real terms. They are even more effective as symbolic resistance, articulating dissent and noncompliance with official dictates on sexuality, morality, and state power.

My research during this period proved challenging. As a foreigner, I was faced with infiltrating what seemed to be an underworld of illicit activities and associations, and in many cases success eluded me. Some people were too afraid to speak to me at all, a fact that in itself speaks volumes. Most of the interviews included here were done without the aid of my voice recorder, because my informants feared that a recording could be traced back to them should it fall into the wrong hands. Some interviews required careful negotiation and references from mutual contacts who could vouch for my trustworthiness. Where I could not obtain interviews or other kinds of access, I have had to be more circumspect in my conclusions, but the portrait of relations of power between state actors and institutions—which, it bears mentioning, is also frequently masculine—and an informal, unspoken alliance of young people who resist its sway over them is nonetheless striking.

"LA SANTA POLICÍA"

On a warm evening in April, I have plans to meet some friends, fellow foreigners, for a night off to relax on the Malecón *a lo cubano*. Leaving my house, I go to meet my Australian friend Allison at the Habana Libre, and we are joined shortly afterward by Aoife, who is from Ireland. Continuing down La Rampa, it seems eerily quiet for a Friday night. We stop to get some drinks from a café near where Calle 23 meets the Malecón and then find ourselves a spot on the seawall. The Malecón, too, is quiet—a shadow of its usual self. Knots of people are gathered here and there but nothing close to the usual thronging weekend crowd. Almost immediately, my eye is drawn to the police officers monitoring the crowd in twos and threes all along the Malecón, which usually has virtually no police. This, I think to myself, explains the relative quiet. We try to ignore them and return to our conversation.

Around nine o'clock, two acquaintances of mine, friends of a friend—both young black Cuban men—appear a few meters away, and we exchange a friendly wave, but no sooner have they begun to approach us than the police descend. The two are taken aside, surrounded by four officers, asked to produce their carnés de identidad and to justify their presence on the Malecón. My friends and I look on in silence. The officers gesture in our direction as they speak, and while I can hear every word, I know I cannot intervene without making the situation far worse. I breathe a sigh of frustration. This is nothing but harassment, and it's because of me. I've endangered these two young men simply by being here.

Eventually, both are allowed to go, and they carry on past us with wan smiles and a nod. The police, for their part, also disperse but for one, who remains nearby and seems to stand sentinel over us. He seems agitated, and eventually he crosses the pavement to speak to us directly.

"Who are you?"

Aoife and I explain that we are students who have come to Cuba to learn Spanish.

"What are you doing here?" He sweeps his arm to indicate the Malecón.

Laughing, Aoife tells him we came to make friends, to chat and to dance to the music playing nearby. The Malecón is a part of the Cuban experience, she says. The officer is plainly unmoved.

"You shouldn't be here. You really should go home," he says earnestly.

I thank him for his concern, and he seems pleased.

"It's important for us to protect foreigners in Cuba, especially foreign women. That's my job."

This seems perplexing to me, so I ask if it isn't his job to protect everyone in Cuba.

"No."

I hadn't expected him to answer so bluntly. We spend an awkward few seconds in silence, until Aoife interjects to tell him again that we're fine and there's no need to worry. Finally, he says in a confidential tone, "I will stay close. Tell me if you have any more problems with these *negritos*."

He retreats to the curb and remains there, feet planted and hands clasped behind his back, casting his gaze up and down the promenade. Allison, who hasn't understood the conversation, asks what was said. It takes me a few seconds to put aside my swirling thoughts and translate for her. All the while, our chaperone keeps his eye on us, and so we continue for more than an hour, the watcher and the watched. The merriment continues all around, but no one dares speak to us as long as the officer is standing there. For a while, I debate asking him more questions, but I decide in the end that I can't risk it. He watches us with a look of benevolence. We watch him with what I can only assume is too thinly veiled exasperation.

At last, perhaps satisfied that we are in no immediate danger, the officer saunters off down the waterfront. Perhaps it's my imagination, but it seems that everyone around us breathes a collective sigh of relief. Allison remarks that she thought he'd never leave.

Within minutes, we're drawn into the party around us. Aoife and Allison find dance partners, and I find myself chatting with two young men named Juan Pedro and Oscar about spirituality in Cuba. Juan Pedro tells me that he believes santería is a guiding force in Cuban lives and personalities and should be important for my research. When Allison needs to use a bathroom, Oscar goes to find one with her, and Juan Pedro and I continue our talk while Aoife carries on dancing. Looking out over the waves in the darkness, he tells me about Yemayá, the oricha of the sea, tempestuous and sensual—and who Juan Pedro says governs jineteras.

"Daughters of Yemayá are passionate, you know? They're willing to use that passion to get what they need in life." He laughs. "And they're putas!

All putas. But hey, they'd be having sex anyway, right? Might as well make it work for you."

He tells me that Cuban sensuality is rooted in santería, since each oricha is associated with a particular style of movement or dance. Just as I begin to think that I should have brought my recorder, I feel a hand on my shoulder. The police officer has returned, but this time he seems distressed.

"Where is she?" he asks urgently. "Where is the other girl? There were three of you before."

Juan Pedro sinks back toward his group of friends while I stammer a reply, asking why he wants to know where Allison went. I feel so incredulous that I nearly laugh, but he just grows more insistent and even aggressive.

"It's not safe for you here. This is a dangerous place. There are bad people all around here. Tell me where she went. Was she with someone? Tell me!"

I can feel the color rising in my face. He stands over me now, gripping my arm and speaking sternly. Thoughts race in my head—that he's out of line, no right to demand information, rude, invasive—but I bite my tongue. Then Aoife slips an arm around my waist, drawing me away from the cop, and tells him merrily that Allison is a big girl and can handle herself. We appreciate your concern, she says, but we've got everything under control. Cool as a cucumber.

He stares helplessly first at her, then at me, and then releases my arm. Before he carries on once again, he takes a moment to check Juan Pedro's carné. And then he leaves, never to reappear for the rest of the evening. Allison returns, safe and sound, a few minutes later. The police presence on the whole dies down as the night wears on. From around 11:00, our little plot on the Malecón floods with gay Cubans, travestis, and drag queens—as sure a sign as any that the PNR has retired for the night.

I thought about that encounter many times after that night. It exemplifies the difficulties of trying to understand police practices: they are institutional, but they are also individual. This officer seemed earnest and well intentioned, confident that he was doing the right thing, and I felt unable to press him to explain why he felt that way. He spoke with conviction about the need to protect foreigners from Afro-Cubans, but it was impossible to tell if this was policy, institutional culture, or personal prejudice. García writes about a strikingly similar incident during her time in Cuba, when a police officer on La Rampa told her she was in danger and must leave the area.[2]

In the vast majority of cases, the PNR acts as the primary point of contact between individual Cubans and government policy on jineterismo, sexual or otherwise. These policies originate in multiple high-level organizations and ministries that include the FMC, the Unión de Jóvenes Comunistas (UJC), and MININT, but officers of the PNR are almost always the filter through which such ideas are enacted. They have served as the chief vehicles of what has been called a "crusade" against a perceived resurgence of prostitution in post-Soviet Cuba, carrying out thousands of arrests by virtually all accounts.[3]

Throughout the 1990s, the PNR swelled its ranks in Havana. New recruits were brought to the capital from the eastern provinces, known as Oriente, to deter an anticipated swell in criminal activity during the economic crisis. In 1996 alone, around fifty thousand people arrived from the eastern provinces, looking for a better life at the height of the Special Period. Oriente is home to a much higher proportion of black Cubans, and white anxiety led to a perception of Havana-bound migration as a "black assault on the city" that would necessitate a stronger police force.[4] In reality, it seems that these racist fears were unfounded, as rates of violent crime still remain quite low in Cuba, and especially in comparison to neighboring countries, for reasons including stiff sentencing practices and strong community solidarity.[5] Sierra Madero argues that it was, in fact, the bringing of new police recruits from the east, which is more rural and conservative, into diverse and bustling Havana that caused a kind of "cultural shock" and led to tensions between police and overlapping communities of urban youth, LGBT Cubans, and Afro-Cubans.[6] Talking to most of my Cuban friends and contacts, it was clear that there is a very low level of trust between the PNR and the population it governs; it is with no small measure of irony that Osmany Horta Mesa calls them "la santa policía."[7]

It is difficult to imagine how PNR officers, many (if not most) of whom are people of mixed or Afro-Cuban descent themselves, could view Cubans of color with such suspicion and even contempt. Conducting an official interview with a PNR officer proved to be, perhaps unsurprisingly, impossible. Most Cubans I met regarded them with a mixture of fear and disdain and avoided dealing with them at all costs, advising me that I do the same. I can therefore venture only speculations as to their thoughts or motives each time I interacted with them. There is also, of course, the problem of differentiating the voices and actions of the individual officers from that of the institution they represent. It also bears remembering that officers receive the same inadequate wages as other Cubans working in state-sector jobs and suffer the same privations and scarcities as everyone else. In order to gain access to the luxuries and necessities of the dollar economy, PNR officers must invent their own means of acquiring convertible pesos. In that sense, it is understandable that they would seek to augment their earnings outside of their usual jobs, for themselves and for their families; in a way, the police seem to have simply arrived late to the same party as all the other people who regularly engage with tourists as a means of improving their own lives. They are living and working in the same world as the so-called jineteras and the other people populating the Malecón or other meeting places in Cuba—on that night and every night. They are constrained and produced by the institutional setting in which they work, the expectations placed on them, and their colleagues.

As the pages to come will show, individual PNR officers engage with the world of jineterismo in a variety of ways. Some see advantages to working with hustlers of all kinds, accepting kickbacks in exchange for their silence or even their protection. In his exploration of sexual commerce and corruption, Valle recounts many different instances of police officers beating and sexually assaulting jineteras, but he also affirms that many offer protection to certain jineteras in exchange for regular cash bribes and sexual services.[8] While bribery is quite a predictable part of this world, and one that fits in with the general need for access to convertible pesos, the power—both personal and institutional—that police possess over marginalized people colors these interactions, mutually advantageous though they may be.

Whether because of institutional practice or personal prejudice, Cubans of color find themselves coming into contact with the PNR on a day-to-day basis. Men are routinely suspected of selling contraband rum or cigars, hassling tourists, or possibly theft; young women, on the other hand, are accosted for their (real or perceived) associations with tourists—that is, for their perceived sexual deviance. Allen also describes how his black and mixed-race Cuban contacts are forced to develop "personal strategies for dealing with police aggravation," which they face every day.[9]

This fact of life for Afro-Cubans has even been immortalized in music. In a song titled "La iyabó de la felpa azul," the Cuban reggaetón artists Baby Lores and Insurrecto cast a police car as the antagonist.

> Se unieron dos zonas residenciales,
> el Canal y el Romerillo.
> Si andas en Varadero a golpe de
> Tul [turistaxi], cuidado con la
> iyabó de la felpa azul.
> Con demasiadas latas en
> el Infotul [Infotur], cuidado con la
> iyabó de la felpa azul.
> Siempre está vestida con la misma
> ropita, le encantan los chamacos
> de la piel oscurita . . .

> Two residential areas got united,
> El Canal and Romerillo.
> If you go around Varadero in
> taxis for tourists, be careful with
> the iyabó with the blue scrunchie.
> With too many cans in
> the Infotur, be careful with the
> iyabó with the blue scrunchie.
> It is always wearing the same
> clothes, it loves dark-skinned
> boys . . .

The car is called an *iyabó* in a nod to santeros, who frequently dress in all white, with the addition of the *felpa azul* (blue scrunchie) to stand for the light on top of PNR cruisers. The car is said to be "fond" of "dark-skinned boys," and, as Nora Gámez Torres notes, the mention of tourist taxis is a coded nod to the jineteras.[10] Encounters like these, which single out Afro-Cuban youth, are facilitated both by the law (and individual PNR officers' interpretations of it) and by officers' power to act extralegally with little consequence. PNR officers' position of authority, combined with the inscription of so-called jineteras as deviant, troublesome, promiscuous bodies, makes a range of potential scenarios of repression possible. The violence of the discourse of prostitution is one that acts through, above, and around the law.

NO RIGHT TO BE HERE

Partway through my stay in Cuba, I spent a few weeks with my friend Yusmara and her extended family at their sprawling home in Santiago de Cuba. For days I heard stories from Yusmara and her husband about Evan, who had lived with them for a year while studying Spanish six years ago. He was the son they never had, they said, and he had visited them every year since, bringing gifts and necessities for their home with him from Canada. They hadn't been expecting him, so it was with barely contained glee that Yusmara slipped into my room to tell me that Evan had just arrived. There were certainly better circumstances for an interview—I was recovering from a bad case of food poisoning—but here he was, and Yusmara was insisting. I tore myself away from the air-conditioned safety of my room to join him at the wrought-iron table in the courtyard, under the stifling heat of Santiago in June.

Slight and wiry, he can't be more than thirty years old—if that—but since living in Santiago six years ago, he has become a successful estate agent in Toronto. Evan's manner can only be described as bombastic, but he's congenial and easygoing nonetheless. Instantly, he begins regaling me with stories about his year in Santiago, when he moved here on a whim to remedy what he felt was a lack of direction in his life. His girlfriend, a wispy Cuban girl named Karla who also looks young for her age, silently listens and picks at her food. I wonder if she's heard all of this many times before.

As he devours the lunch Yusmara has prepared for him, Evan tells me at length about his classes, his friends, nights out, the girls he dated—all the standard adventures of a year spent studying in a foreign land. "I will always come back to Santiago—always. It's like another home to me. People say Havana is the place to be, but they don't know what they're fucking talking about—pardon my French—because Santiago is just . . . special, you know? The people are incredible, so nice, like they've known you their whole goddamn lives. They invite you into their homes. They have priorities. Havana? Havana's just another big city. They'll eat you up and leave you behind in that place."

Evan presides over the table like a grandiloquent prince, gesturing with his fork and knife. He pauses for a moment to chew and swallow, then drinks deeply from his glass of water. Glass still in hand, eyes on his plate, he waves his fork in my direction. "I have a story for you," he says.

Now I am forced to admit, to myself at least, that I hadn't taken him seriously enough. My patience is strained by illness and heat, and Evan's stories of beaches and parties, his overwhelmingly rosy impressions, and his big-talking demeanor were making it difficult to resist rolling my eyes. But now, as his story unfolds, I check myself and sit up to take notice.

On a typically gorgeous day in Santiago, Evan tells me that he was making his way down Avenida de las Américas with his then-girlfriend, a Cuban girl named Teresa. He doesn't recall exactly where they were going, but he remembers taking notice of a man rapidly approaching them from the left and wondering what he could want. The man gripped Teresa by the arm and murmured, "*Ven* [Come]," trying to lead her away. Evan says he held onto her other arm and demanded to know what was going on. More plainclothes officers drew near, flashing their badges too quickly to read their names. Again, they attempted to lead her away and she resisted. Evan found himself in a sort of tug-of-war with the officers over Teresa, digging in his heels and protesting loudly as they tried to take her away.

"I looked around, and I was like, 'Holy shit—this is a fucking *operativo*,'" he says, referring to the mass roundups of young women routinely carried out by the PNR since around 1996 in an effort to combat prostitution. "They were herding girls onto this big Astro bus, and there were all these faces looking back at us from the windows and shouting. The cops were all around us, asking Teresa stuff like—like, 'What are you doing on this street? What are you doing near the hotel? You have no business being here' . . . et cetera, et cetera, you know? She kept telling them, and I kept telling them, that she was a student and her art school was on that street. And it was, it was right there! But they wouldn't believe us. I didn't let go of her either, or I knew she'd be gone."

Incredibly, he says, the officers eventually gave up and left Teresa behind. He stares off into space for a few seconds, chewing and mulling it over. "And you know, I swear I saw two girls we knew on that bus. I definitely saw them. And we didn't hear from them again for two years," he says, jabbing the air with his fork.

The experience sounds profoundly unsettling. He says the two women were sent to prison, though he had never known them to be jineteras or otherwise involved in anything that could be considered criminal. Evan describes feeling like he somehow put his then-girlfriend in danger simply by being who he was—a foreigner. While they had demanded that she account for her presence on the same street as the Hotel Santiago, it was he who was the foreigner, the outsider.

These days, he says, he and Karla are very careful. When he comes to visit and they travel around Cuba, staying in hotels, they are required to justify their relationship at every turn to hotel staff, car rental employees, and beat patrol officers. Karla carries a copy of Evan's passport and a letter describing and validating their relationship that is signed by Evan, herself, and her family. These documents are a sort of talisman to keep her safe when she is questioned by the police.

They get up to leave, exchanging fond goodbyes with Yusmara and her family. As he straps his motorcycle helmet on and heads for the door, Evan turns around and calls out, "Hey!"

I look up from my notes.

"You're not going to print my name, are you? No? Good. I don't want them to know I talked to you about this shit. The last thing I need is to get on their bad side," he says, slipping an arm around Karla's shoulders and looking pointedly at me. Then, with a wave, they're gone.

Evan's story highlights the ways in which the idea of some women as jineteras permits repressive acts against them. What is more, the events he described to me were perfectly legal and shed light on the mechanisms in place for violence to occur through (and sometimes above) the law. The operativos, or mass arrests, that Evan describes have become a quite commonplace feature of the PNR's approach to prostitution, beginning in 1996 in Varadero and in 1998 in Havana with Operativo Lacra. I heard reports of such events across Cuba time and time again, in Havana but also in Santiago and Camagüey. Large numbers of police officers surround a heavily touristed urban zone, usually after dark, and sweep through the streets, stopping all of those who fit their profile and whom they decide ought not to be there.[11] What happens next can range from simple questioning to indiscriminate arrests, as Evan witnessed. Questions of who is stopped, who is interrogated, and who is arrested are determined by the judgment of police officers and their understanding of superficial characteristics as indicators of a proclivity toward sexual delinquency. The UN

Special Rapporteur on Violence against Women, following an official visit to Cuba in 2000, also noted accounts of many women receiving "blows to the head" during the course of their arrest.[12] Dark-skinned young women, and especially those dressed for a nightclub or walking alone, are overwhelmingly targeted in these mass arrests.[13]

These arrests are enabled by provisions in the Cuban Código Penal, namely, Articles 72–74, which deal with something called the *estado peligroso,* or the dangerous state. It is also commonly called *peligrosidad* and is said to have made its first appearance in the 1979 version of the Código Penal.[14] The integral text of Article 72 reads as follows: "A dangerous state is considered the special proclivity in which a person is found to commit crimes, demonstrated by their conduct which is seen to be in manifest contradiction with the norms of socialist morality."

It then lists alcoholism, drug use, and "antisocial conduct," including the practice of "socially reprehensible vices," as indicators of peligrosidad, going so far as to specify that even the developmentally disabled are not exempt from its remit.[15] It is up to individual police officers to decide who qualifies for the estado peligroso on a case-by-case basis, and given that peligrosidad does not refer to any committed crime but rather to "pre-criminal security measures,"[16] its application has been arbitrary at best and requires little in the way of evidence. In fact, the attorney general of Cuba, Juan Escalona Reguera, referring directly to the prosecution of prostitution in Cuba, described the provision for peligrosidad in an interview published in 1996 as a "sack into which all kinds of people are put."[17] It is often used to prosecute public drunkenness, failure to maintain a steady job, rebellious or atypical fashions, campiness and *mariconeria,* or any other behavior that is not against a specific law or that simply cannot be proven. The Cuban sociologists Graciela González Olmedo and Teresa Díaz Canals suggest that part of the reason suspected jineteras are processed under the rubric of peligrosidad is precisely because prostitution is such a difficult accusation to prove: Article 72 enables arrest and prosecution while lightening or even removing the burden of proof.[18]

Arbitrary arrest and detention are nothing particularly novel in Cuba, nor is Cuba unique in this regard, but it is an explicitly enshrined fact of Cuban life: even the Constitución de la República de Cuba forbids the exercise of individual rights in any way that may prove detrimental to the ends of the socialist state.[19] Nonetheless, Article 72 represents important augmentation of state power in that it specifies a form of crime that is not explicitly political in its use of denotations such as "antisocial conduct" and "socially reprehensible vices." It is a vague legal category that drastically widens the range of behaviors that can be treated as criminal and, in practice, puts unprecedented power to arbitrarily arrest and detain in the hands of the PNR. Thus while prostitution is not listed as a crime in the Código Penal, it can be used—and regularly is used—as grounds for punitive measures against suspected prostitutes.

As Cabezas also discovered, Article 72 allows for individuals deemed by PNR officers to conform to a stereotyped profile to be arrested under "highly variable circumstances and conditions,"[20] often in the absence of any kind of juridical or even circumstantial evidence. In fact, arrests are rarely made in the presence of a foreign date or partner, presumably for the sake of appearances: it would portray Cuba in a bad light to have tourists see their companions harassed or arrested. This means that the majority of arrests take place by necessity in the absence of any proof of association with foreigners, let alone of sexual intimacy or financial transactions with them. This profile is that of the jinetera, that figure whose production and reproduction are the culmination of interlocking histories of race, gender, and sexuality.

The determination of which individuals are suspect and will be rendered subject to state-led intervention is imbued with understandings of black and mulata female sexuality as deviant. The perception in official circles that a crisis of values has swept Cuba in the Special Period, a crisis that the PNR was expanded to address, enables the police to actively use the profile of the jinetera to seek out deviant social elements, even in the absence of victims or witnesses to any crime. Stuart Hall and his colleagues describe this kind of crisis as a moral panic, which occurs across governmental structures and media and facilitates raced and gendered profiling.[21] Race, gender, and even social class (or the perception thereof) inform the distinction, made on the ground by the police, between wholesome and deviant, affectionate and transactional when it comes to sexuality and sexual relationships.

As Kempadoo argues, "Lines seem to be drawn around definitions of sex work that emerge from different locations within structures of power in the sex trade around not just gender, but also ethnicity, 'race,' and class."[22] White Cubans, or those with greater socioeconomic capital (a kind of raced code for professional-looking), are often able to evade the perception of disreputability, remaining "invisible and undistinguished in the world of *jineterismo*";[23] black and mixed-race Cubans, on the other hand, have a much harder time avoiding routine scrutiny by the police and assumptions about their sexual and moral proclivities. Viewed from the outside, then, whiteness is associated with romance and blackness with prostitution, but more to the point, money and status whiten, while poverty and perceived "bad" behavior darken.

This speaks to some deep-seated social prejudices, as many white Cuban men persist in believing that black women are not suitable partners and thus that any woman of color seen with a white man must be a jinetera with a tourist. This mind-set informs the rationale for arbitrary arrest in many cases, as darker-skinned women are far more likely to be targeted by police officers in mass arrests as well as day to day. Even those young men who actively and explicitly seek out sexual-affective relationships with tourists, whether those tourists are men or women, are by and large not treated as prostitutes; Gisela Fosado's study of self-professed pingueros who pursue male tourists attests to this.[24] Men of color are often stopped for identification checks, but the existence (or presumption) of a sexual or romantic liaison between a Cuban man and a foreigner can often serve to *avert* police attention, rather than attract it, as was my experience with Ricky, and as I discussing in more detail later. Cisgender men are very rarely, if ever, accused of prostitution because the staggering majority of criminalization and pathologization measures have been directed at women. It is thus women of color who bear the brunt of stigma and discipline in the exercise of Article 72 for prostitution, restricting their movements in public spaces accordingly, and it is women of color who shoulder the burden of circumventing the prostitute/jinetera identity while state institutions like the PNR enforce it.

In practice, those young people who are arrested in the tourist zones of major cities or close to major hotel and resort installations are taken to the police station and given cartas de advertencia. After receiving three such cartas, these women are taken into custody and brought before a judge, who may then institutionalize them to receive rehabilitative treatment for prostitution. Such sentences are for an indeterminate period of up to four years. This is a process that is confirmed by my own conversations with Cubans and with the FMC, which helps operate the rehabilitation centers, as well as by the work of the Cuban journalist Rosa Miriam Elizalde.[25] In the case of the operativos, however—and, it seems, in the case of Evan's two friends whom he spotted on the Astro bus—the system of warning letters can sometimes be bypassed and detained women can be brought directly before a judge.

For thousands of women, these sentences have been carried out at rehabilitation centers located across the country rather than regular prisons. The centers are shrouded in a certain degree of mystery for outsiders like me, as well as for most Cubans, who are unable to gain any kind of access to them and must learn about them second hand. They did, however, play a prominent role in the UN report by Coomaraswamy. The report describes how, at Coomaraswamy's request, she was taken to visit the Centro de Rehabilitación in Pinar del Río province, which is located in a former penitentiary and still bears the old sign. Only recently founded at the time of Coomaraswamy's arrival in 1999, the center was run by MININT and staffed by uniformed women with special social and psychological training. The report states that the fenced-in facility held thirty-five women, living in dormitories with bunk beds and performing six to eight hours of agricultural labor per day. The women were not allowed to leave the center except for organized group excursions, and they were permitted only two hours of visiting time every fifteen days with family members on a preapproved list. Tellingly, Coomaraswamy was not allowed to speak to the incarcerated women in private. She was also told that while no work training was offered for the women as yet, there were plans to institute such courses for the women confined there.[26] In an interview in 2001, Coomaraswamy reflected on seeing posters and other materials displayed that exhorted women to love themselves and improve their self-esteem, qualities, it had been decided, that these women lacked.[27]

In 2000 Cabezas interviewed a trainer employed at one of the rehabilitation centers. According to this testimony, detainees receive workplace skills training in what Cabezas calls "socially acceptable and gender-defined careers," such as hairdressing and secretarial work. The trainer also echoed the messages of self-esteem seen by Coomaraswamy. "The problem," this informant lamented, "is that these women do not value their bodies and do not love themselves."[28]

The experience of this rehabilitative process, however, seems to be a far cry from these outside accounts. One young woman named Yonilys, with whom Cabezas spoke in 2001, described being subjected to mandatory gynecological examinations and blood tests after her arrest.[29] Another woman, Marianita, who was interviewed by Amir Valle, described her experiences as follows:

> I was one of the first to go in the big round-up in 1997 and they sent me to work on an agricultural compound. It was a concentration camp and no one can tell me that the people at the top didn't know what was happening to us, all the mistreatment, all the abuses and even the hunger they made us go through, because these country girls [*guataquitas*] that you see here had to swallow the words of so many shit-eaters who used to come from their offices at the top to tell us that we had to pay, and pay well, for our faults. You're going to think I'm crazy, but there were days when I wished I could have gotten AIDS and instead of being a prisoner there, I could have been sent to a sanatorium: they treat whores well there, with a psychologist and everything.[30]

Despite Coomaraswamy's report, there has been little public outcry by human rights organizations or women's rights advocates, or even by the Cuban American expat community in Miami, which is usually very vocal on human rights issues in Cuba. The centers have, however, come to constitute a constant menace to many Cuban women, and very few seem willing to declare themselves in support of these kinds of rehabilitative measures.[31] Despite the fact that prostitution does not appear in the Cuban criminal code, these centers continue to operate. It is argued in official circles that they play a pastoral or therapeutic, rather than disciplinary or punitive, role by providing care in the women's own interest; however, the paternalist self-help messaging, the sentences of indeterminate confinement and labor, and the forced gynecological exams and blood testing directed at a crime that is no crime in Cuba speak to a form of violence that operates not through but rather outside, and even above, the written letter of the law.

These forms of violence are exercised against young women of color because of a widely held understanding that they are deviant, promiscuous social elements. The sexuality of black and mulata women is tacitly accepted as dangerous in and of itself, and a threat to social order, to the revolutionary ethic, and to the stability of Cuban society. Supposed jineteras are engaged in sexual-affective relationships that sometimes defy traditional, monogamous, heteronormative relationships, that may flout old-fashioned and gendered notions of how romantic and sexual relationships ought to occur—who is an appropriate partner, who must be the pursuer and who the pursued, and how many partners one should have in a given period of time. To a deeply conservative police force, these women are easily read as morally degenerate, which translates quickly into repressive racist and misogynist police practices.

The Cuban government has a history of persecuting sexual dissidents, which is mirrored in the PNR's problematic history vis-à-vis gay and lesbian Cubans: from the UMAP camps in the 1960s, covered in chapter 1, to the spike in homophobia around the time of the 1980 Mariel boatlift, to the arrests and harassment seen each weekend on the Malecón since the 1990s, gay and transgender Cubans' history has been fraught with similar perceptions of their sexual identities as hazardous to Cuban society.[32] Likewise, the assumption that all interactions between white foreign men and Cuban women of color must necessarily be both sexual and transactional is a fundamentally racist and sexist position that enables violence on the bodies of Afro-Cuban and mixed-race women. It constitutes an attempt to control the presence—and presentation of self—in public spaces of these women. Even more forms of everyday violence, however, are possible for those with the power to abuse, bend, and break the law, as Isabel's story reveals.

AFRAID OF WHAT COULD HAPPEN

My meeting with Isabel was the product of several weeks of negotiation and messages passed through intermediaries. Finding someone who is willing to share his or her experiences of the violence of police corruption and abuse is a delicate process, one that involves a convoluted network of contacts and the careful cultivation of trust, not just of the individual in question, but of everyone in the chain that leads to him or her.

Isabel had left school after the ninth grade because, while education is free in Cuba, her family needed all of its members to pull their weight if they were to stay afloat. So, at fourteen years old, Isabel began going out to the heavily touristed zones of Havana to strike up conversations and make new friends where she could. She went to the historic old city, to the busy center of Vedado, to the beach, and along Havana's iconic seafront, the Malecón. The tourists—mostly Italians, she says—were more than happy to meet her; often she would be approached by them rather than vice versa. Isabel is very pretty, with sparkling eyes, a curvy silhouette, golden brown skin, and curly dark hair. She cultivated friendships with lots of interesting new people—some were short-lived, but others lasted weeks or months, and some returned to Cuba several times to see her—and she saw her standard of living grow by leaps and bounds through gifts of cash, clothing, and items for her home.

It wasn't long, though, before Isabel began to attract a different kind of attention. As a young, attractive mulata woman, she could not visit tourist neighborhoods without being stopped for random—that is, targeted—identification checks by police patrols. Some days it ended there, but on others Isabel was brought to the station and issued a carta de advertencia. She was now officially established as a jinetera in the eyes of the police, and once these letters appeared on her record, Isabel became far more vulnerable. She had caught the eye of one particular officer, a beat cop in the area of Calle 23, who began to regularly threaten her. Given her record, he needed no justification whatsoever to arrest her, no matter what she was doing. With no money to pay him off, Isabel was forced to repeatedly have sex with him to buy her freedom. By this point, her eventual arrest seemed almost inevitable. Late last year, Isabel was arrested while passing by Café Sofia on Calle 23. She was sent to a rehabilitation center with an indefinite sentence, which, as it turned out, would last six months.

On the day I meet her, Isabel has been out of prison for five months. I have been waiting all day for a call from a mutual contact who has arranged it, and when it finally comes around five o'clock in the afternoon, I hurry along the busy thoroughfare of Calzada de Infanta to our meeting place—a nondescript fast-food joint called Pollo—where Isabel and her friend, Mirtica, are waiting for me. A few minutes later, sitting in a small park near the Carlos III shopping center, I try to get the conversation started, but Isabel is visibly nervous. She looks over her shoulder frequently and scrutinizes every passerby, saying that even being overheard by the wrong person could result in her being charged with antisocial conduct. This clearly won't work.

Fast-forward another twenty minutes, and Isabel and Mirtica are settling into the couch in my landlady's front room. Isabel seems far more relaxed and begins to describe her life as a jinetera, a term she readily embraces, but her voice is flat and her eyes averted as she talks about the abuse at the hands of the police, her arrest and sentencing, her time in custody, and how much she missed her young son, who is six. Of the center, she says it was an institution specifically for women deemed to be prostitutes but that nothing else set it apart from a prison in her opinion.

Asked how she feels about that experience, she shrugs and looks out the window, but her attention returns quickly when I ask if she believes that what she did constituted prostitution. Firmly, emphatically, she replies, "No. When it comes to jineterismo, the first thing is to build a friendship, to get to know each other. It's the first concern, the most important thing!" Mirtica nods along, smiling sagely.

Today Isabel lives near the airport with her mother and her son. She works in a hospital as an administrative assistant. When I ask if she likes the job, she smiles wryly, saying, "That's beside the point." Times are hard, she is again pregnant, and she worries that as she ages she won't be able to support herself, two children, and her mother on her salary. It's not surprising, then, that she's considering going back to jineteando, despite the obvious risks. "I don't want to get arrested again," she worries. "And I can't lose my children, but I'm afraid of what could happen." She still fears one particular police officer, but that dread stays with her whether she returns to Calle 23 or not. "If I could go back to before the police and the letters, my life would be so much better."

But was she happy then? She laughs at my question, gazing off somewhere above my left shoulder with a look of wistful nostalgia. After a long pause, she says, "Yes. I loved it. I was so happy."

Isabel's story is far from unique in a setting where PNR officers possess a measure of impunity when it comes to people who they can successfully class as social deviants or problematic elements. What is more, it amply demonstrates the abuses that are possible for those with social and struc-

Figure 11. Calzada de Infanta, Havana, where I went to meet
Isabel, 27 July 2010. Photo by author.

tural power. It is not at all uncommon to hear stories of physical and sexual violence perpetrated against young black and mixed-race people by
officers of the law, a phenomenon that is described by some as gratuitous
and by others as part of a wider regime of intimidation and discipline.
While it can be argued that corrupt practices depend on the individual
PNR officer, they are widespread enough to posit a truly systemic level of
extralegal repression within the PNR as an institution. For women, whose
raced and gendered bodies render them marginal and often vulnerable,
this violence is frequently sexual. Cabezas's research supports this. She
asserts that "state violence against women exists in a continuum that

encompasses everything from harassment and verbal abuse to rape."[33] For Isabel, and many others like her, the menace posed by PNR officers with very real power over her manifested itself in repeated instances of extortion and rape, as disciplinary measures and as an affirmation of the personal power of individual police officers.

Extortion of cash and goods has become an everyday reality for so-called jineteras, as more and more police officers have begun to demand bribes and to accept them when offered—almost always in convertible pesos. Many of the people I met argued that this led the officers to accost even greater numbers of people in the streets, so that they could bring home even more hard currency for themselves and their families. Some, like Isabel, find themselves trapped in cycles of abuse wherein their freedom must be purchased from the police over and over again. As a foreigner, I saw this burden brought to bear many times on my own informants and friends, as being seen with me regularly flagged them for scrutiny by beat patrol officers in the vicinity.

One day in May, as I was walking down Calle Heredia in Santiago with Yancel, a twenty-nine-year-old mechanic, we were stopped by two PNR officers. Instead of asking Yancel to see his carné de identidad, as I had come to expect, one of the officers took him ever so slightly to one side and flatly muttered the words, "A pack of cigarettes or you go to the station." This I readily provided from a nearby snack stand, slipping the box into Yancel's hand for him to pass along, and we were left to continue on our way. Yancel could not have easily afforded the cigarettes on his own, had the officers accosted him after we had parted ways for the night, but he would have had to find a way or suffer the consequences.

This was not an exceptional incident—for me, for Yancel, or for many young Cubans I would meet. On many occasions, Cuban contacts and friends reported receiving verbal harassment from PNR officers who had seen us walking together, a thinly veiled form of intimidation. Similarly, a Canadian named Peter recounted to me how his friend had brought two Cuban women to their casa particular one night, one of whom was intended to be Peter's date. When he told the girl that he was not interested and that she should probably go home, she began to cry. Peter felt sorry for her and pressed her to tell him why she was so upset. To his horror, she told him that there was a police officer waiting outside, and without money to pay him, he would likely beat her. Looking out the window, Peter saw the uniformed officer, waiting patiently, so he gave her the money and watched from his balcony as she handed it over and fled.

Valle's interviews show that many police collaborate with young women, so that they can continue seeking out tourist men and moving through public spaces unmolested. While some young people make calculated decisions to participate in these kinds of deals with police officers, the disparate power relations between them are undeniable and imbue the arrangements with a forceful inevitability. Systematic extralegal violence against the sexualized bodies of women of color is made permissible for police officers, morally and institutionally, by racism, sexism, and structural vulnerability. The discourse of prostitution writes these women out of the safety the PNR purports to provide and renders them available for sexual assault, physical violence, and extortion. This further violence, operating around and between legal structures and against young women of color, cannot be erased.

BUT, OF COURSE, THEY'RE NOT REALLY ALONE

Not all the forms of extralegal violence made permissible by the discourse of prostitution are enacted by agents of the state. The phenomenon of the chulo is a troubling element of the sexual-affective economy. There are those who argue that sexual commerce in Cuba is a "freelance" venture and that the women concerned all engage in it for and by themselves,[34] but chulos have been a reality for many women for some time already, and their role is only becoming more significant with the passage of time. Since the crackdowns of the late 1990s, chulos are said to have grown in number and importance. It is now much more difficult and dangerous for Cuban women to interact with tourists in public spaces, like city streets or the Malecón, so many have come to rely on a chulo to make contact on their behalf. While some of these men, like those who feature in Valle's journalistic study, *Habana Babilonia*, fall in line with what would elsewhere be called a pimp—managing transactions for multiple women and taking a specified percentage of earnings—others facilitate their own wives' and girlfriends' interactions with foreigners. In fact, many people told me that this was the very defining feature of the chulo: he maintains a romantic and sexual relationship with the woman whose tourist relations he makes possible, whereas this is not necessarily the case for a pimp, or *proxeneta*. In the years after Operativo Lacra in Havana, chulos have made it possible for some women to continue to hook up with tourists, either by staying close in public spaces and stepping in when the police are near so the woman does not appear to be alone or by actively setting up meetings on her behalf; however, the growing involvement of chulos in Cuba's sexual-affective economy gives them a degree of power over what goes on and clears the way for yet more coercion. They remained one of the more elusive facets of my study of sexual jineterismo, as people seemed to speak of them in hushed tones and often to deny their existence. Raúl was one of the few who spoke candidly about the chulo role.

Walking along the Malecón after dark, voices ring out from all directions. It's a busy night and the promenade is packed with people: elderly women selling roses, candies, and little bags of popcorn; fishermen tending their lines; families out for an evening stroll; and everywhere, young people in couples and in groups perch on the seawall and enjoy the cool evening air. I've had a long day. Stepping outside for some fresh air and a solitary walk seemed like a great way to clear my head, but of course, as a foreign woman in Havana, I am never alone for very long.

"Hello? Hello? How are you? Where are you from?"

I've heard these kinds of lines so many times and from so many different people in the past few months that it hardly registers. I walk on.

"Hello! Hello!"

He persists as I continue walking for close to a city block before I finally turn to have a look at this young man. He is of slight build, with close-cropped hair and studded ears, and he is simply dressed in a black T-shirt and jeans. I think to myself that I suppose I've got nothing to lose talking to him, so I begin conceding responses as he peppers me with questions, and we carry on past the forest of flags outside the U.S. Interests Section, the de facto embassy of the United States in Cuba.[35]

He asks me my name, my age, where I'm from, what I do for a living, whether I have a boyfriend, when I arrived in Cuba. When he asks why I've been in Cuba so long, I tell him I'm interviewing young Cubans who pick up yumas, and he laughs. "What do you think all of these girls are doing out here tonight?" He sweeps his arm to indicate the entire Malecón.

We sit down near the monument to the sinking of the USS *Maine*, where Línea meets the Malecón. Now it's my turn to ask the questions. He tells me his name is Raúl and he's twenty-seven years old. Born in Camagüey, he moved to Havana at eighteen to look for work. At first, with nowhere to stay, he squatted in an abandoned building with several other newcomers from the countryside. Quickly, though, he learned that he could get a decent meal, new clothes, or even cash by accepting propositions from the European women who approached him looking to fulfill their tropical fantasies. Laughing thinly, he says he was desperate and could not afford to be choosy, so he wound up with women who were often more than three times his age, but they were kind to him and wanted to provide him with things that he needed. I ask him how he feels about it now, but he just shrugs and looks out over the crowded Malecón, where hundreds of young people are mingling, chatting, and carousing.

"I did what I had to do. It's over now."

The topic appears to be closed now, so we sit side by side and just watch the crowd for a bit. Eventually, I ask him if he really thinks all of the young women on the Malecón are hustling.

"All of the girls you see sitting alone," he says, glancing at me briefly before adding, "But of course, they're not really alone."

How so?

"Their boyfriends are somewhere nearby, keeping an eye on them."

Chulos, I say.

"Exactly," he says. "The chulo takes care of the girl. He doesn't sit with her, because then the tourists won't approach her, but he's close. If the police come, he'll go talk to her so that she doesn't seem to be alone and they won't think she's *jineteando*. That way the police leave her be. He's not sitting next to her, but he's in charge."

Why?

"Because he's the man! Cuban women expect that. Men are the bosses. They make the decisions and they hold the money."

This all sounds quite troubling to me, and I feel I have to ask how much coercion is involved. Do chulos oblige their female partners to go out looking for tourists?

"Yes, yes, of course! And they have to do as they're told, or—" Raúl mimes a sharp slap to the face. He speaks flatly and frankly. None of this seems to unsettle him.

I can feel myself reacting to what he's telling me, much as I try to remain detached. With more emotion in my voice than I had intended, I hear myself ask how these chulos differ from ordinary pimps.

"Well," he says slowly, "pimps aren't in a relationship with the girl, are they? So they would share the money with her. A chulo is her boyfriend or her husband, so he keeps the money." He shrugs again. "They do it to benefit both of them. Sometimes she wants to do it. Sometimes she doesn't. She does it so he won't leave her."

Another long silence.

"My best friend's wife is a jinetera and he's her chulo. It's quite common." He pauses again. "Six months ago, they met a tourist who just wanted to watch her with someone—but not with her husband. My friend asked me to do it. He said, 'If it's going to be someone, I want it to be you.' He shared the money with me."

After taking a moment to absorb this revelation, I ask Raúl how he feels about it.

"I was just worried she was going to fall in love with me."

And her? How does she feel about it?

He just shrugs in reply.

After yet another lengthy silence, I ask Raúl if he thinks there are many girls without chulos along the Malecón tonight.

"Few," he says. "Very few."

We parted ways shortly thereafter. Raúl's story left me feeling very ill at ease, having shown me yet another form of repression that the discourse of prostitution has made possible. Since the late 1990s, women can no longer feel safe approaching foreign men in public spaces like the Malecón or along streets like La Rampa, so many have come to rely on middlemen of some kind. Part of a chulo's role is to help the young woman with whom he works to avoid police scrutiny, but this places women in a position of vulnerability, and the potential for coercion and violence is high. Cabezas posits that this development has led to a strengthening of patriarchal control of sexual jineterismo, as state repression against young Cuban women of color has effectively expanded networks of male brokers.[36]

Chulos have emerged from a network of actors that includes taxi drivers, hotel staff, waiters, tour guides, and even police officers to take on a far more prominent role. They represent a form of resistance to the violence of practices like arbitrary arrest and rehabilitative confinement, allowing women who do seek relationships with foreign men to continue doing so amid growing state repression. However, chulos are as blurry and indeterminate a category as any other on the scene, and who qualifies as a chulo is often unclear. I would later be told by a representative of the FMC that being a chulo is among the most reprehensible and harshly punished crimes in Cuba, but when I asked how they are detected, I was told that state institutions look for older Cuban men who have no "valid" reason to be in the company of young women. This seems both conceptually problematic and ridiculous, given that chulos are often meant to be in relationships with the women they manage and thus have every reason to be in their company. It seems that many such chulos would be undetectable via that logic. What is more, the exact set of activities that constitute *chulería* is also imprecise. A number of my own contacts might qualify as chulos, depending on the definition, as they acted as middlemen and liaisons for various young women who wanted to meet male tourists. Some run interference with the police on behalf of women who were already in the practice of seeking out tourists; others coerce or cajole their girlfriends or other women into taking up the activity in the first place. The chulo is nearly as indeterminate a marker as the jinetera, but the effect of increasing male control of the sexual-affective economy is nonetheless very real.

Valle's interviews with self-proclaimed jineteras and chulos also paint a bleak picture of intimidation, abuse, and retribution. Physical and sexual violence is a commonplace feature of the accounts, and women who leave their chulos are beaten and even mutilated—practices that the law forbids, but fear of arrest, further abuse, and revenge prevent reporting in most of these cases.[37] This violence is gendered in that it takes place between intimate partners and in that it almost exclusively affects women, since young men hooking up with foreigners are not subject to the same punitive framework. The notion of a chulo who works with male jineteros is completely unheard of. It is also raced, in that women of color are more likely to attract police attention and thus to need the protection and facilitation that a chulo purports to provide. White women can operate under the radar with regard to the police and therefore are less vulnerable to the potential violence of the chulo relationship.

The police crackdowns have exacerbated women's exposure to these kinds of violent practices, however, serving to insert middlemen between Cuban women and foreign men and giving them a direct role in selecting would-be suitors and controlling the interaction—overall, an increasing level of male control over Cuban women's sexual relationships. By framing sexual-affective relations with foreigners as a free and selfish choice that individual women make, the state-centered position on jineterismo serves to erase this violence and to ensure that the voices of women who have been genuinely coerced are not heard in formulating the official response to jineterismo.

It is also important to keep in mind that the police and chulos are not completely discrete entities. Some chulos, much like other people involved in the sexual-affective economy, maintain relations of bribery or collusion with individual police officers; others *are* police officers. It is the long-term relationship between a chulo and a jinetera that seems to define it rather than the official professions or positions of either of them. The potential for (or even expectation of) sexual or romantic intimacy between them is also a distinguishing characteristic. While many young women pursue foreign dates and partners in the interests of boyfriends, husbands, even parents and siblings, whose lives might also be improved by a foreign liaison—interviews done by César confirm this[38]—such a level of simultaneous intimacy and coercion marks the chulo role as different from any of these. They are facilitators of resistance as well as sites or sources of extralegal repression at the same time. There are, however, many more subtle and everyday means of resisting state-centered power and violence. Some of these may seem insignificant, but they contribute to a wider symbolic resistance to and critique of state socialist discourse.

A GOOD FRIEND TO HAVE

On a sweltering evening in Santiago, I was on my way to meet my Norwegian friend Anders at El Piropo, a bar-café in Plaza de Dolores. By now, I've become accustomed to my own conspicuousness as a foreigner in Cuba, and especially in Santiago, but next to Anders I blend in easily:

he is tall, with golden-yellow hair and an easygoing smile on his fair, sun-burned face. He seems blithely oblivious to the looks we receive as we find a table, and he heads immediately to the bar. By the time Anders returns to our table, he's carrying four beers and has already made the acquaintance of two very beautiful young women. With a wink at me, he sits down and invites Cristina and Olivia to join us.

Cristina, we learn, is a seamstress at a clothing factory here in Santiago, and Olivia is a nursing student. From the outset, it's clear that Anders is the reason they've joined us, as both girls vie for his attention. My attempts to interject are all rebuffed, until finally some wordless signal passes between the two women: Olivia leans forward, chatting ever more intently with Anders, while Cristina turns to me with one raised eyebrow and a sigh. She doesn't seem pleased to be stuck talking to me, so it looks like I have my work cut out for me.

Cristina is nineteen years old. She quit studying two years ago in order to start earning money for her family, but she only makes $200 MN (around US$8.50) per month. She has caramel skin, and her dark hair is pulled smoothly back into a knot at the back of her head. She's dressed casually, in stark contrast to Olivia's high heels and dress, in a tank top and jeans. That's all I can really manage to learn, though, since if I'm going to insist on conversation, it seems Cristina would prefer to ask the questions. We cover my age, nationality, occupation, and relationship status in rapid succession, but it is when she asks me why I am in Cuba that her interest is finally piqued. I tell her I'm here to talk to young Cubans who have, or want to have, relationships with foreigners so that I can better understand jineterismo and its effects. She stops fiddling with her can of beer for a moment, then resumes it in earnest, nodding to herself as she processes this new information, chewing it like food in her mouth. Finally, she sets the can down and leans across the table.

"Why?"

Her gaze is piercing. I tell her I'm interested in how people feel about relationships with foreigners, what it means for young Cubans, and what it means for Cuba. Cristina nods thoughtfully.

"What are you going to do with what you learn here?"

I reply that I want to write a book and include all of the stories that people have told me.

"Are you against us?"

I answer no, and suddenly it seems I've earned some further confidences. She glances quickly around her, before beckoning to me to move closer. "Look, European men come here because the girls are cheap, you know? Havana has blonde girls and they're more expensive, but in Santiago it's all darker girls [*morenas*] like me. Italians especially."

And they pay you?

"They give us presents—it's better that way. It's just what we do. We come here and see who we meet. So I can help my family and so Olivia can continue studying."

I ask if the two of them come here alone, if any of the men seated around us are their boyfriends, brothers, or friends, but she shakes her head. She tells me about a number of the men she's met here but asks me not to record the details.

We're interrupted by Olivia, who hisses sharply to Cristina and then gestures pointedly with her eyes toward the wrought-iron fence that rings the bar. In the darkness just beyond the patio, I can just make out the form of a lone police officer, eyes locked on our little group. Before I have time to wonder what is about to happen, Cristina and Olivia slip away from our table and go to speak to him through the fence.

"What's going on?," Anders mutters, as much to himself as to me, but all I can do is shrug. So we wait, but not for long, as the girls return shortly.

"We've been friends since we were kids," says Cristina, jerking her head in the direction of the cop as he disappears under the unlit neon signs of Calle Enramada. "It pays to know a cop in Santiago."

They're gathering their things and taking their leave of us. I ask them if we can meet again to talk some more, and Olivia smiles, but her wide-set eyes remain expressionless. She's impossible to read. The three of us make plans to meet again the following afternoon in that same place, but I can already sense that the meeting will not come to pass. Anders and I say goodbye, and the two girls hurry away.

Twenty minutes later, as Anders and I continue to lounge on the terrace of El Piropo, the streets around us suddenly flood with police officers. Feeling rather electrified, I watch as each Cuban under the age of around thirty is systematically stopped and questioned for blocks in every direction. Then the pieces fall into place: it's an *operativo*.

He warned them.

Figure 12. Calle Enramada leading away from Plaza de
Dolores, Santiago de Cuba, 10 June 2010. Photo by author.

The next day, sitting in the sun and waiting, I watch a lone police officer
saunter slowly past, and I'm not surprised that Olivia and Cristina do not
appear. Theirs is one of many ways young Cubans have found of averting,
subverting, and co-opting the gaze of the police, and likely one of the most
valuable, since, as far as I could tell from our brief encounter, it cost them
nothing. This officer simply chose to protect Cristina and her friend in the
name of their shared childhoods. Many, if not most, are not so lucky, however, and must find other means of evading police power. Some of these
means are predictable, but others indicate a great degree of ingenuity in
the face of adversity.

Unsurprisingly, in a setting where being seen with foreigners can be a
very risky proposition, one of the simplest and most straightforward ways
to dodge trouble is not to be seen with them at all. Since police officers
rarely enter venues where tourists congregate, such as hotels, nightclubs,
bars, and restaurants, young Cubans know they must be wary as they exit
these types of establishments and frequently tell foreign friends and dates
to follow at a distance when they leave together. In and around the nightclubs of Havana in particular, I heard this same plan reiterated again and

again by young Cubans to the foreigners they had picked up. Some extend the logic so far as to take separate taxis when traveling over longer distances, preferring to arrive separately at their destination. Similarly, there is a growing trend toward the on-line world among young Cubans, who create profiles on dating and matchmaking websites looking to meet non-Cubans. Given the high cost and limited availability of Internet connections, this outlet is available only to those who already possess a degree of relative affluence, but it is nonetheless a growing trend that is now readily observable in hotel Internet cafés around Havana.

On the other hand, as discussed above, some young women make the calculated decision to enter into arrangements with individual police officers as a way of staying safe. Damarys, a thirty-one-year-old teacher I met at Café Sofía along La Rampa, told me she has to be careful choosing which men to leave the bar with, because once she is seen walking with them in the street she will have to pay the officer on duty for his silence. While bribery is usually the extent of these deals, sexual services may also be provided and even expected, particularly if cash is scarce. This brings to mind Peter's story of watching a young woman give money to the police as she left a tourist casa particular. Given the unequal relations of power inherent in any interaction between the police and a suspected jinetera, issues of consent to such practices can be blurred. In the face of police power, many of these women have extreme difficulty articulating and enforcing their will. Nonetheless, co-opting police power in such a way helps many young women avoid criminal records, arrest, and internment in rehabilitation centers while continuing to resist state-centric ideas about moral behavior and sexuality.

Cubans in long-term relationships with foreign partners face a different set of challenges and thus have developed distinct practices for refusing the jinetera identity. Danielle, a twenty-two-year-old woman I met on the beach in Varadero, told me she had chosen to take the bull by the horns. In the face of constant identification checks and threats of warning letters, she visited her local police station and asked to have her relationship with her Italian partner officially noted on her record. This way, when she was questioned by police and her details were run through their system, they would see that she was in a committed monogamous relationship and thus, presumably, not a jinetera. Several others reported attempting several times to do something similar, however, and being met with refusal and even derision.

Where registration fails, the right paperwork seems to go a long way toward subverting criminalization and legitimizing relationships. In Ricky's case, featured in the previous chapter, a photocopy of his marriage certificate sufficed to obtain the virtual blessing of the police for not just his relationship with his English wife, Sarah, but also with other tourists and foreigners. Evan and Karla's experience also speaks to the importance of documentation: Karla carried a copy of Evan's passport and a letter describing their relationship in the hope that these would help her prove that she was not a jinetera. Establishing one's sexual-affective relationships as legitimate, honest, and wholesome seems to directly influence one's perceived right to mobility in public space in the company of particular people.

It is fascinating (and very instructive) to note, as I have mentioned, that young men in Cuba can avoid police scrutiny in very different ways from young women, as I learned with Ricky. Men fulfill many different roles in the illicit, tourist-oriented economy—from acting as liaisons for restaurants and casas particulares or procurers of cheap cigars and rum or unofficial tour guides to platonic friends or even romantic and sexual companions. Women, on the other hand, are assumed to be performing only one possible role: the provision of sexual services and romantic companionship to foreign men. Therefore, when a Cuban woman is seen with a male tourist, she is assumed to be engaged in some kind of sexual relationship with him, and that relationship is itself deemed problematic. If, on the other hand, a foreign woman is seen with a Cuban man, the existence of a sexual relationship between them—made evident by displays of affection such as holding hands—serves to absolve him of suspicion of other criminal activities, such as selling black-market cigars, and thus to legitimate the interaction. I found this ploy mystifying when I first arrived in Havana and I was asked to hold male contacts' hands when we were in busy tourist districts. Over time, however, I learned that this simple trick produced marked results. My male Cuban friends and contacts were rarely questioned if we walked arm in arm rather than simply side by side as friends or colleagues.

Again, this illustrates the ingrained raced and gendered edifice that informs understandings of transnational relationships between Cubans and outsiders. Foreign-Cuban pairings are overwhelmingly categorized by racial markers, and thus Cubans of color (particularly young women) and white foreigners (particularly older men) are rendered most visible. Women are seen to have nothing else to offer a foreigner besides her sexualized body, and as women of colour, that sexuality is automatically marked as deviant, even criminal. Black and mixed-race Cubans are made detectable in their relationships mostly with white foreigners, but for men, the existence of a sexual liaison is the solution to the problem, whereas for women, the sexual nature of the interaction is the problem in and of itself.

These tactics of evasion and co-optation are just a few of the ways that contemporary Cuban youth have found to protect themselves against repression. For the most part, they constitute only a feeble counterweight to the overwhelming power and presence of the police in most of Cuba's urban areas, but they demonstrate resilience and ingenuity in the face of oppressive disciplinary measures and a way in which individual subjects can confront and resist state power on the only level that is available to them—the level of their own bodies, lives, and relationships. Scott calls these types of tactics the "weapons of the weak," or "small arms in a cold war": forms of minimal compliance and "false deference" to powerful elites that refuse and reduce the effects of power in small ways without directly attacking it.[39] In his study of everyday forms of resistance in the rural Indonesian village of Sedaka, Scott observes the following:

> Everyday forms of resistance make no headlines. Just as millions of anthozoan polyps create, willy-nilly, a coral reef, so do thousands upon thousands of individual acts of insubordination and evasion create a political and economic barrier reef of their own. There is rarely any dramatic confrontation, any moment that is particularly newsworthy. And whenever, to pursue the simile, the ship of state runs aground on such a reef, attention is typically directed to the shipwreck itself and not to the vast aggregation of petty acts that made it possible. It is only rarely that the perpetrators of these petty acts seek to call attention to themselves.[40]

This is not intended to romanticize the struggles of the marginalized against power structures but rather to show how resistance can take many forms and often happens, as Scott notes, "between revolutions." Subjects made vulnerable by the raced and gendered knowledges produced about their lives, their bodies, and their sexualities have everything to lose in a true confrontation and thus are safer pursuing ad hoc, piecemeal forms of resistance that smooth their paths and reduce the risk inherent in their lives. As Scott notes, it is an unspoken dispute over the definition of justice—what ought to be permissible within a shared social setting—and the many singular acts of resistance that compose it function in a truly anarchistic way: "If they are open, they are rarely collective, and, if they are collective, they are rarely open."[41] The forms of resistance enacted every day by young Cubans of color in response to disciplinary power do not directly challenge state authority, nor do they seem to be overtly political, but they contribute to a growing refusal of state-centered ideals of behavior and morality.

CONCLUSION: SMALL ARMS IN A COLD WAR

> For a while we were hungry and we suffered, until I got tired
> of being so poor and I came to a decision. One afternoon I
> grabbed Luisa and got right down to business. "Alright,
> enough of this sitting around and being hungry. You're going
> to the Malecón to hustle!" I made the right decision. For a
> while now, that mulata's been bringing home up to three
> hundred dollars a week.
>   At last. To hell with poverty!
> Pedro Juan Gutiérrez, *Dirty Havana Trilogy*

The discourse of prostitution, and the production of the figure of the mulata/jinetera to bear its effects, enacts a kind of violence against young black and mixed-race women in Cuba, a violence that is symbolic but also physical and sexual. Police practices since 1996 have demonstrated that prostitution has effectively become synonymous with black and mixed-race women on the streets of Cuban cities. Mulata sexuality is read as deviant and troublesome, requiring police intervention, which enables the exercise of power through and—in the case of the rehabilitation centers run by MININT and the FMC— above the law. Practices such as arbitrary arrest, detainment, interrogation, mandatory gynecological and blood tests, and rehabilitative incarceration are enacted against individuals accused of a crime that is not one under Cuban law. Furthermore, these practices put women suspected of being jineteras in a vulnerable position, relative to the police, who form the most direct point of contact between state policy and the public, as well as to chulos, who seek to enable their activities and at the same time profit from their vulnerability. Silenced by the illicitness of their activities and identities, women who participate in the tourist-oriented sexual economy are exposed to a potential violence that operates around the law and can take the forms of extortion, physical violence, sexual assault, and—as Valle's study suggests—pimping arrangements and retributive brutality.[42]

Speaking openly about jineterismo with a police officer, or even a representative of the PNR as a policing institution, was out of the question. It is impossible to guess from the outside the motivations and circumstances of the people who work within the PNR, and thus a degree of mystery remains in my understanding—and circumspection in my conclusions—when it comes to the overlapping spheres of individual and institution. It is possible to say, however, that these practices occur on a scale that suggests a systemic nature, certainly one that cannot be explained by individual officers' decisions alone, and that they have profoundly reshaped the way young Cubans interact in public spaces and go about their daily lives.

In light of these forms of violence, young Cubans have evolved ways and means of resisting. They engage in false deference toward police and other authorities, display the most minimal levels of conformity to state institutions and ideals, and, most important, find ways of averting and subverting the gaze of the law. Yakelín, whose story featured in the preceding chapter, regularly attends her local CDR's meetings and pays her dues to the FMC, all the while rejecting the ideals of socialist solidarity that these institutions put forward. Ricky carries his marriage certificate wherever he goes. Yanet, a self-professed jinetera who was interviewed by Valle, put herself forward as an ideological officer for the board of her local CDR, thereby cementing her position in the community as an upstanding citizen.[43] Many—like Lili, Cristina, and Olivia—continue working and studying on a day-to-day basis, though often with a near-total lack of enthusiasm that dampens their contribution to the socialist system or its economy. Attending one's place of work or study becomes simply a form of minimal compliance, which keeps other activities from drawing unnecessary attention.

Meanwhile, young people avoid disciplinary practices by co-opting the police through bribery—financial and sexual—and by engaging in various forms of subterfuge. These "weapons of the weak" are important daily means of carrying on in the face of repression. In the broader scheme of things, such "Brechtian forms of class struggle"[44] may appear insignificant and self-serving—and on an individual level, they are—but false deference and even symbolic resistance both work to enable a wider political critique of state socialist ideals, building Scott's "political and economic barrier reef."[45]

The discourse of prostitution makes these forms of repression permissible and, subsequently, makes these kinds of tangible and symbolic resistance possible and even necessary. The PNR in particular has been an instrument of the suppression of sexual interactions between Cubans and foreigners and thus has served to enforce the category of prostitute, a category that—as I argued in the preceding chapter—is nebulous and indeterminate at best. It is left to young women themselves, whether or not they identify as jineteras, to contest and resist the prostitute identity that is imposed on them, while the PNR's role in exacerbating the very phenomenon it purports to combat can be nearly invisible to outside observers. Their many means of averting, subverting, and co-opting the gaze of law enforcement officials show a resilience that resonates in many other aspects of Cuban society.

From here, having seen the effects of the state-centric discourse of prostitution and the image of the jinetera, I set out to trace the structural roots that enable these kinds of disciplinary practices. Legal provisions such as Article 72 on peligrosidad and penal practices such as rehabilitative confinement and discretionary arrest originate in state-level policy, which is then interpreted on the ground by individual agents of the state. Sierra Madero argues that the Código Penal itself—and in particular Article 72 on peligrosidad—has a "prophylactic and hygienic function, [granting] to the authorities certain powers over those subjects considered lazy or antisocial."[46] State policy on jineterismo/prostitution and frequently the provisions of the Código Penal itself derive not from any one overarching institutional body but from a variety of organizations that operate separately, but never truly independently, and that propagate a by now all too familiar discourse of prostitution—one that posits very particular notions of good and bad women, right and wrong sexuality, and the proper, virtuous, healthy way of being.

4 There Is Only One Revolution

STATE INSTITUTIONS AND THE MORAL
REVOLUTION

For though it is not actually said, honour is not something
you can touch, or see, it is only something you lose.

Mirta Yáñez, "We Blacks All Drink Coffee"

The Revolution is a developing, dynamic process. But there
is only one Revolution.

Fidel Castro, speech of 23 March 1959, quoted in Fernandez,
Revolutionizing Romance

In the centralized Cuban system, state-centric ideas about prostitution and sexuality circulate not just at the level of the streets, where jineteras, tourists, chulos, and police officers interact, but also at the very top. They find expression—perhaps in ways and to ends not previously anticipated—in the hands of the ubiquitous police force, which interprets, applies, and circumvents state dictates according to a mixture of organizational and individual will. The ideas and governmental policies that underwrite these daily practices, however, originate in places far removed from the Malecón. Indeed, while the discourse of prostitution is a global phenomenon, this particularly Cuban incarnation of prostitution as an idea—what it means and what constitutes the most appropriate response to it—comes from the various institutions that make up the government of Cuba. They are separate but overlapping, and while they are far from a monolithic state apparatus, they share many of the same imperatives and all of the same allegiances.

Fidel Castro himself has said that there is but one Revolution, and it is an ideological framework and a governmental structure bundled into one. In one sense, he is correct—Cuban state socialism *is* the Revolution—but the Revolution is also fraught with internal tensions and external restrictions, not least of which is the U.S. embargo. In a society where jineterismo-as-sexual-practice sees reasonably high degrees of acceptance and support, understandings that paint the jinetera as deviant or problematic seem at times to emanate almost exclusively from the state and its supporters.

The state's investment in this discursive terrain is admittedly high. The campaign to eradicate prostitution in Cuba holds special significance for the people and institutions who took part in it. As Stout notes, it is an "allegory" for the fight against capitalist exploitation, which forms the foundation of the Revolution's legitimacy.[1] For those who participated in the campaign to end prostitution in the early 1960s, and certainly for those implicated in the struggle against the jineterismo of today, this is a narrative for which the stakes are high indeed. It is a sort of parable about the vindication of a country after years of exploitation, symbolized by the abuse of the bodies of its women: it is a claim to fame, a proud achievement, a legitimating genesis story to be defended and carried forward. There is also an atmosphere in Cuba's mass organizations, whether they be the FMC, the UJC, or the CDR, that any equivocation or softening of rhetoric will be seen as counterrevolutionary, which further entrenches accepted discourses.[2] The success or failure of the campaign to eradicate prostitution is not at issue here; rather, this chapter focuses on the roles of these state-affiliated institutions in the process of categorizing and disciplining young women of color as dissident sexual subjects.

I had been cautioned time and again by friends and contacts to be wary of revealing my research to state institutions, so I conducted this research toward the end of my time in Cuba, when I had already achieved most of my other interviews and had less to lose. To access this sector of society, I requested interviews with officials from the institutions that have been most instrumental in state policies on the jinetera. Many declined to return my calls. Where I could not get interviews, I read what they had published in archives and libraries around Havana. It was as difficult a world to enter as that of the streets, and at times it was even more opaque.

When Valle began his study of jineteras in the early 1990s, his key informant—the self-styled queen of the jineteras, Loretta—gave him this advice: "Don't look for the official voice." She added, "In Cuba, as we all know, each person has a double moral code, a double face: the official and the private, and this happens at all levels, including amongst those in power."[3] Here, Loretta is describing the expectation in all the various ranks of government that employees maintain an inviolate party line. Regardless of an individual bureaucrat's perspective, he or she will always parrot the official stance on a given issue, passed down from the uppermost echelons. This admittedly does not set Cuban officials apart from those in many other settings, and cannot be held against individual officials and bureaucrats, but it was nonetheless frustratingly true: at the FMC, the Centro de Estudios sobre la Juventud (CESJ), CENESEX, MININT, and even the newspapers and the University of Havana. The interviews I managed to conduct felt one-dimensional and constantly ran up against walls, and my account of them reflects this.

I did, however, discover a number of threads of tension running through the discourse presented to me. While Loretta is right to say that one story would be seamlessly presented across sources—and, indeed, that the various offices and functionaries would be unresponsive and even hostile—their understandings of precisely what the supposed rise of a thing called jineterismo means are not always the same. Valle notes that the official discourse holds that a very small number of women are jineteras and that these women are rejected by Cuban society at large—a story I heard again and again.[4] Asked to reflect on the issue, however, different people—and, by extension, the organizations they represent—offered their own readings of why they think jineterismo occurs, what it means for the young women involved, and what it means for Cuba.

There are tensions not just among institutions but also between institution and individual, practical and ideological, generalized and specific. The people I interviewed for this chapter spoke to me as representatives of their institutions, so their answers speak to broader institutional commitments rather than individual opinions. They are invested—ideologically, professionally, and quite likely personally—in the milieu in which they operate, and what they could tell me was governed by institutional norms, though it cannot be known to precisely what degree. Themes of antimaterialism, morality, and self-respect were woven through the recurring core narrative of a few benighted women who had lost their way and been rejected by their families and colleagues. Together, they reveal an idealism regarding how—and why—relationships should be conducted and the possibilities for desire and even love across borders.

"THROWAWAY FLOWERS"

If there is one voice that has been heard more than any other on jineterismo in Cuba, it is that of Rosa Miriam Elizalde. The consummate Cuban journalist, Elizalde writes articles for a variety of publications—both print and online, at home and abroad—and always displays an unflappable and optimistic faith in the ideals of Cuban socialism. She is a regular columnist for *Juventud Rebelde*, once a daily newspaper that has been reduced to a weekly since the Special Period, and her columns on the jineteras of Cuba have been collected into a slim volume titled *Flores desechables: ¿Prostitución en Cuba?* It was published in 1998 and has been cited in virtually every piece of writing on the topic, whether academic or journalistic, making her the foremost commentator on jineterismo. I found a copy of her book at the Biblioteca Nacional José Martí, near Plaza de la Revolución. Its evocative title, which means "throwaway flowers,"[5] speaks volumes about the author's take on jineterismo. Its cover bears an image of the Mona Lisa with a wad of American cash peeking out of the neckline of her clothes, an image whose meaning was difficult to decipher even after I had read the entire book.

The story presented in the book is one of moral weakness, of allowing the material to overshadow the ideological. Elizalde criticizes so-called jineteras for pursuing frivolous and unworthy goals while dismissing poverty as even a potential motivation. No educated and healthy Cuban woman, she argues, could be reduced to prostitution by mere economic necessity. According to her own interviews, Elizalde concludes that the jinetera is induced by the prospect of material gain—money, luxury gifts, hotel stays, and emigration—as a result of their scant moral and spiritual values.

Foreign men, she asserts, are good for "going to all the best places, for wearing a different outfit every day, for matching the purse to the shoes, for spending money without a care in *el shopping* [the dollar stores] and, above all, for not working."[6] In another instance, she argues that these jineteras seek only to live "like every day is a party."[7] To cement her point,

Elizalde not only casts aside the idea that love and affection might exist between jineteras and their foreign dates and partners, but even argues that these women are losing the very capacity to fall in love or find satisfaction in relationships: "in every locale, the market for pleasure is a bazaar of dissatisfaction."[8] In her estimation, jineteras are engaged in purely transactional affairs in order to feed an appetite for frivolous and unnecessary material goods. Her book stands as a scathing criticism of what she sees as an evolving relational ethics that cannot result in anything other than false happiness.

Elizalde is not alone in this regard: Elaine Morales Chuco, one of the vice directors of the CESJ, also writes that young women who date foreigners pursue partners based only on their ability to provide material benefits, to such an extent that their capacity for stable relationships and love is compromised.[9] The influx of comparatively affluent tourists, Morales Chuco stresses, has created new "necessities" for Cubans of all ages but especially young people who want to dress stylishly and carry the latest cell phones and music players, items that have become "axes in the process of alienation" from the mainstream of Cuban society.[10] Adhering closely to Elizalde's understanding of the economics of jineterismo, she argues that "necessity can be constructed individually under an illusion of survival. In Cuba no one arrives at prostitution because of need."[11] Morales Chuco argues that this lifestyle gives rise to a "stunted individual happiness"—and to a loss of modesty, stability in relationships, and the capacity for true intimacy—resulting from "moving away from the behavioral models accepted by the Revolution."[12]

The Cuban journalist Mirta Rodríguez Calderón and Jan Strout, an American writing for the socialist magazine Cuba Update, concur.[13] Strout writes that "these modern-day sex workers are frankly trading their bodies for consumer goods and recreational opportunities otherwise unavailable to them," to the detriment of their emotional well-being and their potential for healthy, loving relationships.[14] According to Rodríguez Calderón, young women in Cuba increasingly "reject work as a way to make a living" and "don't link love with sexual relations."[15] Rodríguez Calderón and Strout paint a stark picture of transactional encounters that inhibit young women's capacity for love and sexual satisfaction, providing the empty joys of material luxuries in return.

What is most noticeable about Elizalde's accounts of jineterismo, however, is its tone. The book is markedly disdainful, noting that streets and nightclubs that had been the sites of major roundups of young women had "alleviated themselves of the bitter taste of the laughter of jineteras."[16] She decries not just the purported commerciality of the jinete and the implied lack of a socialist work ethic but also the implied promiscuity, bringing women's sexuality at its most elemental level into the realm of deviance. Promiscuous sexual relations, Elizalde says, are "the anteroom of prostitution."[17] Sexual relations with foreign men, she goes on to note, are a way to divest oneself of the values instilled by the Revolution through health care, food subsidies, and education. To that end, Elizalde fully supports the use of discretionary arrests under Article 72, as well as the supposedly rehabilitative actions taken by the police, MININT, and the FMC in Varadero and Havana beginning in 1996, around the time the book was published.

My attempts to contact Elizalde and request an interview were met with silence. I sent her numerous emails at *Juventud Rebelde*, receiving no reply, and my queries to the other journalists I encountered were met with sympathy but little else. My meeting with the woman whose mission seemed to be exposing the "network of delinquency that wove its cloak around the jinetera"[18] was not to be, but her extensive writing nonetheless conveys a clear message on its own. Her book builds up a narrative of jineterismo that is emotionally empty, that is purely commercial to the point of damaging young women's ability to establish and maintain loving relationships in future. Her aversion to the jineteras themselves, while certainly stemming in part from a distaste for their sexual proclivities, likely also stems from Elizalde's belief that they shun revolutionary values, which she so firmly supports.

> The jineteras are used time and time again to attempt to demonstrate the debilitation or the inviability of a system that succeeded in eradicating sexual commerce from its social spectrum. The grand plan is to disillusion those in the world who admire the social advances of a Revolution that counts, among its many conquests since 1959, an ascendant effort for the dignification of women. . . . But anyone with a minimum of intelligence and proximity to our reality notices that the majority of prostitutes in this poorly apportioned world have little in common with a Cuban jinetera. Not even in

a relationship like this that commodifies and humanly devalues women can Cuban women who dedicate themselves to sexual commerce clear their minds of the values that the Revolution instilled in them.[19]

She interprets sexual relationships with foreigners as a rejection of the Revolution and its humanist, egalitarian mission. Elizalde's voice is a populist one and a very public one. Her writing firmly places sexuality within the realm of morality, and national morality at that, arguing that sexual relations with non-Cuban men impact directly on one's revolutionary credentials. She precludes any space for the women she discusses to decide their own identities or meanings: "It is prostitution, without dressing it up; it is attached at the root to this term and I would say, as well, to its worst and most cynical expression."[20] Hers is a hard-line voice but one that is evidently welcome in Cuban state media.

A PLURALITY OF SEXUAL BEHAVIORS

In contrast, the Centro Nacional de Educación Sexual is known in Cuba and abroad as a progressive bastion with a very liberal attitude toward sexuality and sexual health. The Centro articulates its mission as one of coordination among various organizations implicated in sex education in Cuba, and of direct provision of sex education and sex therapy, in order to allow the individual to "live his/her sexuality in a safe, full, pleasurable and responsible way."[21] Under the leadership of Mariela Castro Espín, the daughter of Raúl Castro and FMC founder Vilma Espín, a connection that is not without significance, CENESEX has taken a high-profile role, working to socially normalize homosexuality and transexuality.

The liberalization of Cuba's stance toward gay, lesbian, and transgender people is certainly far from complete, and homophobia is still commonplace. Landmark steps have nonetheless been taken, particularly at the institutional level: where once gay Cubans were considered counterrevolutionaries by nature and imprisoned in the UMAP camps, today Havana hosts a festival of pride events and, since 2008, the government has begun to provide hormone replacement therapies and sex-reassignment surgery to transgender Cubans through its national health care system. Same-sex relations have been decriminalized since 1979. CENESEX, which took its current form in 1989, has played a central role in bringing issues of homosexuality and sexual diversity to the fore and raised Cuba's global profile as one of the most liberal countries in Latin America toward its LGBT population.

Mariela herself—usually known by her first name, like all members of the Castro clan—has gained a reputation among people in the capital especially as a benevolent protector of LGBT Cubans, as legends swirl around the city of her appearances in local police precincts to argue on behalf of transwomen, drag queens, and gay Cubans detained arbitrarily. One Cuban transwoman named Wendy Díaz recalls in an interview how Mariela once chased a young man who had thrown rocks at a group of transwomen outside the CENESEX headquarters, finally catching him after five city blocks.[22] It is through stories like these that Mariela and, by extension, CENESEX have gained such a larger-than-life profile. The organization enjoys an uncommonly positive reputation among Cubans, virtually unique among state institutions, and its efforts are well known throughout Cuba, not just at the corner of the Malecón and La Rampa, where hundreds of gay and trans Cubans gather on weekend evenings.

With this liberal approach to sexuality in mind, I began my research on CENESEX. It surprised me to find that the organization has been largely silent on the jineteras. In the annals of *Sexología y Sociedad*, CENESEX's in-house journal, I could find only one article that dealt with prostitution at all, and even that was from a historical perspective, through admittedly their archive was incomplete. The rest of its collections were closed while its headquarters underwent a major renovation. The first time I visited CENESEX, in fact, I thought the entire organization was closed. Painters and plasterers abounded, but none could tell me where I could find any CENESEX staff or temporary offices. I walked away discouraged. I tried again periodically and also phoned their office line, until finally one day I met a doctor who worked occasionally on the Centro's master's program in sexuality. He gave me a different phone number, and sure enough, my call was answered on the first attempt. I was given an appointment for a meeting.

CENESEX, like so many other Cuban institutional offices, makes its home in a stately, almost cavernous mansion dating to the prerevolutionary upper classes. It is midafternoon when I arrive, but the building seems quiet, so I sit down to wait on the hedge-lined front steps. Sacks of cement lie here and there, and the smell of paint pervades the place, but there are only one or two people toiling away. Soon, a diminutive woman rounds the corner and makes her way up the path from the street. She has dark hair pulled tightly back from her face and is casually dressed. I wonder if she has come from home to see me. I stand up to introduce myself, and, after shaking hands and exchanging pleasantries, she motions for us to take the two whitewashed iron chairs on the veranda as the workers carry on around us.

Julia wastes no time. As she settles into her chair and sets her bag to one side, she is already telling me, "First of all, jineterismo in Cuba is not a real social problem. There aren't many people who do it. It's really not an issue. And second, the people who do it are people who have reached the age of majority." She holds both hands up, signaling that these facts are incontrovertible. "There is no child prostitution in Cuba. Of course not! How are they going to do it? They're in school! The idea is absurd, right?"

I have no idea how to respond, but from there somehow we fall back into a more preliminary mode, and I find myself asking Julia about her work with CENESEX. She tells me she is a researcher, conducting studies and writing papers on a variety of topics related to human sexuality. In return, she asks me about my work, so I tell her that I am trying to learn more about jineterismo as a cultural phenomenon and about sexuality in Cuba in the context of the economic crisis and the growth of tourism.

"What an odd question," she says, furrowing her brow.

She seems genuinely perplexed, so I ask her what I've said that is so strange.

"Well, the economic crisis has affected the family, I suppose, and through it the ways that people go about forming relationships," she replies. "Every member of a family now has to direct their efforts to the family's economic well-being. The economic function of the family is the most important. That affects the decisions people make and their relationship choices. There are fewer marriages."

It's clear that she thinks even that connection between sex and the Special Period is a stretch. I ask if she thinks that this logic—that is, that each must do what he or she can to support the family—applies to people who form liaisons with foreigners.

"You mean jineteras? No, I don't mean that at all. They aren't doing productive work, work that's good for society or even for themselves. We all need productive work, something that we improve upon and that improves us as well. These girls—" She shakes her head. "What are they going to do with their lives?"

I ask her what the term *jinetera* means to her, and without hesitation she replies, "Prostitution. It means making yourself into an object. Making yourself inactive. It has to do with the system of values!"

Julia is speaking very quickly now. She seems annoyed, so I start trying to frame my questions differently. Trying to improvise, I tell her briefly about some of the people I've met in Cuba, about Yakelín and Lili and how they saw their relationships and their lives. There seem to be a lot of people who have relationships with foreign tourists, I say carefully, but who don't necessarily consider themselves prostitutes—

"Not a lot," she interjects, shooting me a warning look.

Some, I say.

"Yes, some."

People who are looking for love with partners who can make their lives easier, the same way one would expect to see in any country around the world, I add.

"And that's not prostitution?" She raises her eyebrows pointedly.

I hadn't expected such a direct answer, and for a moment I'm at a loss for words. Julia seems to be casting any relationship in which there is consideration for economic well-being as prostitution. Suddenly, most of the questions I had prepared seem pointless. She sighs and rests her cheek on one hand while I scan my notes nervously. As the seconds drag on, my eyes come to rest on the full name of CENESEX, scrawled at the top of my page of notes: Centro Nacional de Educación Sexual. Looking back up, I ask her about sex education in Cuba. She seems to soften somewhat, and begins to speak once again.

"The way we teach sex education is based on an idea of sexual diversity. We touch on themes of values, respect, cohabitation, sexual health, and partnered life, but also about transsexuality, homosexuality—behavior that diverges from normality. The plurality of sexual behaviors."

Steeling myself, I ask if jineterismo could count as an element of this sexual diversity.

"Yes," she says hesitantly, glancing up to the ceiling as she considers the point. "But it's an unaccepted element. One that we don't accept. It has to do with our vision of the human being, of never making an object of oneself. It's even in our Constitution, you know."

Before even telling me that she has to leave, Julia begins stirring as if to go. For one last question, I ask her about attitudes toward sex in Cuba today. Pausing briefly, she describes sexual liberty as one of the greatest achievements of the Revolution, particularly with regard to gendered understandings of sex and sexuality. She says that increasing women's presence in the various spheres of public life, and thus deemphasizing reproduction as the principal role of women, has changed the way people think about women, sex, and even promiscuity. This, in combination with liberal sex education and access to contraception, has helped to narrow the stigma gap between men and women. "People think differently about men, women, and sex in other places; however, in Cuba, they're not so different. It has been a slow change, bit by bit, since the Revolution."

With that, Julia takes her leave of me, telling me as she goes that she hopes our conversation has been useful to me. I barely have time to thank her for her time before she's gone, and I can't help but think that we're both glad the experience has come to an end. The interview had felt shallow at best. Where in my other interviews I could rephrase, follow up, make jokes, and share experiences in an effort to overcome uncertainty and get the conversation flowing, with Julia I could do none of those things. She seemed guarded and apprehensive, her answers felt rehearsed, and she left before I felt like we had really gotten started.

What struck me most in the immediate aftermath of this interview was that, despite its liberal attitudes and its activist reputation, CENESEX remains a state-affiliated institution—the only kind of institution generally allowed to exist in Cuba. Julia made sure that we began with the two most-cited institutional talking points: only a small number of women practice jineterismo, and all of those who do are of age. From there, however, her story took on a markedly different tone. She expressed concern for the dehumanization and objectification of young women who use their sexualities as tools to transcend economic adversity. This concern is also taken up by Ana Isabel Peñate Leiva, of the CESJ, who writes that prostitution—and this included its present-day incarnation, jineterismo—

represents the most blatant expression of the gender binary, in that prostitutes (assumed to always be women) "assume a preestablished role: subordination."[23] Later she asserts, "In the world of prostitution, the human is dehumanized, sex is commodified, the woman receives a double discrimination: by gender and 'profession,' and from the point of view of sexual satisfaction, it is a long way from being gratifying, and love does not intercede, and the risks that are run in this 'delivery' turn out to be great and very dangerous."[24]

Julia, like Peñate Leiva, seemed preoccupied with active subjecthood. They see it as incompatible with relationships in which one partner provides for the other. They echoed socialist feminist ideas about the incorporation of women into the world of work. Peñate Leiva argues that commercial sex constitutes a "concrete manifestation of exploitation, violence and disrespect for the dignity of the human being," that these women are deprived even of their names in becoming so-called prostitutes.[25] Julia expands the remit of this degradation to any kind of financial support in a relationship. Both also seem to credit this objectification to the women themselves: Julia claims that one makes oneself into an object, while Peñate Leiva says it is young people's "decline [resquebrajamiento] of moral values and ethics that incentivizes the philosophy of possession [filosofía del tener]"[26]—and, as Julia notes, they seek to avoid "productive work" in the process. As educated and capable citizens, young women are morally responsible for their own objectification, or for its prevention.

Julia also raised the idea of productive and worthwhile lives. She wondered aloud what jineteras will, or even can, do with their lives. While it is certainly true that not all of my informants had great ambitions for their careers, travel, or even their families, many—if not most—did possess such aspirations and were working and studying at the time I spoke to them. For many of them, liaisons with foreigners were both means and ends in this regard: they found sources of funds and stability to accomplish their other goals, and some found a supportive relationship, a goal in itself. On the other hand, Julia may have believed (as others certainly do) that they were either otherwise unemployed, as the stereotypical understanding of the jinetera would have it, or that nothing they did would count as long as they continued as jineteras. This last point is an even more stringent association of a "proper" sexuality with fashioning a "worthwhile" life. Her very liberal ideas about sexual mores and declining sexual stigma against both men and women (particularly compared to neighboring countries and even to Cuba's own expat community in Florida[27]) suggest that sexuality must play a part in a productive and happy life. This culture of acceptance and liberalism can, however, apparently only be stretched so far. Their inclusive ethos does not extend to the jinetera.

To understand why it is that CENESEX lobbies the state for an aperture with regard to queer Cubans, once considered sexual dissidents, but not with regard to jineteras, it may be helpful to look more carefully at its policies and programs. The Cuban government has framed its ongoing change of heart on the issue of homosexuality as part of the evolution of its humanist mission, a righting of wrongs in its revolutionary ideology. Fidel Castro himself has called the UMAP camps and other forms of discrimination against gay, lesbian, and queer Cubans "a great injustice," taking personal responsibility and linking it to an as yet incomplete Revolution that had carried forward prerevolutionary forms of prejudice.[28] Carrie Hamilton calls this the government's "desire to set the record straight" on one of their most controversial policies ever.[29]

However, Sierra Madero argues that CENESEX operates under a very traditional understanding of gender roles as a binary relation between the masculine and the feminine. This binary thinking, Sierra Madero points out, is more evident in the support CENESEX offers to transgender Cubans, which encourages transgender people to work toward sex-reassignment surgery as the ultimate goal.[30] One is expected to go through the process of transition and, afterward, fulfill one's properly gendered new role. Transgender people who situate their identities somewhere between or outside the points of the usual gender spectrum, or who do not conform to masculine or feminine roles, defy these kinds of models of gender and relationships—much the way that jineteras are read as improperly feminine. CENESEX's liberal approach to gay and lesbian couples, then, is based on the idea that the heteronormative model of stable, monogamous, nonpromiscuous relationships can be transposed onto same-sex couples, who can then be considered as revolutionary as any other workers and citizens. Homosexuality becomes acceptable when it is legible through the lens of "normal" relationships.

By this heteronormative logic, women are meant to be passive, the pursued rather than the pursuer, and to embody values of monogamy, commitment, and faithfulness; promiscuity and lust, in this sense, are the preserve of men. The image of the jinetera as a woman who (supposedly) rejects long-term relationships and pursues sex actively and licentiously, for pleasure or for material gain, exists outside this framework. By this measure, CENESEX is a comparatively liberal institution but one that still operates within traditional models of gender and heteronormative relationships. I argue that the jinetera as imagined does not and cannot fit into that model. This goes back to Julia's concern for productive lives: a sexuality that is lived outside the bounds of the accepted blueprint for relationships cannot count as worthwhile, or even permissible.

A COMMENDABLE UNDERTAKING

By the time I finally spoke to someone from the Federación de Mujeres Cubanas, I had spent weeks sequestered in its reading room, on Calle 10 between Avenues 3 and 5, combing through its archives. The FMC is one of Cuba's mass organizations, which are meant to speak on behalf of a broad sector of the population—like the UJC, the Central de Trabajadores de Cuba (CTC, a kind of monolithic workers' union), and the CDRs. The Federación is dedicated to engaging and incorporating Cuban women into the revolutionary project through the pursuit of such lofty ideals as gender equality and the emancipation of women. It was founded by Vilma Espín, wife of Raúl Castro and a high-ranking revolutionary guerrilla in her own right, in 1960, and she remained its president until her death in 2007. At the FMC's first congress, held in 1962, its explicitly declared goal was "to elevate the ideological, political, cultural and scientific level of women, in order to incorporate them en masse into the process of constructing the new life."[31]

Ideologically, the FMC operates under a specifically socialist feminist paradigm, as Noelle Stout has noted.[32] Accordingly, its mission in its early years took a classic Engelsian form: working toward the integration of women into the workplace and other areas of public life while simultaneously building an edifice of legal rights to structure both the public and private spheres, which Sheryl Lutjens describes in great detail.[33] In this respect, the FMC's concrete gains have certainly been profound: the Federación has played a crucial role in advocating for such legislative projects as universal child care, parental leave, equal pay for men and women, reproductive rights, and even the Código de Familia of 1975, which mandated that housework and child care should be equally shared between male and female spouses in a family household.[34]

Today, the Federación is a powerful and evolving organization. It maintains several day-to-day functions that grant it visibility in the lives of Cubans, and especially Cuban women. It maintains a small army of volunteer social workers who work with families against a range of social ills, including alcoholism, truancy in schools, and public hygiene. Indeed, it was this very mass of volunteers that, in its infancy, played such a pivotal role in the postrevolutionary push to eradicate prostitution. Since those days, however, the Federación has greatly expanded and now runs regional guidance centers known as Casas de Orientación a la Mujer y la Familia that offer workshops and seminars on themes such as self-esteem, values, and gender roles, in addition to vocational training in hairdressing, dressmaking, and secretarial work.[35] It also publishes a weekly women's magazine, *Mujeres*, with articles on news, politics, relationships, and parenting from a perspective of "ethical, revolutionary journalism."[36] As an institution, the FMC is self-financed and claims to be totally independent, although its allegiance to the government is what underwrites its authority in women's affairs in the country. It holds consultative status with the Economic and Social Council of the United Nations and has a membership of more than four million women—nearly 100 percent of the female population of Cuba.[37] Maintaining one's membership is considered an important part of espousing proper citizenship and revolutionary womanhood.

Since the beginning of the Special Period, the FMC has arguably become at least somewhat more responsive to the diversity of its constituency—whether by design or by obligation—than it had been previously. The very real privations suffered across the island in the 1990s forced the Federación to recognize that gender inequalities persisted despite its own considerable accomplishments: women suffered most from the shortages and cutbacks and frequently bore the burden of making ends meet for their families. The FMC also began to admit to the existence of divisions and inequities among women themselves, differences of education, employment, and access to hard currency that strongly colored how individual women variously experienced the crisis. It was also during this time that the FMC first began to tentatively refer to its work and mission as feminist, a term it had previously rejected as bourgeois, and to address thorny issues such as rape, sexual harassment, and domestic violence—previously seen as divisive and likely to alienate the support of Cuban men—with more vigor.[38]

Nevertheless, the FMC remains a conformist and conservative institution. The dissident writer Reinaldo Arenas reported that the FMC maintained a ban on lesbian members as late as 1984.[39] Given this, and the FMC's role as the authority on women's issues in Cuba, it should come as no surprise that it has played a central role in the state's response to jineterismo. In the mid-1990s, however, it came under fire from a new grassroots women's organization called Magín, made up of communications professionals and journalists. Magín decried the FMC's "moral conservatism" on the issue of jineterismo. *Maginera* Georgina Herrera even went so far as to claim that "the FMC has a completely bourgeois concept of moral values."[40] For this and other controversial stances, Magín was closed down by the Central Committee of the Communist Party of Cuba in 1996, after only three years of operation.[41] The FMC's own founder and then-leader, Espín, had the following to say about jineteras in a 1995 article in the national newspaper, *Granma:*

> Painful are those cases of prostitution which have appeared among weak people, families without ethics, girls who are a great disgrace to the country and do not recognize the moral degradation into which they fall. . . . The majority come from homes with little in the way of ethics, or simply very depraved people who accept that their daughters live that way because they also benefit. Many are young people who are estranged [*desarticuladas*] from home, and a few [do this] without their family's knowledge. At least those have a minimum of morality, feel some shame.[42]

Espín shows little sympathy for the jineteras in the face of the crisis, nor does she concede any agency or independence to them in their choices. Her sentiments would be echoed in many FMC statements still to come.

The FMC's focus remains largely, then, on propagating revolutionary ideals to its members and equipping them to act as good socialist citizens, even as some of its recent moves would seem to suggest a growing acceptance of the plurality of opinions, identities, and desires among women.

From the mid-1990s on, the FMC has spearheaded what Fusco has called a "crusade" against young women perceived to be jineteras or prostitutes.[43] The organization has been pivotal in the creation of the reeducation centers, to which young women can be sent for an indefinite sentence of up to four years under Article 72 on peligrosidad.[44] Its role has been nothing if not controversial: Julia O'Connell Davidson and Jacqueline Sanchez Taylor argue that the FMC is toeing the "party line" on sex tourism and failing women in the process, and likewise, Cabezas judges the organization complicit in the criminalization of "dissident sexual citizens."[45] Others, however, such as Rodríguez Calderón and Strout, view the FMC's work with young women as a necessary and compassionate response to a deep social ill.[46]

The FMC has been a flashpoint of debate, and in fact, much of what has been said about jineterismo centers on the FMC, its perceived obligations, policies, ideological grounding, and practices. Stout notes that it might be incongruous to expect the FMC, which is a socialist organization and not an explicitly feminist one, to support or advocate for the so-called jineteras; its role as a proponent of revolutionary ideology takes precedence over feminist sisterhood.[47] Nevertheless, the Federación's power over the state's response to jineterismo is undeniable, as are its influence and esteem in other areas of Cuban life. Indeed, when I first set out to learn about the FMC, I visited the dean at the University of Havana to get a letter of introduction, as I did with all of the institutions I visited, and that day I watched as he fastidiously amended his form letter from the usual *estimados compañeros* to a reverent and appropriate *estimadas compañeras*.

I spent many mornings and afternoons at the FMC archives reading official accounts, or *memorias,* of the organization's eight congresses held over the course of fifty years and combing its archives for other studies and reports. The archive staff, bemused by my requests, retrieved and dumped stack after stack of files and books in front of me, shaking their heads and leaving me alone in the stale reading room. The memorias revealed an organization preoccupied with its claim to the complete eradication of prostitution, an accomplishment on which it has built its authority with regard to Cuban women. Time and time again, the abolition campaign takes pride of place among the most important goals and proudest achievements of the FMC. The memoria of the second congress of the FMC in 1975 states:

> After 1960, the Revolution undertook a work of fundamental importance to the edification of a new society on different bases: the elimination of social vices inherited from capitalism. The degrading and dolorous profession of prostitute would practically disappear in a year. The mere fact of the triumph of the Revolution had awakened in many of these women the desire for a different life. Others required reeducational attention to show them the new possibilities that were opening before them, rescuing them from this lamentable form of subsistence that they had had to take up.... The Federación, together with other organizations charged with this task, contributed to channeling all of these unfortunate women toward dignified and useful work. It provided them with medical attention and self-improvement courses [*cursos de superación*], while FMC members [*las federadas*] cared for their children and found solutions to their most urgent problems. The campaign was a total success.[48]

This was the first congress after the FMC and the government had together declared victory in the struggle against prostitution in 1965. Though paternalistic by today's standards, at that time the FMC's campaign was widely lauded as a compassionate and progressive solution to the social scourge of prostitution.

After this point, there is little mention of prostitution, as it was considered a closed chapter of the history of Cuban society after 1965, no longer imaginable or intelligible as a possibility in women's lives. The memorias turn their attention to literacy campaigns, education opportunities for girls, socialized child care, and strategies for alleviating women's double burden of home and work. Even at the fifth congress in 1990, there is no mention of the issue, but by 1995, Cuba was five years into the Special Period and the FMC turned its attention once again to prostitution. This time, however, it took a decidedly different approach. The memoria of the sixth congress sees the FMC lamenting the resurgence of prostitution on the island but at the same time assessing it—and, in turn, the women involved—much differently than before the Revolution.

Figure 13. A field office of the FMC in Baracoa, Guantánamo Province, 14 June 2010. Photo by author.

We have conferred special priority on the treatment of the problem of the prostitution of women insofar as it entails one of the most serious forms of discrimination and self-discrimination [*autodiscriminación*], essentially opposed to the ennobling condition that the women of our Nation have achieved. This proves a complex undertaking, keeping in mind that the causes and characteristics of the people who practice it today are different from those of the first years after the revolutionary triumph, which enabled us to eradicate it in a short time period. . . . We have carried out studies that show that a great proportion of these girls have been neglected in various ways by their families and are characterized by a lack of ethics and moral values in the broadest sense, which in the majority of cases they draw from their upbringing [*formación familiar*].[49]

Cuban women of the 1990s and 2000s are educated and possess the same rights and freedoms as men, the FMC reasons, and thus they ought not to have to resort to an activity as base as prostitution in order to survive. To that end, the resurgence of prostitution is attributed to a flawed value system and poor upbringing—and thus responsibility is made individual rather than structural.[50]

At the sixth congress, in 1995, the FMC proposed a multipronged response that includes lobbying the government to remove all sexualized images of Cuban women from its tourism brochures and posters, a source of tension within the state machinery and one that the FMC argues portrays women as a "salable object [*objeto de venta*]" and "[foments] the idea of a sex tourism totally at odds with the principles of our society."[51] The sixth memoria also includes resolutions to create pedagogical materials dealing with topics such as self-esteem, love, relationships, and cultural and political values; to continue the work of its volunteer social workers with prostitutes and their families; to collaborate with other organizations on a comprehensive plan; and to bring the theme of prostitution into the public sphere using a variety of media, noting that "in times like these, the authority of the Federation on the subject is of vital importance in the community and in society as a whole."[52]

This is the period in which the FMC began in earnest its program to stop young Cuban women from getting involved with tourist men. By the next congress, which took place in 2000, the campaign was well under way and the FMC cast itself in a quasi-religious moral role.

> Today, a great part of our delegations and blocs decide their plans based on the problems that confront the women of their localities; develop preventative-educational efforts with the people and families that require it; confront those with tendencies to live from frivolity [*facilismo*], vice, or illegality; denounce and prevent wrongdoing [*impide lo mal hecho*]; endeavor to save those women who, having lost their way, have submitted to moral degradation; develop important materials for the health and education programs; contribute to the search for solutions to difficulties and realize important work of persuasion in their community, explaining the real causes of problems and the enormous advantages of our system.[53]

Elaborating on this message, the memoria recounts that since 1995 the FMC has carried out national studies and written a brochure for young women under the evocative title, "La dignidad se prueba en tiempos difíciles y no la cambiaremos por nada" (Dignity is tried in difficult times and we will not trade it for anything), along with other educational materials for distribution to schools and the Casas de Orientación. On a grand scale, the memoria reports that the FMC social workers have worked for the "social rehabilitation [*reinserción social*]" of young women suspected of prostitution, enrolling them in classes at the Casas de Orientación or at work centers in order to "modify the behavior of youth engaging in prostitution."[54] Here, the FMC also acknowledges its own "systematic participation" in the rehabilitation programs being carried out in centers across the country, where its social workers conduct educational training for detained women.[55] Moving forward, the Federación vows to continue to dedicate its resources and efforts to quashing sexual jineterismo as a top priority.

By 2009, when the eighth and most recent congress was held, the Federación makes mention of an "accord" between itself and the police. The two institutions now collaborate to determine the best individual course of action—work, study, or detention—for each woman who comes into their shared custody or is deemed to be "at risk [*en riesgo*]."[56] The FMC's efforts were ongoing in programming for the rehabilitation centers, profiling of detained and "at-risk" girls and women, meetings and "ideological debates" with other mass organizations, and collaboration with members of the CDRs.[57] (Interestingly, the existence of young Cuban men who also seek the company of foreign tourists is recognized for the first time, but there is no indication given that any of the FMC's efforts would be expanded to include them as well.) This last memoria closes with plans for an updated study of the nature and causes of prostitution, to be completed in the coming years. All in all, these memorias reveal the core convictions of the FMC: a faith in the self-evidence of socialist precepts, demonstrated by talk of awakening women to a better way of life and explaining the true causes of sexual commerce, but also firm confidence in its own role as a benevolent arbiter of social values and caregiver to a population.

My reading of the memorias complete, I approached the Dirección Nacional of the FMC to request an interview. I had been advised repeatedly to tread carefully in making myself known to the Federation, an organization with considerable influence with the government and a clear political stake in controlling the way jineterismo is discussed, at home and abroad, even if that stake was at times in conflict with Cuba's tourism promotion. At the Federation's headquarters, I was given a contact name and a phone number. I called every morning for nine days before I managed to speak to Yuris herself, and, graciously, she cleared some time to meet with me.

The Dirección Nacional of the FMC is housed in a stately prerevolutionary mansion, which sits on the tree-lined thoroughfare of Paseo, between Calles 11 and 13. The shrubbery that divides the sidewalk from the palatial buildings along the boulevard gives way at the open gate to number 260 and reveals Yuris, waiting on the veranda in a rocking chair, shaded by the pillared roof. She turns and takes me in as I make my way up the steps, smiling cordially and rising to take my hand. We sit down in the rocking chairs, which is when I notice the reporter's notebook in her hand.

Yuris is a high-level functionary with the FMC, having worked there for many years, and she exudes a confidence that is both kindly and severe. When I tell her that I am hoping to conduct an interview with someone from the FMC on the subject of transnational sexual relationships, she smiles and benevolently ignores the question. Flipping open her notebook, she asks for my full name, my address in Cuba, my home address in Canada, my university affiliation, my level of study, and the subject of my research, jotting my answers down one by one and nodding. Finally, she stops and meets my eye again.

"I won't be giving you an interview myself," she says, looking askance at the digital recorder in my hand. "But I will help you with what I know. What do you want to find out?"

I tell her I'm interested in the idea of jineterismo—what it is and what it means for young people and for Cuba. She nods slowly, digesting this information, and then she begins to speak at length.

"Look, the elimination of prostitution in this country—after the Revolution, you understand?—was a commendable undertaking [*trabajo meritorio*]. The Federation was founded in 1960, immediately after the triumph of the Revolution, with Vilma Espín as its president, and it directed the fight [*la lucha*] against prostitution in the 1960s—this all happened before 1965, of course."

Yuris goes on to describe the brigades of young revolutionary women who volunteered as social workers, going into the most notorious neighborhoods and into the brothels themselves to bring the gospel of

Revolution to Cuba's benighted prostitutes. The story unfolds seamlessly and easily, a founding legend passed from one generation to the next. I've heard this story repeated so many times that I feel like I could tell it myself now. She draws the narrative to a close with the declaration of victory in 1965.

"Well, what else? What else do you need to know?" Blankly, I repeat my desire to arrange an interview, but this time she dismisses the question directly, saying, "That won't be necessary. Is there nothing else I can do, then?" It dawns on me as she looks at me expectantly that she is not going to arrange any further interviews for me, as we had discussed on the phone—that this is, in fact, all I am going to get. She gestures at my notebook. "What else do you want to know?"

Realizing that this has suddenly become my only chance to ask my questions, I ask her bluntly about jineteras. How does she understand what they do and who they are?

"It's prostitution—they're one and the same. Before the triumph of the Revolution, women were desperate, poorly educated, powerless. The difference is that today, in this day and age, Cuban women are better developed, educated, with opportunities. They don't need to do what they do."

I ask her why the FMC considers jineteras such a problem. Do they think these young women pose a threat to the achievements of the FMC?

She shakes her head, almost flippantly. "It's a challenge, but it doesn't endanger the Revolution."

I press on, asking why the FMC then specifically opposes jineterismo.

Yuris looks at me sharply and incredulously. She doesn't speak until I venture a clarification, saying that I simply want to understand the issue as the FMC sees it. This seems to satisfy her.

"Jineterismo is prostitution, and prostitution is violence—it's exploitation. The prostitute is a victim, that's why. It is not penalized under the law—it's not illegal at all. *[No es sancionada por la ley—no es ilegal para nada.]* She is a victim."

I ask her to describe the procedures for finding and rehabilitating suspected jineteras in practice.

"Our greatest success has been in prevention [*nuestro éxito es en la prevención*]," she tells me with a look of pride. "In Cuban society, there is always a neighbor in the street, someone who can see how a young girl is dressed or in what car she arrives home—it's a community effort [*trabajo comunitario*]. Within the community, there are three elements to our approach: the neighbors, the schools who report a young girl's absences, and the family doctor who can tell what she has been up to. Then, we have community social workers, volunteers from the neighborhood, who go to visit the homes of these girls who are practicing prostitution or who we think are at risk [*en riesgo*]. We work with them, and we work with their families as well when we can.

"These girls are naive, for the most part. Many of them come to Havana from the countryside. They want to be singers or actresses or dancers or models," she says, shaking her head. "They follow a boyfriend to the city, or find one when they arrive, and often it's he who pushes them to prostitute themselves."

I ask her how it is possible to tell who is and who is not a jinetera. To illustrate, I describe for her some of the young Cubans who have told me that they see their relationships with foreigners as completely normal and healthy. How, then, can one tell which relationships are "real" and which are prostitution? Yuris stares at me blankly in response. What I had thought was a valid question clearly was not. I begin to rephrase, but she motions for me to stop. Yuris carefully tells me that no healthy relationship can exist between a Cuban woman and a foreign man, because these liaisons are always and inevitably mediated by material gain. They are all jineteras.

I'm taking great pains to record her every word in my notebook, and I notice that she has also filled several pages with densely packed writing as we talk. I wonder if that should make me nervous, but there is no time for that now. I ask her what happens next, after a young woman is deemed to be a jinetera or at risk of becoming one.

"They are brought to our Centros de Reeducación," she says matter-of-factly, "to convince them of their own value [*para convencerlas de su proprio valor*]."

Nodding and writing, I ask what the centers are like. Are they prisons for jineteras?

"No, not prisons." Yuris describes them to me at length as places where young women receive education on proper moral and ideological grounding, career training, and help for their perceived problems with self-esteem. When I ask about jineteros, young Cuban men who might equally be engaging in relationships with foreign tourists, she concedes that such a phenomenon also exists but denies that it requires the same attention. There are fewer of them, and the problem is not as serious. She seems unconcerned about that issue.

I ask her how it is decided which young women will be sent to the centers.

"The Policía Nacional Revolucionaria is in charge of identifying them [*La PNR es quien las detectan*]. After that, there are legal mechanisms which she must pass through [*hay órganos legales que debe pasar*]."

Courts?

"Yes."

And can women leave the Centro and go home when they want?

"No, of course not. These girls need to recognize the situation they are in, they need to recover their values [*rescatan sus valores*]—they're victims, are they not?"

Yuris describes these measures matter-of-factly. She seems utterly confident, and in this moment I feel—somewhat absurdly—that I am looking the disciplinary state machinery in the face. I feel I am facing something of a brick wall, where disagreement is out of the question. I ask her—slowly, carefully—if these women are educated and empowered, if they are making a choice that the FMC abhors but is nonetheless freely made, then of whom are they victims?

"Themselves!" she says frankly, and I sense once again that my questions are ridiculous to her. "We have to protect them from themselves. There are many different paths to take—none are easy. [*Hay muchos caminos para andar—ninguno es fácil.*] We cannot grow tired in this; we are not going to grow tired in this effort. [*No nos podemos cansar; no nos vamos a cansar en este trabajo*]."

From here, Yuris begins to reflect on the Fourth World Conference on Women in Beijing in 1995, a topic she seems much happier to discuss. She tells me about Cuba's role at the conference and about the national action plan that came out of it as a mechanism for eliminating discrimination.

She again mentions the Casas de Orientación, which seem to be community outreach and resource centers—an FMC initiative of which she is particularly proud. I ask if it would be possible for me to visit one. She happily obliges, disappearing into the building to call and arrange an introduction for me. When she returns, I thank her for her time and assistance, and she waves her notebook, saying we'll be in touch.

I leave the front porch of the FMC's main office with contact information for the nearest Casa de Orientación and distinct mixed feelings. I am conflicted about the interview, and I genuinely cannot tell if I have said or done anything over the course of the conversation that will flag me as a cause for concern—for surveillance, perhaps, or for increased scrutiny at the airport as I leave Cuba. In the interview itself, as with Julia, I had felt unable to break through the veneer of professionalism with Yuris. While this is understandable—she was, after all, speaking to me in her official capacity—it only heightened my sense that I was receiving preprepared answers to my questions. Yuris did not seem at all disingenuous, however, and I came away from my conversation with her with the impression that she wholly believes in the efforts of the FMC. This staunch pride in the Federación's ideological crusade is echoed in the memorias, and in statements like that of Sonia Beretervide, a member of the national secretariat of the FMC quoted in *Mujeres* magazine: "There is no country in the world that makes up its mind and has the courage to discuss a topic like prostitution at the community level [like Cuba has]."[58]

The theme that arose most readily out of my conversation with Yuris, and out of my impressions of the FMC in general, was that of morality. Yuris spoke of a crisis of values and of the need to cultivate and refurbish the morals of young women in the face of jineterismo. Similarly Beretervide argues, "It is not the country's economic crisis that brings them to behave this way, it is that, faced with difficult situations, the tools of the immense strength of the majority of our youth do not appear readily at hand, because there is deformity in the family, there is a deficiency of values, and this negatively influences appropriate upbringing in this difficult time that is adolescence."[59]

The U.N. Special Rapporteur's report also noted, in consultation with the FMC, that "dysfunctional families" are often blamed for prostitution.[60] Likewise, a study conducted by the Instituto de Medicina Legal

(Institute of Forensic Medicine) with young women incarcerated under Article 72 cited "debilitation of . . . moral values" and "poor development of the personality" in childhood as the main causes of jineterismo in young women.[61] (The study's cover also featured a cartoon mocking a jinetera for seeking recourse from the police when she has been robbed. The woman decries what she sees as the thief's moral deficit, while the officer regards her quizzically, evidently because she, a jinetera, must have no "moral values" herself.)

It is interesting to note here that absolutely none of my interviewees recounted abuse in their childhoods, which seems completely at odds with the FMC's characterization of supposed jineteras. This notion of "deficiency" in families and in the rearing of children appears repeatedly, and in the Cuban context—as elsewhere—this translates easily into deficient motherhood, since mothers are charged with the majority of child care. It also invites a particular idea of what a functional family must be—that is, a socialist one that produces children who wholeheartedly support the Revolution in its vision for the individual and for society—because the only proof of dysfunctionality provided is behavior that diverges from acceptable morality.

Acting as a moral compass and a conservationist refuge in difficult times, the Federation addresses itself to those who have shown possible weakness during the economic crisis. In so doing, the FMC is locating morality in poverty, and excluding young women from the realm of the moral based on either financial security or sexual promiscuity—or both. Poverty is defined as outside the government's hands, obscuring a structural analysis in favor of a focus on individual women's choice.[62] In the absence of structural excuses for immoral conduct, ostensibly removed by the Revolution and its reforms, the responsibility for upright conduct is put on the shoulders of individuals. Women, who are expected to be the moral centers of their families and who are judged for their sexual behaviors in ways that men are not, bear the brunt of this situation.

A language of path selection appeared repeatedly, in the memorias and in my interview with Yuris, of there being many paths to take and of losing one's way. This suggests the notion of a true path to becoming a good citizen, a good socialist, and, in the context of the FMC's work in particular, a good woman. As discussed in chapters 1 and 2, Cuban womanhood has been constructed since the Revolution around images of strong, resilient, and powerful figures—around hembrismo rather than marianismo, a concept that is not necessarily endorsed by the FMC but that fits well into the organisation's ideas about proper womanhood. The FMC takes this notion of the Cuban hembra and imbues it with images of the mother, the worker, and the revolutionary, creating a sort of revolutionary New Woman. It is a moral standard for women, as Guevara's New Man is for men and for Cubans in general, but one that depends in part on a moral sexuality.

This New Woman could perhaps be a counterpoint to the imagined jinetera, or to Elizalde's throwaway flower, and is as much a caricature as either of these as well. She is a mother and a wife (not single), a full-time worker, and active in her local CDR and FMC branches; in the current climate, she and her family frequently go without, but this in itself is a source of virtue. Romance often imbues nationalist mythologies such as these, and for Cuban women, sacrifice is a central part of the story.[63] The New Woman would find more than mere subsistence in work but rather fulfillment and vindication—an hembra, perhaps, and a luchadora, certainly, though one who conceives of la lucha differently.

In keeping with its mission of compassionate interventionism, the FMC also repeatedly shows concern for the health and well-being of young Cuban women, under the conviction that a happy and healthy young woman cannot engage in the sexual-affective economy. Yuris decries the violence and victimization she sees as inherent in jineterismo; likewise, Beretervide characterizes jineterismo as a form of self-harm, or *autoviolencia*, and the Instituto de Medicina Legal's study calls jineteras self-destructive and without respect for themselves.[64] In an interview, UN Special Rapporteur Radhika Coomaraswamy recalled posters and other materials exhorting young women to love and respect themselves and to improve their self-esteem when she visited a rehabilitation center in Pinar del Río.[65] The assumption here, evidently, is that women detained as suspected prostitutes must by nature lack these qualities, a hypothesis that certainly did not hold with the majority of my informants who were actually involved in the sexual-affective economy. Nonetheless, this understanding of jineteras as sad, self-harming, and victimized plays into both Elizalde's claim that they are diminishing their capacity for love, now and in the future, and Yuris's assertion that no "real" relationship can exist between a Cuban woman and a foreign man.

The foreignness and the maleness are also important in themselves, for that matter. In our interview, Yuris paid only lip service to the idea that there were young men dating tourists who might warrant the same concern from government organizations. Granted, the FMC is an organization specifically for women, but the very fact that addressing jineterismo has fallen so heavily on its shoulders speaks volumes about the state's understanding of what prostitution and jineterismo-as-sexual-practice *are*. Promiscuity and perceived low morality become problems when *women* do them. Other sources in my search seemed to echo this sentiment, as most were willing to acknowledge the existence of supposed jineteros and even pingueros, but no one seemed to think it required action. This was reflected, as the previous chapters have shown, in the divergent experiences of young women and men on the ground and the different ways they were treated by police and other authorities. Furthermore, in all of the documents and files I read, never once was any concern expressed over the possibility of commercial sex aimed at a so-called Cuban market—this is not seen to be a problem, so it seems that the foreignness and the maleness of the tourists are crucial to the equation. As I noted in previous chapters, men's liaisons with foreigners are seen as an affirmation of Cuban masculinity, as domination of the foreign interloper; women's, on the other hand, activate nationalist fears of invasion and defilement by foreign influence.

On the whole, the FMC's position among the various state institutions that are addressing jineterismo seems to be a maternal one. The Federación knows what is best for women, and it employs—or attempts to employ—methods of supervision and surveillance, through neighbors, schools, and family doctors, in its pursuit of its interventionist strategy. It cultivates and encourages its constituency to embark on the path to good citizenship and womanhood and rebukes and rehabilitates those who stray. However, I found Yuris's conviction, echoed many times in the congress memorias as well, that young women such as these are rejected by society to be inaccurate. In all of my interviews, no one expressed feeling shunned or pitied, and certainly none reported having been questioned by their family doctors or teachers or even receiving visits from one of the

FMC's volunteer social workers. As one informant put it to me, "We only see them when there is a hurricane." In practice, the PNR would appear to remain the primary means by which young women are brought into the process of rehabilitation offered by the FMC. Its narrative of moral degradation, self-victimization, and low self-esteem, however, certainly colors its approach to the young women who are brought under its care, as well as its framing of the issue to the Cuban public and to the world.

THE CLAMORING SILENCE OF RACE

What is most starkly absent from all of these institutional and public accounts is the question of race. While it was much easier to discuss, or at least to observe, race in action in my other interviews and encounters, here it was missing, and glaringly so. In conversation with Cubans, I found race conspicuously absent and manifestly present at the same time—rarely explicitly mentioned, but always there. Lumsden describes a "destigmatization" of racial terminology in Cuba, where it is quite common to hear people refer to one another, often with affection, by words such as *negrito, blanquita,* or *mi chino*—sometimes regardless of the person's "actual" racial background, divorcing phenotype from heritage.[66] As Nadine Fernandez notes, this easygoing approach to racial language does not necessarily empty it of its marginalizing power, since Cubans still operate within frameworks where *mulato adelantado* (advanced or light-skinned mulato) or *mulata blanconaza* (almost-white mulata) are considered complimentary remarks, and the concepts of *pelo bueno* and *pelo malo* (good/straight or bad/kinky hair) persist.[67] Once, an elderly man told me that because he was old-fashioned, he would describe himself as *negro teléfono,* or dark as the plastic of an old-style rotary telephone. While even these terms are often used with a typically Cuban irreverence—*blanco cubano,* for instance, indicates a person whose ostensible whiteness likely belies a concealed degree of mixed heritage—their power is still considerable.

At the same time, and paradoxically, the sensitivity of the issue of race is palpable in conversation with Cubans. Many people, when they want to mention race, will say nothing at all; rather, they touch the skin on their forearms to signal skin tone or use one of a variety of euphemistic stand-ins like *chocolate* or references to sugar, rum, tobacco, or coffee. There is so often a telling weight in even the briefest conversational interlude about race, reliant on gestures and looks, at least until one could be certain of being among friends. Thus, even in those moments when I felt I could not raise the issue myself, I could still observe it in action and feel it everywhere. That silence can be traced back to official circles such as these, where talking about race is taboo. As such, it has just as many discursive effects as the other axes of marginality—gender, sexuality, class—which are discussed at least somewhat more openly, if not always critically. Indeed, Foucault argues that such silence is "less the absolute limit of discourse, the other side from which it is separate by a strict boundary, than an element that functions alongside the things said, with them and in relation to them within over-all strategies."[68]

In Cuba, this silence around race has its roots in the very beginning of the Revolution, when all of the legal and structural barriers to people of color's full participation in the Cuban political, economic, and social spheres were lifted. In 1966 Fidel Castro announced, "Discrimination disappeared when class privileges disappeared, and it has not cost the Revolution much effort to resolve that problem."[69] Linking racism to class, and thus to the now-banished capitalist world, absolved the Revolution from the responsibility to act. There would be no public examination of the privilege enjoyed by white Cubans. No mass organization was founded to speak to the needs and interests of Afro-Cubans, much less for Chinese Cubans or any others, and from the 1960s on, race was only discussed in terms of cultural pursuits like music and dance and in reference to racism in other parts of the world, especially the United States.[70] For many years, Cuba did not collect race-related information on its census forms, and Cubans had very little reason to ever tick a box to choose which of the many identifiers best described themselves and their experiences. It is a kind of anxious refusal to engage, with race and by extension with racism, that denies the possibility of confronting oppression and discrimination. The paradox of Cuba's official silence on race was that calling out acts of racism, and thereby implying that the Revolution had not eliminated them, was considered as serious a counterrevolutionary act as racism itself.[71] Issues of race were subsumed under the rubric of class struggle, even more so than questions of gender and sexuality had been, and any kind of organizing around race was considered to run counter to the goal of national unity.

Today, the most common way of deploying racism in Cuba is to couch it in terms of *nivel de cultura*, or cultural level, which is used to assess a variety of attributes like cultural tastes, style of speech, accent, appearance, and professionalism. Unsurprisingly, characteristics such as colloquial language, kinky hair, dark skin, and accents from Oriente are associated with low nivel de cultura. On the other hand, more formal forms of speech, paler skin, straight and especially blond hair, and accents from Havana are considered to be of the highest level. It is a form of thinly veiled coded racism that has real effects when it comes to who gets selected for scarce but lucrative jobs in the state-sanctioned tourist sector. This standard of assessment in the tourist industry as also known as *buena presencia*, where whiteness is valued for front-of-house, "professional" positions, while blackness is reserved for exoticized jobs in entertainment or behind-the-scenes maintenance. These practices contribute to what Mark Sawyer calls a "pigmentocracy" amid constant claims to a society free from racism.[72] As I highlighted at the beginning of this book, Afro-Cubans are less likely to receive remittances from family abroad, less likely to be able to obtain jobs in the legal tourist sector, and more likely to be read as exotic, sexualized attractions in themselves for tourists—by the police, by other Cubans, and even by their own estimation.

The clamoring silence surrounding race in the institutional setting is then both surprising and expected. There is no mention at all of race in the FMC's memorias, nor is there in any of the texts I managed to obtain that were produced by MININT, the CESJ, or CENESEX. In my interviews with Yuris and Julia, I was reluctant to raise the issue—and, in doing so, challenge the accepted narrative of racial equality—as I felt I was already treading on thin ice and feared losing the interview entirely. Cuban institutions have cultivated, as de la Fuente puts it, a "powerful national discourse of racial fraternity that posits that all Cubans are equal members of the nation, the existence of overwhelming evidence to the contrary notwithstanding."[73] One of the most powerful effects of this discourse is not just to effect a silence in official circles, but to discipline others—myself included, in these interviews—into doing the same.

CONCLUSION: THE POST-PROSTITUTION WOMAN

> They've got it in for the jineteras here, because no one is more
> machista than the Cuban, and because everything is matter
> of image: the jineteras were finding ways to make ends meet
> with the tourists, and if they left them alone, in a couple of
> years our beautiful little Cuba would go back to being called
> the Great Brothel of America, as those who came before used
> to say, because there was no whore or fag in the world more
> prized than the whores and fags of this country. But don't
> even think about it, child: they wouldn't let that image screw
> up the idea they want to give to the world that here, it's
> already a long time since we left heaven to the Big Guy
> Upstairs. Paradise is here in Cuba, the Cuban society.
>
> Celeste, twenty-six-year-old gay Cuban, quoted in Valle,
> *Habana Babilonia*

After my interview with Yuris, I called the Casa de Orientación to make an appointment but was told that I needed official permission from the national headquarters before that could happen. Undeterred, I called Yuris, who told me that the Casas are independent and do not require permission and that, regardless, the Dirección Nacional does not give such permission. I called the Casa back, only to be informed once again that I could not visit without the proper permission. This back-and-forth continued for close to two weeks, until I was forced to concede defeat. The experience felt in many ways emblematic of all my encounters with state institutional bodies in Cuba: they were difficult to navigate and often frustrating, for me and for the other Cubans I knew.

My experience is not unique to Cuba either; on the contrary, defeats such as these characterize most fieldwork, no matter where it takes place. What is more, regardless of their ideological allegiances, most of the people I met in the offices of the FMC and CENESEX, and to whom I spoke over the phone, faced the same professional and personal constraints as everyone else in Cuba, much like the officers of the PNR. While they may have been apathetic or uninterested in helping me, they may also have been overworked, ill equipped, or simply had their hands tied by a variety of institutional, ideological, or personal commitments.

For many people who have found their careers in the state institutions of Cuba, the postrevolutionary eradication of prostitution holds immense discursive weight. The "fact" of the eradication of prostitution is frequently held up as proof of the Revolution's commitment to a humanist mission of social justice and to the building of a society free from prejudice and discrimination. For the Federatción in particular, there is much to be gained (and lost) in this new struggle against resurgent prostitution. As one of the first goals and founding myths of the Cuban Revolution, this political investment is one of the reasons Cuban socialism has always carried with it an ideal of sexuality. Where Marxist theory has shouldered criticism for the "aporia" that is sexuality within its canon, its Cuban variant has always concerned itself with the sexuality—and thus the potential sexual deviance—of the people.[74] The centrality of prostitution as an idea to Cuban socialist rhetoric, the campaign against prostitution in the early 1960s, the persecution of gay, lesbian, and transgender Cubans in the post-revolutionary years, and today's repression of jineterismo are testaments to this ongoing confrontation with sexuality. The state does not ignore but rather engages directly with its citizens on the issue of sex and sexuality. The identities and activities of sexual dissidents have been a matter of concern throughout Cuba's history—and elsewhere—but it has been a particular priority in the years since the Revolution.

Admittedly, as Stout argues, it cannot be expected that Cuban institutions, least of all the FMC, would necessarily defend the jinetera.[75] It is far more acceptable in the Cuban institutional setting to portray women who pursue foreigners as emancipated actors with a range of choices who act out of emotional immaturity, greed, moral underdevelopment, and, ultimately, a lack of revolutionary consciousness; to do otherwise would be to imply that their emancipation was incomplete. It is this perceived authority to determine and control social mores that is most interesting. Implicit in many of the texts and both of the interviews presented here is the natural role for the state, and particularly the socialist state, in cultivating and programming the social and cultural life of the people.

This is not necessarily unique to socialist settings either: as Rose and Miller argue, government-led social programs of all kinds serve to "make the objects of government thinkable in such a way that their ills appear susceptible to diagnosis, prescription and cure by calculating and normalizing intervention."[76] Foucault notes a global "policing of sex: that is, not the rigor of a taboo, but the necessity of regulating sex through useful and public discourses."[77] This interventionist role, however, finds especially succinct expression in the inherently collectivist socialist paradigm. Julia noted that so-called jineteras constitute one of many different nodes on the spectrum of sexual diversity but "one that we don't accept." Embedded in this statement is the understanding that it is up to institutions like CENESEX to decide which sexual behaviors are permissible for the individual. Yuris also spoke of the need to save young women from themselves, to take corrective measures and show them the error of their ways. Particularly in the context of an activity that law does not prohibit, this interventionism is striking.

What is even more arresting, however, is the idealism that runs through the state discourse on prostitution, which really amounts to an idealized—and perhaps revolutionary—notion of love. It is Elizalde's conviction that a true relationship cannot exist between a Cuban woman and a foreign man, which Yuris attributes to the almost unavoidable economic differences between them. Julia counts any relationship in which one party seeks financial support or security from another as prostitution. Natividad Guerrero Borrego, director of the CESJ, shares this view and avows that love cannot exist for a couple wherein any kind of economic interest exists.[78] By ostensibly removing the need for economic interest in romantic and sexual relationships, the Revolution seems to have tried to create a *post-prostitution woman* who practices a form of revolutionary love that is free—from coercion, from economic interest, and from immoral influence. In equating economic *difference* with economic *interest*, however, this narrative describes a normative setting in which no love is possible where there is any economic inequality: one must not love a richer person for the sake of money, certainly, but for no other reason either. It is an impossible, idealized meeting of complete equals who not only seek nothing from their partners in the way of material support but also accept nothing—and this in a context of growing inequalities. This brings to mind once again the notion of locating virtue in poverty.

This narrative of sexual morality and revolutionary love has profound ramifications for women, and in particular for those women whose relationships and sexualities do not fit with such an ideal. This is not a discourse without tensions or ambivalences. The state needs tourists and the revenues they bring, and a sensualized, exotic image of Cuban women can be very effective in attracting business, as the incident of the FMC complaining about sexed-up brochures and posters demonstrates. The Cuban government is finding itself in more and more of an impossible bind, both desperately needing and vocally rejecting tourist dollars for itself and for its people. This is the *eterno Baraguá* of Cuba since the Special Period.[79] The FMC and CENESEX seem to function almost as islands within a state system that is still fundamentally machista, and which needs reminding now and then that it is not supposed to be objectifying its *compañeras*. Across the spectrum of institutions, however, there is a unifying theme: it is up to women to act as the gatekeepers of sexuality and sexual morality.

Bringing together these conceptions of gender, sexuality, race, and economic difference, we can see the jinetera as a caricature and as a "regulatory fiction," to use Judith Butler's term.[80] It allows state anxieties about foreign invasion, as well as its ambivalent and conflicted engagement with the international tourism industry, to be displaced onto the bodies of young black and mixed-race women. This discourse speaks volumes about power, sexuality, and the politics of marginality in Cuba today, and it imbues the sexual practices of a certain sector of the population with political meaning and the possibility of resistance—a resistance that entails a contestation of these very ideals and ways of being that underpin revolutionary ideology.

5 Conduct Unbecoming

BODILY RESISTANCE AND THE ETHICS OF THE SELF

> Mes enfants, you mustn't go at things head-on, you are too
> weak, take it from me and take it on an angle. . . . Play
> dead, play the sleeping dog.
>
> Honoré de Balzac, *Les paysans*

> Maybe the target nowadays is not to discover what we are,
> but to refuse what we are.
>
> Michel Foucault, "The Subject and Power"

Cuba's sexual-affective economy has implications that go beyond stereo-types and categories, police practices, corruption, or the jurisdictions of any one state institution—beyond the state and the Revolution it repre-sents. The emergence of the jinetera (and, to an extent, the jinetero) in Cuba in the past twenty years signifies a much broader dynamic of nego-tiation and subject formation. Jineterismo can be read not only as a nebu-lous category of people, as I argued earlier, but also as a practice of resist-ance to a pastoral power that has become suffocating. In turning away from the values and ideals set out by powerful elites and refusing the con-cern and care offered by paternal state institutions, young Cubans disin-vest themselves from prescriptive norms and resist subjection. What makes this particular practice of resistance distinct, however, is its locus in the body. Using sex, sexuality, affect, and even love as tools of resistance, jineteras engage in a kind of aesthetic self-creation, which pointedly challenges the operation of power and subject formation in Cuba. This is especially significant in a system where conventional channels for political activism are closed, as it becomes increasingly important to find ways to "do politics" outside the traditionally *political* sphere of activism and governance. As Deleuze points out, "Life becomes resistance to power when power takes life as its object."[1] The mere act of living life, freely and happily despite the risks, becomes a mode of resistance and self-creation.

ARE YOU AGAINST US?

Andre, who appeared briefly in chapter 2, is my very first interview. We sit down to talk on a warm night in March on the steps of the Banco Financiero Internacional. I had met Andre through a mutual acquaintance, Javier, who now sits on the step above me and watches the proceedings eagerly. A busy shopping street by day, Avenida Salvador Allende—known locally by its pre-Revolution name, Carlos III—is surprisingly quiet, and I feel as if we're utterly alone.

My voice recorder, meanwhile, is refusing to record. Javier is overbearing, looking over my shoulder and brushing off my feeble intimations that he should leave Andre and me to chat in peace. As I'm becoming more flustered and stressed, however, Andre is palpably at ease. He leans back, lithely resting his weight on his elbows. Finally, I toss the recorder back into my bag and resolve to transcribe the interview by hand.

To begin, I ask Andre about his family and childhood. Born and raised in central Havana, he lives with his mother and has one sister, who is married with children. He recounts a happy youth filled with friends, parties, and trips to the beach. After finishing school, Andre studied computer science at college. Today, however, at twenty-five, he says he doesn't work in that field. I ask if he has an official job of any kind.

He shakes his head. "Not right now."

When I ask him to tell me about meeting foreign women in Havana, his face breaks into a grin. He seems slightly bashful at first, but that quickly fades.

"I go out a lot, sometimes alone and sometimes with my friends. To Habana Vieja or around here, in Vedado, where there are lots of foreigners. Just try to chat them up, you know. Sometimes it's better to be with my friends, because we can meet groups of girls and go to a nightclub. The girls pay for us to go."

And what happens then?

Smiling, he says, "We might go home together. See how it goes. If we like each other, then we spend more time together. Maybe stay in touch. Maybe have a relationship."

I ask if he's involved with any foreign women at this moment, and he nods. I ask how many.

"Eight."

My eyes widen, and I look down at my notes to conceal my surprise. He seems pleased at my reaction and goes on to tell me that of the eight there are two who know that there are others. All of them return periodically to visit him, and some send him gifts of money from abroad.

"One of them is 25 years old, and another one is 52—but she doesn't look 52," he says, grinning and exchanging looks with Javier. "The rest are between 30 and 45. That's the ideal age, when they're old enough to have good jobs and some money but young enough to still look good. Some people go for the really old ones—little old ladies and old men, you know— because they have money and they can get you out [of Cuba] sooner, but I want someone I'm really attracted to."

While I struggle to grasp the reality of eight separate but simultaneous romantic attachments, I can see why European and North American women take to him. Andre chooses his words carefully and articulately. He speaks English, Italian, and German. Though he's slight of build, he's well groomed, with dark skin and large brown eyes, and he's simply but nicely dressed in a crisp white shirt and jeans—a far cry from the embellished, bright styles favored by many young Cubans. When I struggle to find the right words, or to jot down all of his comments, he pauses patiently. He's genuinely pleasant, particularly against the back-drop of Javier, who laughs awkwardly and interrupts throughout our conversation.

"Some of them send me money or give it to me when they're here, and that helps me take care of my family and support myself," Andre tells me. "But I really do prefer foreign women. They're more interesting to me, even if they don't know how to move like a Cuban girl. Foreign women don't know how to move—not on the dance floor and not in bed."

Amused by this last comment, I ask him if he would ever consider a relationship with a Cuban woman anymore, since he tells me he's been dating foreigners for three years.

"Maybe, but just to fuck [*solamente para zingar*]. Cubans girls ask you for money, they have no shame at all, but foreigners don't do that. I want to get married and leave Cuba, so tourists are the ones for me. It's not just about money—I want to fall in love. My cousin was a *jinetera,* and now she's married and living in Europe. She really paid her dues before she got out [*Luchó mucho antes de casarse*]. She was a real *jinetera de clase.*"

I ask what he means by that, and Andre explains that he sees certain jineteros and jineteras as more upstanding, more noble, more genuine than others. The ones who are looking for love, he says, are the jineteros and jineteras *de clase*—the ones with class. "I'm a *jinetero de clase,*" he says emphatically. "In fact, I don't like that word, *jinetero.* It's what people say, but I think it's a bit vulgar. I call myself a *candelero.*"[2] He goes on to tell me that he thinks there are more women than men occupying the lower ranks of jineterismo, and this he attributes to greater economic need among young women, some of whom may already have children or who may have migrated to the city from the countryside, leaving behind their families. They're looking to make some fast cash, Andre posits confidently, and to them, falling in love is a sign of weakness.

"I want a real relationship. The women I date—they're not ugly, not ugly at all, but I guess no one looks at them in Europe [*quizás nadie las mire en Europa*]. And they like me. They like black men, you know, because we have bigger dicks. And you know, if you fuck well, you're a good jinetero [*Sabes que, como zingas bien, estás buen jinetero*]."

Again, he and Javier glance mirthfully at one another. Javier grins and slaps his friend on the back. They take evident pride in this belief in their prowess as black men. Over time, it also becomes very clear to me that Javier envies his friend the language skills and easy manner that help him to meet and charm foreign women.

Moving on, I ask Andre if he's ever had any problems with the police. He considers the question for a moment, looking up toward the trees along the boulevard. "Yes, lots of problems. Talking to tourists is practically illegal [*Hablar con turistas es como ilegal*]. They ask me for my *carné de identidad* a lot, and I know it's just to bother me. But I'm lucky—I've never been arrested."

He smiles wanly, and I ask him how he feels about it. In response, Andre puckers his lips and leans forward, with his arms on his knees and his chin cupped in one hand. "Wanting to talk with people or travel doesn't make you antirevolutionary. Being a *jinetero* is something bad, according to the government. It's not in their interest. But Cuban society has adapted to the *jineteros* [and *jineteras*]. Here, everyone is *jineteando*. There's fear, the government is afraid, but everyone does it. Tourism is the principal source of funds that we have." He notes how young Cubans tend to refer to tourists and tourism as *el fuego*—the fire—and then, sardonically, "We're all in the fire. Cuba is on fire."

I'm struggling to write all of this down, so Andre pauses and relaxes back onto the steps. He seems to be thinking, and when I look back up at him, he starts speaking again immediately. "Look, me, I'm revolutionary, but I think that in Cuba, now, the Revolution doesn't get us anything [*no gana nada la Revolución*]."

When I ask what he means by "revolutionary," Andre replies that he supports the Revolution, that he's not a Batistiano or a dissident. He tells me that he agrees with the Revolution's ideas, and he believes that Cuba is a better and fairer place to live than it was before 1959 but that the government has lost sight of its ideals in the present atmosphere of scarcity and repression of dissent. Life has become harder, and, in the process, racial discrimination has resurfaced.

"When you're black, being a *jinetero* is the easiest thing. It's not difficult to find work, [but] it's difficult to find work with the same benefits. Jineterismo has sex, money, and travel," he notes, counting emphatically on his fingers. "The most important things."

Asking Andre about his dreams for the future produces a more subdued response.

"One day," he says, "I'll leave here. I'd like to live in England. I've met a few English girls and I liked them. I think I would like it there."

Anything else?

"No, just that. I just want to make my life there."

Closing my notebook at the end of our interview, I thank Andre for his thoughts. I tell him I've exhausted my questions and ask if he has any for me, but he just shrugs. It isn't until we've stood up to say goodbye that he catches my eye with a pointed look.

"Are you against us?"

For the first time, he looks a little concerned. No, of course not, I reply. Looking to reassure him, I tell Andre that his story is fascinating and that I want to learn more about people like him and what it's like to be a young person in Cuba, dealing with hardship, shortages, travel restrictions, and political repression, all the while surrounded by foreigners whose lives seem easy by comparison. I ask him what is bothering him. Is he worried that I will report him to the police?

"No," he says. "I just wanted to know what *you* think of us." Andre smiles and seems satisfied. Javier, with one arm thrown around Andre's shoulders, is growing more and more boisterous, so Andre says goodbye, waving as they turn to head down the street together.

I saw Andre many more times over the course of my stay in Cuba, but we never talked in such detail again about jineterismo or political life in Cuba. My conversation with him prepared me well for the interviews that would follow, since his sentiments were echoed over and over but not often as eloquently. He had clearly given much thought to his own agency and what it meant in his life. He also seemed to understand some of the subtle work-ings of power that shaped his experience, which he demonstrated amply through the very conscious way he negotiated his own identity amid multi-ple pressures. While his goals of sex, money, and travel may seem material-ist or even frivolous, they become much more relatable when set against a backdrop of deprivation. Andre wants to live like foreigners do, without worrying about making ends meet or having to forgo new experiences.

Political power in Cuba, as elsewhere, is diffuse and pervasive rather than instrumental. It takes the form of discourses and regimes of knowl-edge that shape individual subjects and condition their behavior. On an everyday basis, the power of government institutions functions by manag-ing and cultivating the population rather than by outright force, using a range of tactics from subtle to unabashedly corrective and interventionist to nudge them toward the "right" kinds of education, health, careers, rela-tionships, families, and opinions. Those who reject this pastoral care in order to pursue other goals or identities are classed as dissidents or anti-social elements in the eyes of Cuban state power. This, I argue, is what

Michel Foucault termed *biopolitics,* also called *biopower,* which he describes as follows:

> By this I mean a number of phenomena that seem to me to be quite signifi-
> cant, namely, the set of mechanisms through which the basic biological fea-
> tures of the human species became the object of a political strategy, of a
> general strategy of power, or, in other words, how, starting from the 18th
> century, modern Western societies took on board the fundamental biologi-
> cal fact that human beings are a species. This is what I have called biopower.[3]

In effect, this meant that the old right of sovereign power "to take life or let live" was joined by the biopolitical imperative to "make live and 'let' die"—to care for and foster life.[4] Biopolitics is the process by which power cultivates and invests life, taking the governance and production of the population *as species* as its "central core."[5] The production of healthy, pro-ductive citizens in keeping with a prescribed notion of the good life is readily apparent in attempts to correct and manage young people's—and especially, though not exclusively, young women's—sexualities.

When he formulated such an idea of power, Foucault had in mind the modern, liberal-democratic Western world, but Sergei Prozorov adapts his reasoning to the study of socialist settings, describing biopolitics as the displacement of outright violence with the "power of the norm," which compels individual subjects to conform to acceptable values and behav-iors.[6] Much like in the twilight days of the Soviet Union, in which Prozorov locates his analysis, many Cubans are resisting the power that is pervasive in their lives by engaging in various kinds of disinvestment. They are rejecting governmental care in favor of new means of supporting them-selves and their families, resisting the system as former Soviet bloc citizens once did through absenteeism, pilfering from state institutions, on-the-job corruption, and participation in shadow economies of all kinds.

These are not practices unique to socialist contexts by any stretch of the imagination—they are common wherever remuneration is not seen to be in keeping with labor—but they are particularly significant in centralized economies where individual insubordinate acts congeal more readily into systemwide effects. By its collapse in 1991, according to Prozorov, the USSR was a shell of its former self, no longer the nucleus of biopolitical socialism but rather a "ritualistic form of Soviet sovereignty."[7] Small-scale strategies like nonparticipation or insubordination in the workplace had become formidable "barrier reefs" of resistance, to use James C. Scott's term,[8] that eventually slowed the vast, lumbering centralized economy to a near-standstill.

Today, as young Cubans increasingly find ways outside of the state-controlled sectors to support their families and themselves, many—like Andre—leave their jobs entirely and others simply waste their time on the clock. Their disinvestment from the system makes it more and more difficult for the socialist economy to survive. In Cuba, more and more people are getting at least some of their income from remittances from abroad and black- and gray-market activities of some kind, and those who participate in the sexual-affective economy are certainly among them.[9] Many, if not all, continue to offer varying degrees of what Scott calls a "command performance of consent"[10]—maintaining official jobs, staying in school, attending meetings of the mass organizations, voting in elections, paying lip service to revolutionary ideals and figures, and marching in the massive rallies that take place on important national holidays. On a few different occasions, Andre mentioned attending meetings of his local CDR. Yakelín also spoke about her unfailing CDR attendance and her membership in the FMC. Amir Valle wrote about one young woman named Yanet, a self-proclaimed jinetera, who even acted as *ideóloga,* or ideological officer, of her local CDR.[11] Lili carried on her state job as a social worker, despite having grown disillusioned with it; likewise, Cristina and her friend Olivia continued studying and working despite meager pay and few prospects for advancement. All of these individual acts taken together form what Scott might call a *public transcript,* or an outward veneer of consent and obedience, which helps each of these people avoid the attention of the police and other state-centered institutions, and also helps the powerful maintain their claims to control.[12]

Meanwhile, behind the scenes, a "shared critique of power" is articulated through a *hidden transcript* of dissent and criticism, shared and reinforced in secret among oppressed people as an outlet for their frustration.[13] In Cuba today, these hidden transcripts that Scott describes take the form of codes and conventions that can be confusing to an outsider. Cubans often refer to prominent figures by nicknames, some of which are secret codes among friends and others more widely used: "el papa" for Fidel and "el chino" for Raúl were among those I heard quite commonly.

Many will also touch their chins, miming stroking a beard, to evoke Fidel without speaking any name at all. These tactics are at most a code for expressing dissent and at least an element of plausible deniability. Many of the Cubans I met preferred to avoid speaking of politics entirely unless they knew they were among friends; some would even espouse beliefs they did not hold when they were in public as a form of cover.

The hidden transcript does not need to be purely based on speech as a transcript either; it can include acts and even work, that most sacred of socialist institutions. Workplace expressions of nonconformity can include pilfering, poaching, evasion, foot-dragging, and intentionally shabby work, all of which are open secrets and common on-the-job practices in Cuban state-sector workplaces.[14] Patrick Symmes documents how, on a microlevel, Cubans buy and sell materials meant for major construction sites and use them to expand or improve their own homes; this practice is echoed across the centralized economy in those who steal goods from the shops in which they work, or office supplies, or food from the kitchens of the major hotels and restaurants.[15] It is evident in the way items like packaged foods and building materials are bought and sold, more often under the table than through official shops or legal suppliers.

This also brings to mind Homi K. Bhabha's notion of *mimicry*, whereby oppressed people in colonial (and even postcolonial) contexts reiterate the practices and identities of the powerful. In so doing, however, their mimicry "must continually produce its slippage, its excess, its difference."[16] The performances of work, study, community engagement, and political support produced by individual actors are never as authentic and effective as the political elites had intended; rather, they manifest, in Bhabha's words, "a difference that is itself a process of disavowal."[17] In this sense, mimicry is a means by which the colonized can return and co-opt the gaze of the powerful through acts that are not ostensibly political but that nonetheless undermine the grip of power—admittedly a somewhat heretical reading of Bhabha, who seemed to envision this resistance as unintentional. In showing up at CDR meetings month after month, Andre does not abandon his criticisms of power; rather, he approximates what he believes the organization's leaders want to see, so that he is not marked as a troublemaker. Yakelín, too, in her active membership in the FMC aligns herself with the organization and may be able to thereby avoid its scrutiny.

In Prozorov's words, "It is the sovereign decision that establishes whose life the government must foster and support."[18] Andre was among the many I met who engage in sexual-affective relations with foreigners and who are actively finding ways to refuse what Prozorov calls a power "whose paradigm of intervention is indeed not decapitation but the loving embrace."[19] In our interview, Andre made it very clear that since he had not chosen the path of the upstanding citizen—he had no official job, he consorted regularly with tourists and accepted their gifts of cash, and he had frequent encounters with the police—he was outside the realm of the lives to be celebrated, encouraged, and supported. He knew that many things about his life flagged him as deviant. Andre situated himself firmly within the realm of disinvestment, of turning away from the pervasive power of subjection disguised as care. He did not rely on a state-sector job or state social programs; he made his own life elsewhere and by other means, maintaining only a veneer of consent to ease his way. Most of the young people I interviewed, however, did not express it so explicitly: their disaffection took the form of a general feeling of alienation and a desire to turn away, to forge something different.

A GOOD GIRL

Even meeting Haydée was an experience. Months after my conversation with Andre, I was in Camagüey where my friend Damarys had arranged for me to meet Haydée. Bustling briskly down the long hallway of her home in the center of the city, Damarys sets the scene for me: "Haydée is a lovely girl, sweet as honey. You want to know how it is for young people in Cuba? She will tell you." She pauses to straighten up various potted plants and knickknacks as we move from the kitchen toward the front sitting room, but then she turns suddenly to face me with one cautionary finger raised high. "But she is a *good* girl. My friends' daughter." The implication is clear: Haydée is not a jinetera. With that, we pass through the door to where Haydée sits waiting.

We chat cordially for a few minutes while Damarys mills about, fluffing cushions and angling picture frames just so. Haydée seems relaxed, sitting back against the couch cushions with one slender leg slung lazily over the other, but her gaze flickers around the room. She tells me she's nineteen and currently studying accounting and computing at college. She's lived in Camagüey her entire life. At first, she speaks mostly in clipped phrases, offering nothing further, but her wide eyes dart up as Damarys makes to leave, waiting almost interminably for the click of the door, and then they fasten onto me intently as she leans forward.

"You're writing a book about jineterismo, right?" I nod. The words come quickly now, but her voice hovers just over a whisper. "Here, it's mostly Italians, you know? They come to Camagüey because there are fewer cops on the streets, not like in Havana or Santiago. And they call out to you as you walk down the street."

To you and your friends?

"All the time. And then you just decide if you like him and if it's worth it. That's how it works."

Where does this happen?

"In the street. And at the disco, Caribe. There are lots of tourists there."

Have you done this yourself?

Instantly, I regret those words and wonder if she'll be offended, but she waves her hand flippantly in the air and says, "Of course I have. The last time I was in Havana, I spent four days with a Russian I met there."

Are you still in touch with him?

She shakes her head. "He wasn't so special."

Needless to say, I'm stunned by Haydée's sudden frankness. She's still watching me steadily, with one eyebrow crooked expectantly. She describes a world where there is virtually no line between those who are and those who are not jineteando, where opportunism reigns as foreign men treat the Cuban women who catch their eyes as available, and young Cuban women see no problem accepting their advances or not as they so choose. I press on and ask her what she takes this notion of jineterismo to mean.

"You could call it prostitution," she says slowly, but then, pursing her lips and thinking, she adds, "but no one does. Because pretty much all of us do it, you know? At one time or another. It's not a crime, not at all. It's a way of looking for easy money when you need it. There's a lot of need [*Hay mucha necesidad*] in Cuba, and going to bed with a foreigner is a way to solve problems."

And none of these women consider themselves prostitutes?

"No. And society doesn't either. It's just another part of the daily struggle [*la lucha diaria*]."

Just like any other?

"The same."

Does it cause you any trouble?

"Well, the police are waiting for you all the time here. That bothers me a lot." Haydée tells me that young people in Camagüey are frequently stopped and asked to produce identification, much like they are in Havana. It's about intimidation, according to Haydée. The police are hoping to frighten young people out of interacting in public with foreign tourists. Nonetheless, she says, they never arrest Cubans in the presence of a foreigner; rather, they wait and apprehend young Cubans as they walk alone in the streets of the city. With stakes so high, it seems nothing short of amazing that young Camagueyanos continue going out to meet tourists.

"Look, they do it out of necessity. And the government lets the tourists come. We all do what we have to do [*Cada cual hace su vida*]."

Looking toward the future, Haydée says the usual things: she wants a husband, a house, a family, and a job. She'd like to travel abroad, certainly, but she'll never leave Cuba for good. "There's more freedom here, I think. There's always parties, outings, everything. I get the impression that in other countries, people always have to work."

With that, Damarys breezes back into the sitting room and our conversation comes to an abrupt halt. Haydée sits back once again, waiting through only another minute or two of small talk before excusing herself. She's out the door quickly, and I see the sandy brown waves of her ponytail bob past the window as she goes. The entire experience feels extraordinary.

I've wondered many times since then why Haydée felt she could speak to me in a way she clearly could not in front of Damarys. What part was I playing for this nineteen-year-old girl? She was so frank and self-assured that it would be naive to chalk up our conversation to catharsis or validation seeking. Maybe, as a foreigner only passing through Camagüey, I was so thoroughly outside her world that it didn't matter what I thought, leaving her free to share anything. Then again, it may have been the opposite: we were of relatively (though not exactly) similar ages, and Haydée had reason to believe that I would sympathetic, as my reputation had begun to precede me in certain circles. What kind of subjectivity I embodied in that

Figure 14. The winding streets of central Camagüey, 5 June 2011. Photo by author.

space of Damarys's living room that day still perplexes me. Perhaps Damarys simply would not have approved. She was, after all, a friend of Haydée's mother. Older generations have always been prone to anxiety over the sexual proclivities of young people, after all. It also made me wonder how much Damarys really knew. These were questions I felt I could not ask either Haydée or Damarys, as to do so would shatter the delicate game being played around me.

Together, Damarys and Haydée demonstrate something more intimate about Cuba—both the actual country and the imagined nation—that mirrors its relation to the international through the lens of jineterismo. As Andre said, *Cuba está en fuego*—Cuba is on fire. Likewise, Haydée herself noted how the state lets the tourists come, because *we all do what we have to do.* Here too, there is a subtle game of control and (open) secrecy at work. Cuba engages willingly with the foreign and makes its own ideological compromises in exchange for hard currency and access to the trappings of a "better" life, but these cannot be honestly acknowledged. Cuba is involved in a jinete of its own but one that cannot be discussed in the open, nor can it be allowed to replicate itself at the level of daily life or of women's bodies.

Something else that Haydée showed me was that disinvestment did not need to be voiced; rather, it could simply be lived. Had we not spoken that day, I wonder if she ever would have put these thoughts into words. She certainly seemed more focused on getting on with things than on pondering her place in the world. That said, though Haydée did not articulate her disaffection in the same thoughtful way that Andre did, many of the same sentiments are evident in what she did say, and, more important, in the way she lived her life. Throughout her story there is an overall feeling of negation, an apathetic shrug at the socialist ideals of self-improvement, voluntary work, and collectivism. Her disaffection from power in the socialist system—which presents itself as care, assistance, and inclusion—evokes Prozorov's understanding of resistance in the sphere of biopolitics:

> If the transcendent aspect of sovereignty is exemplified by the exteriority of the sovereign, who kills but does not care, to the immanence of the life of its subjects, the transcendent moment of immanentist biopolitics may well be embodied by the figure of a living being who does not care so much for being cared by power and puts its life at stake precisely in order to reclaim it.[20]

He describes *biopolitical violence* as that which through its "loving embrace" makes "life itself unbearable"—what Michael Dillon more colorfully calls being "cared to death."[21]

Resisting such violence, therefore, must consist in emptying out the positive content of power by refusing the care offered by state power by embracing new forms of life and living, in the face of real physical danger, and becoming "a being that rebels against being 'cared to death' and would rather die (or kill) than live *like that.*"[22] It is my contention that the young people whom I interviewed are taking a momentous step by turning away from the political system in which they grew up, knowing full well that they may be excluded from their careers or education, that they may be subjected to violence and rehabilitative incarceration, that they may not be able to count on the police, their locals CDRs, or even their family doctors any longer. Prozorov posits that this kind of disinvestment or refusal constitutes a very significant kind of resistance, arguing, "It is all very well to refuse enslavement, domination, exploitation and even work, but to refuse care . . . is a different matter altogether that involves concrete costs and losses."[23]

Haydée, though only nineteen years old, despaired of politics as an arena for change. She did not see political activism or organizing as viable options since in Cuba today these are dangerous and often short-lived undertakings. Instead, she resists austerity—as an experience of economic hardship and as a way of being. As García notes, state institutions in Cuba locate morality in poverty, casting suspicion on those who possess (or even desire) fashionable clothes, comfortable homes, personal electronics, or other trappings of affluence.[24] According to this system of values, young women in particular can be excluded from the realm of the moral based on the perception of either financial security or sexual promiscuity—or both, and today one is often taken to be proof of the other. To this, Haydée adopts an "attitude of indifference," in Prozorov's words.[25] She and others like her are indicating through romantic and sexual practices that they are not willing to live like this, this way, at this price. She takes the possibility of exclusion in her stride and carries on pursuing something different for herself.

Nadia, too, used almost those very words: "I'm not willing to live and die here." Constantly called upon to suffer through and endure shortages and hardships, even as the prospect of a more comfortable and easier life sometimes readily presented itself in the form of romantic attachments, Nadia was frustrated and unwilling to carry on struggling. While she was afraid to court trouble by going back to dating European tourists, she still dreamed of finding a partner who could provide her with the financial stability that she believed would solve all of her problems. Whether it is a long-term relationship that results in marriage and emigration or a series of fleeting affairs that provide temporary escapism, sexual-affective engagements with tourists in Cuba constitute a turning away from a pre-scribed set of values and way of being. It is a refusal of the care proffered by state institutions that seek to educate and rehabilitate young people, socializing them as productive citizens within the system. In refusing this care and pursuing a different kind of good life, Haydée was opting out of the moral system created for her and resisting subjection by a power that tries to shape her in its own image.

By stepping outside prescribed ideals and ways of being, people like Haydée and Andre—and Yakelín, Yanet, and Nadia—go some way toward externalizing biopolitical power. They refuse care and accept the consequences. While they do not challenge its authority directly or openly, they accomplish something more important in turning away: they defuse it and empty out its positive content. From the perspective of state-centric institutions and others with commitments to state socialism, these people have failed as reputable, upstanding citizens—as the New Man or even the New Woman of Cuban socialist lore. However, failure in itself can be a manifestation of resistance to subjectifying power. The queer theorist Judith/Jack Halberstam calls this the "queer art of failure," a form of refusal that undoes and unbecomes, using passivity and failure to disrupt the intended script.[26] By questioning success as defined—out loud for all to hear, or through incremental daily practices—and unbecoming prescribed ways of being, failure can be both politically potent and an effective means to repudiate the logic of rule. Through failure, through refusal and disinvestment, turning away and refusing care, so-called jineteras and jineteros can resist power that is pervasive and productive.

Jineterismo as a sexual practice is one of many observable activities in the tourist-oriented economy that engage in this kind of refusal and failure. There are many different ways to step outside the formal economy and make a life that does not depend on state care, from running illicit casas particulares or paladares to dealing in black-market rum, cigars, drugs, or other contraband. The resistance posed by supposed jineteros and jineteras, however, presents an important facet of the power/resistance dynamic in Cuba in that it is located in the body. Bodily practices of sex, sexuality, affection, and even love are central not only to resisting and externalizing power for many young Cubans but also to confronting the process of subjection that would determine the very identities of these individual subjects.

That the body—the raced, gendered, sexualized feminine body, centuries in the making and continuously evolving—acts as an organizing index for both oppression and resistance is crucial to understanding jineterismo as a distinct and remarkable political practice. Cuba's long and contorted history of inscribing race, gender, and sexuality with indelible and yet changeable meanings creates the body as a palimpsest, to which new meanings can be added but older ones never fully erased, and crafts an image of the nation of Cuba itself as a body.

"FROM THE OTHER SIDE OF THE MIRROR"

Rape and prostitution are central themes of the socialist state's genesis story. As emotional and evocative concepts, they help maintain a sense of urgency and external threat, lest Cuba once again become the victim of exploitation by foreign interests. The story goes that before the Revolution, Cuba—like so many of its women—was abused by outsiders, first Spain and then the United States. The body of Cuba is conflated with the bodies of Cuba's women. Given this tendency to evoke the violated body—for here rape and prostitution are fused—it pays to take a moment to imagine what the body of Cuba might look like, founded as it is on mestizaje and colonial sexuality.[27]

At the top of the sweeping stairs that lead up to the University of Havana, there is a statue of the Alma Mater in bronze. It depicts the classical figure of a woman draped in robes and surrounded by reliefs depicting the various university disciplines. The statue was installed on the stately campus in the 1920s and is photographed by thousands of tourists each year.[28] Her face takes inspiration from that of the daughter of a Cuban official—a virtuous, pure, and pretty young white girl. For the drawn-out process of sculpting the body of the statue, however, the artist used a different model. The figure of the Alma Mater, beloved in the city as a symbol of higher learning and the potential of a nation, is that of an Afro-Cuban woman, a friend of the artist and, it is whispered around Havana, a prostitute.

Cuba, with a pure white face and the sensualized, sexualized body of a black woman, is constantly at pains to conceal her raced heritage and deny the truths produced about her. She carries with her a history of sexual availability and violence, and she has internalized—or, in Fanon's poignant wording, "epidermalized"[29]—her own inferiority. An aspirational veneer of purity and whiteness covers up the difference—and the experience of that

Figure 15. The *Alma Mater* statue outside the University of Havana, 15 March 2013. Photo by Dan Iggers, 2013. Printed with permission.

difference—that underpins, bolsters, embeds itself in Cuba's entire national project across eras. Her face shows what she wants the world to see: a demure, white facade that projects an inviolate sexuality, a pure and irreproachable femininity. Her body, however, betrays an innate sensuality, both prized and condemned. Sierra Madero describes the body of the Cuban nation—the *nación sexuada,* or sexed nation—as akin to a human body, with "carefully drawn contours and defined borders, with its erogenous sites and abject zones."[30] As Gayle Rubin laments, "We never encounter the body unmediated by the meanings that cultures give to it."[31] Cuba's body—one that embodies the mestizaje that founds Cuban identity[32]—is inscribed with cultural knowledge of the mulata as the embodiment of the turbulent encounter between colonizer/white and colonized/black, and the bearer of a powerful, passionate, and dangerous sexuality. She carries with her the evidence of the meeting of cultures, races, and classes that created her.

In the years of the colonial slave society, Cuba was pursued by Spain and later by the wealthy United States, but her own desires never really mattered. She was a slave, or little better, the daughter and concubine of powerful white men in a colonial society where women of color were always already fallen. Her very existence spoke of sexual availability—in the brothel, on the plantation, and in her employer's home. Gazing on Cuba, Mexico might see its own legendary figure, *la chingada,* or the fucked woman[33]—one whose loss of innocence came against her will, or perhaps simply with the wrong man, and who is all but destroyed by it. Her tarnished reputation recalls La Malinche, the Aztec woman who became the lover of the conquistador Hernán Cortés and who stands as a marker for all those native women who were "fascinated, violated or seduced by the Spaniards"—and whose betrayal Mexico has yet to forgive.[34] La chingada haunts the Mexican imaginary to this day as both the mother of the nation, the *hijos de la chingada,* and as a symbol of denigrated femininity, weakness, and moral depravity. Cuba seemed bound for a similar fate at the dawn of the nineteenth century.

Like Cynthia Weber, who describes Cuba and its Revolution as the bringers of a "midlife/hegemonic/masculinity crisis" that threatens the masculine United States,[35] I see the body of Cuba as continuously in opposition to the foreign. (For Weber and, indeed, for Cuba through most of its recent history, this *foreign* and the United States are nearly one and the same.) Through the nineteenth century and into the twentieth, the iconically feminine Cuba played the "trophy mistress" to the militarized yet fretful masculinity of the United States.[36] The hypersexualized object of desire that pervaded U.S. fantasies, Cuba inspired Americans to propose annexation in smitten tones that were nonetheless still tinged with violation.

> [Cuba] admires Uncle Sam, and he loves her. Who shall forbid the bans? Matches are made in heaven, and why not this? Who can object if he throws his arms around the Queen of the Antilles, as she sits, like Cleopatra's burning throne, upon the silver waves, breathing her spicy, tropic breath, and pouting her rosy, sugared lips? Who can object? None. She is of age—take her, Uncle Sam![37]

Cuba was a "ripe pear" awaiting American seduction, an "erotic [bastion] of American security"; indeed, beginning in 1761 and continuing well into the twentieth century, suitors from Benjamin Franklin and Thomas Jefferson to William McKinley made acquisitive overtures.[38] Devastated by two crippling wars, Cuba had finally thrown off the burden of Spanish rule by the end of the century but found herself under the thrall of the United States at last. Her white face and black body made her exotic and accessible for American adventures, so in the first five decades of the last century, Cuba stood for escapist fantasies of secret weekends away, torrid affairs, and debauchery. The wars had left her destitute, but soon American men began to flock to her to "[take] advantage of [President] Batista's pimping of his own country."[39] Her body and her sexuality, as much imagined as real, were once again her defining features and her best means of creating a life for herself. Hyperfeminine, lascivious, exotic, and perpetually available: Cuba was a prostitute. This is the "other side of the mirror."[40]

The Revolution, Cuba was told, would save her. Though foreign capitalist monopolies had raped her, not to worry; she would soon be reinscribed with revolutionary value(s) and elevated from a life of exploitation. Her iconic femininity remained, but it was overwritten by—or perhaps simply paired with—the emblematic New Man that was the Soviet Union. Set on her feet, clad in fatigues, and handed a gun, Cuba was told to hold her head high. Her white face, smiling serenely at the challenges ahead, became the unflinching picture of virtuous socialist womanhood, the new Cuba—and the logo of the FMC, seen across the country—while her uniform concealed the sensual blackness of her body. While she worked to project an inviolate yet voluptuous femininity, pushed and pulled to live up to an impossible ideal of socialist virtue, her body retained the centuries-old narrative of sensuality that would only stay hidden so long. In the shadow of the Soviet Union, Cuba was patiently supported and helped along, even if now and then a Russian attaché made a pass at her, his tropical protégé. For thirty years, she was the picture of virtue: a wife, mother, and consort befitting the nation she embodied.

At the point of crisis, when the Soviet bloc disintegrated, Cuba looked once more to that which she has always been told is her greatest asset: her tropical sexuality. Opening the door ever so slightly to the capitalist world, tentatively, Cuba—the woman and the nation—returned the glances of the foreigners who eagerly looked her way. Today, as ever, Cuba's dance card is

Figure 16. Cover of the newspaper *La Semana* (The Week), 19 May 1926. The caption reads, "The Republic to Uncle Sam: 'Don't try to pull a fast one on me, old man. Keep in mind I'm not a little girl: I'm already twenty-four years old!'" Source: Casa de las Américas.

Figure 17. The original logo of the FMC, showing a faceless woman in fatigues holding a rifle and an infant. After the death of FMC founder Vilma Espín in 2007, this image was replaced with a likeness of Espín. Photo by Nicole Mcdougall, 2006. Printed with permission.

always full. The storied mulata sexuality has always walked alongside Cuba like a tangible presence, and through it the comforts of material wealth as well as enjoyment, pleasure, and even love can be attained. In shedding a military uniform for a red Lycra dress, however, Cuba has drawn derision from would-be rescuers for flouting their hard work, leaving the entire project vulnerable to fears of failure. Claudia Aradau describes how, like a prostitute trafficked into Europe from outside, a body can be seen as both *at risk* and *risky,* both pitiable and dangerous, and all the more so when such a fate is "knowingly accepted."[41] Today, Cuba is incited to show off her exotic sensuality, to be feminine and sexy, and to flatter and flirt. Today, her white face and black body are the markers of a unique cubanidad and a source of pride, unlike centuries past. A white face means elegance and sweetness; a black body speaks of an almost animal passion. Cuba's compañeros never tire of quipping that she—the hot mulata—is the island's finest achievement.[42] This supposedly liberated morale, however, only renders her all the more risky/at risk even as it renders her more desirable. When the tourists come to dance, to flirt, to buy her gifts, to wine and dine her, Cuba knows that saying yes comes at a price.

After centuries of lecherous colonists and slave owners, of hiding demurely behind a fan, of serving as a young white American's rite of passage, of revolutionary beauty pageants and state-sponsored manicures, Cuba is under pressure to become something different, something *better.* Her sexuality is imbued with antirevolutionary content, while her chastity is the measure of the nation's value. The dangerous promiscuity of which Rosa Miriam Elizalde warned, which leads inexorably to prostitution—of the body as subject and the body as nation—is Cuba's.[43] Marx himself admonishes her: "A nation and a woman are not forgiven the unguarded hour in which the first adventurer that came along could violate them."[44] Or, more plainly, in the words of one self-proclaimed jinetera, "Cuba is an old woman with rouge on: the mother country is a whore among whores, full of vices and covering her wrinkles with makeup."[45] Again, her defilement is condemned, and as before, her desire—for love, for prosperity, for security, for sex, for a different kind of life—is seemingly erased. She and her foreign suitor are, as Octavio Paz says of La Malinche and Cortés, more than historical figures: they are phantasms, "symbols of a secret conflict that we still have not resolved."[46]

This image of the body, and of the nation *as* body, is central to understanding jineterismo as a political practice of sexuality and resistance. In the context of a state ideology whose rhetoric embodies the Cuban nation in its women, and whose own stance toward capitalist tourism is ambivalent at best, jineterismo-as-sexual-practice takes this imagery of the body and turns it on its head, using it for purposes other than those intended. Jineterismo is rooted in the body: in bodily practices, sex, sexuality, affect, and love. Politically, the body is then a site of both oppression and resistance. Elaine Scarry and Deepak Mehta posit the body as both corporeal and imagined, two dimensions that are inextricably interwoven. The corporeal body has all the "felt-fact of aliveness" and the "sturdiness and vibrancy of presence of the natural world" that Scarry notes, while Mehta observes that the body as imagined is always already "embossed with a future."[47] The imagined body of the jinetera is the very same body of the mulata, who haunts Cuba's history, and whose race and gender constitute her as an available and enthusiastic sexual object, making these particular bodies a poignant and fitting locus for practices of resistance.

Foucault describes the body as "totally imprinted by history and the process of history's destruction of the body."[48] It cannot be understood outside of this social and cultural inscription or returned to any natural, originary state. Young Cuban black and mixed-race women, and particularly those who are seen as embodying a classic mulata identity, feel at times empowered and at times trapped by the iconic sexuality that is inscribed on their bodies, and which casts them as both desirable and deviant. Isabel recounted happily how foreign men were drawn by her complexion and her curly hair, believing her to be the hot Caribbean temptress of their fantasies. Cristina, on the other hand, felt that the color of her skin made her and the other darker-skinned women of Santiago inferior to the "blondes" of Havana. She resented the white European men who arrived looking to meet black and mixed-race women, assuming they only wanted girls like her because they came "cheap," in her words. It is true that both Ricky and Andre also credit their successes with foreign women to fantasises of the raced Afro-Cuban other, but their experience demonstrates all the more how the sexualities of Afro-Cuban women have been subject to the systematic attempts to regulate and control while their male counterparts have not. The contours of the Cuban mulata/jinetera body are thus as much imagined as they are concrete and real.

The corporeal body is equally important to the imagined one, serving as a physical site of resistance. In a biopolitical system, Foucault argues, sexual resistance constitutes a particular transgression, falling as it does at the nexus of the two branches of governance: the discipline of the body and the regulation of the nation, both as a population and as an idea.[49] This makes it both a fertile ground for practices of resistance and also a lightning rod for oppression. In a similar vein, Allen Feldman highlights how political violence functions through the "mobilization of values through the spectacle of the body," whereby the individual subject's body is used to address the broader population as a sort of "mass article" or "social hieroglyph."[50] Since an approved sexuality has always been central to citizenship in Cuba, discipline and regulation of dissenting sexual subjects have been enacted directly on the body, from regulation of interracial marriage in the 1800s to the casas de recogidas at the turn of the twentieth century to the imprisonment of gay Cubans in the UMAP labor camps in the 1960s to the rehabilitation centers for jineteras of the 1990s and 2000s. Isabel was just one of many, perhaps thousands, who endured police brutality, abuse, and rehabilitative incarceration. Even the simple specter of fear itself conditions many of these young women's lives and restricts their mobility in public spaces. This kind of violence creates their bodies as theaters for performing, policing, and enforcing ideological norms.

In spite of—or perhaps because of—the corporeal body's status as a spectacle of oppression, it exists as an all the more potent site of resistance. It is *because* it is a site of oppression that the body is such an effective instrument for resisting: it is this context that imbues the body and practices of sexuality with meaning. Foucault himself noted that the body itself must be "the rallying point for the counterattack against the deployment of sexuality."[51] This is in large part due, as Foucault also notes, to its ability to feel pleasure. Whereas Scarry argues that the body's physical capacity for pain is unique among sensations—and that "the problem of pain is bound up with the problem of power"[52]—I would like to posit a similar role for pleasure.

Pain, maintains Scarry, is the absolute of lived experience, both undeniable in the self who feels it and unconfirmable in the other.[53] The experience of pain is isolating, erasing everything else including language and becoming almost impossible to express; this "isolating aversiveness" makes it extremely difficult to truly imagine another person, and Scarry argues that this is what enables us to harm other people—and thereby contribute to the unmaking of the world.[54]

> The difficulty of articulating physical pain permits political and perceptual complications of the most serious kind. The failure to express pain—whether

the failure to objectify its attributes or instead the failure, once those attributes are objectified, to refer them to their original site in the human body—will always work to allow its appropriation and conflation with debased forms of power; conversely, the successful expression of pain will always work to expose and make impossible that appropriation and conflation.[55]

These factors are what make pain politically useful, which is the principle behind torture, and what makes it such a destructive force in the world. What is more, pain is simply itself—it is not *for*, *by*, or *to* any actor or action external to the body.[56]

Foucault, in conversation with Deleuze, argued something very similar on behalf of pleasure: it is not subject to the same "grid of intelligibility" as love or desire—it simply *is*.[57] Scarry does not agree with me that pleasure can be put forth as a counterpart or opposite to pain in this way: pleasure, unlike pain, is not isolating.[58] However, this may be in itself the fact that positions pleasure as a counterweight to pain. Scarry notes that in moving against the isolation of pain, "mental and material culture assumes the sharability of sentience."[59] Pleasure is an inherently (though not necessarily) shareable experience, and I argue that the move to pursue and share it can be a radically relational, productive form of (self-)creation, one whose intentionality renders it all the more potent. As an avenue for resistance, it makes refusing biopolitical care that much more inviting, and it raises the possibility of forging a new and different kind of care, more versatile and flowing. Pleasure, therefore, like pain, can be a site of radical relation to the body and to the other, and a kind of resistance to a subjectifying power that would label certain forms of sexuality and sexual practices as deviant. Pleasure, like pain, is bound up with the question of power. Andre and Haydée both gestured at this: Haydée remarked that all young Cubans engage in jineterismo of some kind, while Andre commented, "We're all in the fire. Cuba is on fire." New possibilities for solidarity and community may be emerging, both across and within borders, and taking pleasure as their core.

Cuba's sexual culture is evolving and becoming, if anything, more fluid. While Cubans still undeniably live in a machista culture, the effect of forty years of coeducational schools, more or less comprehensive sex education, and access to (and acceptance of) contraception has been a gradual lessening of the stigmas normally attached to premarital sex in Latin America and the Caribbean, particularly for young women. Young Cubans begin having sex at an early age—many as young as twelve—and soon come to see it both as an essential part of their romantic relationships and a harmless, spontaneous pastime with new acquaintances.[60] In the wake of the economic crisis of the 1990s, Sierra Madero observes, young Cubans have come to see romantic and sexual relationships as transitory or unstable, much like so many other previously dependable aspects of their lives—medicines, school supplies, new clothes, even food—that have melted away before their very eyes.[61] Likewise, Fusco sees sex in Cuba today as a leisure activity for youth with limited options for entertainment and recreation, an "unspoken revolt against both the socialist emphasis on productive labor and the revolution's puritanical morality."[62]

What may seem a cynical sexual ethos to some was more often seen by my Cuban contacts and friends as a kind of radical, progressive openness to love and to sexual pleasure, to new experiences and new connections—though it was not without problems of its own, especially in a machista culture where the new sexual "liberty" was not always permitted to everyone equally. Nevertheless, sex with non-Cubans as a means of acquiring new experiences, sexual and otherwise, fits easily into this paradigm. While some spoke only of their financial need, others recounted stories of autonomy, heightened estimations of self-worth, and even joyful enjoyment of the sex they had with foreigners. They maintained a dynamic openness to new relationships, to themselves and to others, and they were willingly and openly embracing an individualism and a new take on care and community, both completely at odds with Cuban socialist doctrine.

Adopting—and also resisting—Scarry's logic about pain, it is possible to argue that the experience and expression of pleasure speaks to the "expansive nature of human *sentience*, the felt-fact aliveness that is often sheerly happy," which, in turn, "opens into the wider frame of *invention*."[63] It is this capacity for invention and creation that makes Cuba's tourist-oriented sexual-affective economy such a potent field of resistance. Through performances of identity and sexuality, jineterismo as a sexual practice contributes to an ethics of the self: a process of self-making and subject formation with resounding implications for political and sexual subjectivity, both within Cuba and elsewhere.

"THEY'RE NOT BUILDING BOMBS"

Everyone in the neighborhood knows Mariela, it seems. I've come to visit Ricky, who lives here too, and now we're sitting outside with a group of his childhood friends, all of whom live within a few square blocks. They're playing dominoes and enjoying themselves so immensely that one would never suspect it was two o'clock on a Wednesday afternoon. We're in Vedado, just north of Línea and two or three blocks from the sea, and Ricky is preparing me to meet his neighbor, Mariela.

"She was a jinetera, you know"—his friends nod along vigorously—"a big one. Maybe ten years ago? And her daughter is a jinetera now, too. But don't ask her about that. Not directly, anyway. She's afraid to get in trouble, so be careful around that. She can tell you lots of things, though. Lots of things."

His friends chime in, telling me that Mariela will be a key informant for me. They seem to hold her in particularly high regard, and I begin to get the distinct impression that I'm about to interview local royalty.

Later, Ricky and I are sitting in the front room of his family home. The ceiling is high, the only windows placed high above the door and covered by slats, so the air is still and hot. It's a simple little room, with a small refrigerator and a stereo in addition to a haggard couch and a single bed. We've already been next door to say hello and found Mariela in the midst of a manicure, so now we wait at Ricky's until she's finished.

Within ten minutes, there's a quiet tap at the door. Mariela lets herself in without waiting for a reply and then delicately settles herself on the sofa while blowing on her nails. She apologizes for not shaking my hand. As Ricky slips away into the back room of the house to give us some privacy, his neighbor lights up the first of many cigarettes, which she holds elegantly aloft between two fingers. She seems at ease, but when I ask her if it would be all right to record our conversation, she freezes. I find myself backtracking nervously, telling her we can easily do without the recorder, removing its batteries to reassure her that it isn't running, hoping I haven't caused her to clam up entirely. She watches me drop the batteries into my bag and then assesses me carefully. Finally, she draws a deep breath and sighs.

"I'm sorry," she says slowly. "I just don't want trouble. They can find you by your voice in a recording, even without your name, and charge you with antisocial conduct."

I tell her that it's no problem at all and that I hope we can still carry on. She nods benevolently, telling me she's happy to sit with me all day if need be, so that I can jot every detail down by hand. I venture to think that we're back on track.

Mariela is the forty-six-year-old mother of a twenty-six-year-old daughter. She is slim, with a careworn, almost gaunt face, but her innate refinement compels me to imagine her as she must have been twenty years earlier. Like Ricky, Mariela has lived in the district of Vedado her entire life. She tells me that she studied electronics in college, but she has never worked in that field. By the time she completed her studies, she already had her daughter, Ángela, and she stayed home while her husband worked. By 1992, however, Mariela's marriage had dissolved and the Special Period had begun, so she took a job as a chambermaid at the Hotel Presidente. She received good money in tips, but her paycheck was nearly worthless, even early on in the crisis.

"You can't get by on a salary like that [*El sueldo no te alcanza*]," she says, shaking her head as she stubs out her first cigarette and lights her second. Today she works in an administrative position at a local school, but in her years at the hotel, Mariela came into frequent contact with foreign tourists. She preempts my questions and dives straight into the heart of the matter herself.

"The interaction could be completely normal, you're just chatting with them or walking along as two human beings [*seres humanos*], but when they [the police and local CDR members] see you with foreigners, they say you're hustling [*jineteando*]. Here in Cuba, it's common. It's not possible to converse with foreigners, because here we are not human beings. Jineterismo, to me, is to go with foreigners for money or other benefits, but there are all kinds in this world. Not all of them are necessarily jineteros.

"When I go out in my own neighborhood, the police don't stop me anymore because I'm forty-six and I dress like I'm forty-six, but they do stop my daughter, because she's twenty-six and she dresses like a twenty-six-year-old. You couldn't go out all dressed up if you were Cuban either," she says, waving her hand at me. "Any girl who dresses up to go out in this area, who wants to have a good time with her girlfriends, they see her as a jinetera. They say to her, 'Why are you here, near the hotel?' They take her

Figure 18. Avenida de los Presidentes in Vedado, Havana, a few blocks from where I met Mariela, 22 July 2010. Photo by author.

down to the station, give her a *carta de advertencia,* they call her parents. The police never go into the hotels or the clubs, but they wait outside for girls to come out. My daughter can hardly leave the house in her own neighborhood. Her friends have been sent to jail or back to their home provinces. They ask her for her *carné de identidad* constantly. It doesn't matter what she's doing at the time. I wish she could have grown up somewhere else."

Mariela shakes her head, brow furrowed, as I write down everything she has said so far. When I ask her if she ever had the opportunity to leave Cuba, she nods emphatically.

"I had a relationship, just by chance, with an Italian man who I met at the hotel. Maybe sixteen years ago? He asked me to move to Italy with him, and I wanted to go, but I couldn't get an exit visa for my daughter. So we stayed. I think, if we were allowed to do like you people do, to go and see the world and then come back again, not many of us would stay abroad—we'd always come back. If things changed here, that is. Young people have to seek out what opportunities they can find here. It's the only way for them. It's the only way."

I ask her if she thinks it's a normal thing that people do to get by here, and she nods sagely.

"Yes. I see that every single day."

Mariela pauses while Ricky reenters, bringing a rusty electric fan, which creaks to life and brings us some respite from the stifling air in the room. I use this brief interlude to ponder what to ask next. I decide to test the waters with some broad questions about Cuba's current situation, but as it turns out, she's quite willing to talk openly of politics and what she sees as Cuba's biggest problems.

"Food, housing, money to buy the things that children need. It's really difficult to raise children here without access to dollars. It's a safe place for children—no one is going to kidnap them or hurt them—but you can't buy them books or shoes. Since the politics isn't changing, all of that is going downhill [*Como no cambia la política, esto se va abajo*]. The FMC, the CDRs—we don't have their attention. They only come here when there's a hurricane."

Emboldened by her frankness, I ask her if she considers herself a socialist.

"No. The Revolution gave us health care and education, sure, but no money or freedom. If in so many years, this country hasn't been able to resolve those problems, then no, I am no socialist. Jineterismo is a loss of prestige for this country, but it really is the only way for young people. What do they [the government] have to fear from it? Well, you can't criticize the boy across the street for being a thief if you have a thief in your home as well, now can you? It's ridiculous—these people [jineteras] are incapable of threatening the Revolution. They're not building bombs. They're getting by as best they can [*Están resolviendo como puedan*]," she maintains, laying her hand over her heart. "They're good citizens and good human beings like everyone else. If I were a jinetera, it would be because I was thinking about my own financial well-being, my own future. You can't tell me that I'm making a bomb, because I'm not going to accept it."

Half an hour later, walking back with me toward Línea so I can catch a *máquina* (an informal form of public transit) back to my house, Ricky asks me how it went. I play my cards close and say vaguely that it was an interesting conversation. "So she didn't tell you nothing about being a jinetera," he says, glancing sideways at me. I just shrug and smile in reply.

What Mariela did for me was sum up the impact that this atmosphere of fear and repression has had on ordinary Cubans. She spoke of the fear she felt for her daughter, a young mixed-race woman, and others like her, and how this kind of treatment by the police, the media, and the state left them feeling like something less than human beings with rights, dignity, and integrity. She described the link that has been drawn between deviance and young women's sexual expression, and of the need for young people to forge something new for themselves. Mariela was my last interview before I left Cuba, and I walked away from it feeling that she had summed up the essence of resistance in Cuba. It was not about overt, politicized dissent or "building bombs"; rather, it was about ideas, values, and identities.

With her analogy about the thief, Mariela had also revealed the impossible position in which the Cuban state finds itself. The ruling regime has staked its claim as a moral force, in Cuba and abroad, and made the eradication of prostitution central to that claim. Since the dissolution of the Soviet Union and the ratcheting up of the American embargo, however, the Cuban government has found itself in the uncomfortable double bind of abhorring foreign capitalist incursion on the one hand and desperately needing hard currency on the other. While the United States was once Cuba's patron and perhaps its likeliest source of support, today the American position only makes Cuba's position more and more dire. The revolutionary regime is trapped between the moral high ground and the very pragmatic need to survive—both in a political sense and, during the worst years of the crisis in the mid-1990s, in a very real sense. Thus, as Mariela describes, the Cuban state's hand is forced: in a way, it must punish individual Cubans for behavior that it must itself undertake as it pursues foreigners' money, if it wants to maintain the moral high ground. Whether for survival or prosperity, individual Cubans turning to foreigners show up the weaknesses, or the incompleteness, of the revolutionary project; the compromises that the state makes on a systemic level must be stamped out on the ground.

Drawing on Foucault's understanding of power as productive, Butler describes the process by which we—our identities, values, and lives—are shaped and constituted by pervasive and, indeed, productive operations of power. She calls this process *subjection.*[64] Subjectivities are produced by power acting on and through individual subjects. This process is embedded within the paradigm of biopolitical governance, which seeks to generate a productive, wholesome population by designating certain healthy goals, values, relationships, and meanings that are to be followed in order to participate in social life. Foucault concurs: "Confronted by a power that is law, the subject who is constituted as a subject—who is 'subjected'—is he who obeys."[65] Mariela clearly felt this pressure to obey, and to avoid causing trouble for herself and her daughter by speaking out too openly. Knowing well the system in which she lived and what disciplinary machinery existed for outspoken dissidents, Mariela chose to keep her head down, only speaking out carefully and in guarded spaces. This drive for self-preservation is a powerful desire that Butler calls "pervasively exploitable"[66]— the desire to continue existing, to obey, to *be*—and this incentivizes obedience for many. What, then, would resistance to this kind of subjection by power look like? Or, in Butler's phrasing:

> What would it mean for the subject to desire something other than its continued "social existence"? If such an existence cannot be undone without falling into some kind of death, can existence nevertheless be risked, death courted or pursued, in order to expose and open to transformation the hold of social power on the conditions of life's persistence?[67]

Failure to reiterate or reproduce the norms of acceptable social behavior can invite sanction, marking the individual subject for death of some kind. Deliberately taking on this death, then, and pursuing a different kind of existence outside prescribed notions of being becomes a means of resisting subjection. Self-creation entails processes of negotiation and reiteration that must be constantly worked on—what Foucault calls the *technologies of the self*[68]—and it functions as both an ethics and an aesthetics. As an ethics, self-creation is a "true social practice" that shapes not only the relation to the self, but also to the other, constituting the self as the "ethical subject" of one's own behavior.[69] That is, the subject becomes the author and originator of his or her own acts in relation to others. As an aesthetics, self-creation is an "art of oneself," or practice of living one's life as an art form.[70] Timothy O'Leary takes up this point, noting that this is not an aesthetics in the superficial sense, one that "calls on us to make ourselves beautiful," but rather one that "calls on us to relate to ourselves and our lives as to a material that can be formed and transformed."[71] It is an opportunity for innovation, excitement, and creativity, albeit one that, seen from the outside, is often dismissed as mere immorality.[72]

Perhaps unsurprisingly, then, sexual practices can be central to this kind of aesthetic self-creation. In his writing on resistance and biopower, Foucault posits that new subjectivities can be created—rather than discovered—through experimentation with bodily practices, including sexual relationships and drug use.[73] Jeffrey Weeks also argues:

> Self-identity, at the heart of which is sexual identity, is not something that is given as a result of the continuities of an individual's life or of the fixity and force of his or her desires. It is something that has to be worked on, invented and reinvented in accord with the changing rhythms, demands, opportunities and closures of a complex world.[74]

Engaging in pleasurable, passionate relationships with others, regardless of their perceived immorality or diversion from heteronormativity, can thus be a practice of self-creation by which we elaborate our own moral codes and learn to conduct ourselves ethically with others. Cuban women who date foreign men challenge binary understandings of gender roles, which assign a sexual passivity to women, by actively pursuing the relationships they want. Those who have found long-term attachments with foreign men—presumed, nearly across the board, to be white—also defy centuries-old beliefs about women of color and their suitability as marriage partners. In refusing what they are, or are incited to be, young Cubans who carry on sexual-affective relationships with foreigners posit a new form of resistance and self-making, as well as a pointed critique of normative power. The result is not necessarily a better life, were such a thing even possible to prove, but a life that they perceive as *their own*.

Engaging in practices of freedom that include defining and redefining the meaning of sexual relationships and sexual pleasure, instead of adhering to a static notion of one true, natural, or liberated sexuality, is an important part of this process.[75] In fact, Slavoj Žižek says that true enjoyment of sexuality, as something above and beyond mere pleasure, is possible *only* when sex and sexuality exist outside the normalizing idea of a *right* sexuality, as a kind of transgression or a "challenge to the gallows." It is the risk involved that propels a "simple illicit love affair" into the realm of what he calls true enjoyment, or *jouissance*.[76] While I cannot claim to know how Mariela felt about her Italian lover, or any others she may have had, others—Andre, Lili, Yakelín, and Ricky among them—described their relationships with non-Cubans as more interesting, more exciting, more pleasurable, and simply more fulfilling, a fact that some of them openly credited to the element of transgression: these relationships provided an escape, not just from material want, but also from social pressures, machismo, frustrated careers, a restrictive political culture, and a way of life and thinking that they found stifling. This is not about opposition to socialism but rather about (the perception of) freedom from repression and from the exercise of pastoral, prescriptive power. Žižek argues that today's politics is largely a "politics of *jouissance*," not in terms of an incitement to enjoyment, but rather a push to regulate and control it—to manage the threat of dissident sexualities, among which raced women's sexualities can certainly be counted.[77] A specifically relational jouissance, or a jouissance of the other, according to Žižek, marks a "pure expansion into the void."[78] It also recalls Scarry's "sharability" of human sentient experience. Sexuality is thus a potent site for practices of freedom and of self-creation.

The significance of self-creation as a mode of resistance to subjection is great. It extends the logic of turning away and refusal discussed above by providing avenues for living and being *otherwise*. It has also been argued that the most important forms of resistance today are those that "contest a certain form of subjectification."[79] What I find more interesting about aesthetic self-creation as a mode of resistance in Cuba, however, is its *apolitical* nature—that is, it does not address itself directly to the state or state-led institutions. When they did speak of politics, as Andre and Mariela both did, they meant institutional structures of governance (the Communist Party of Cuba, the Council of State, the CDRs and the FMC), and it was in tones of despair and hopelessness. They saw politics as a dead end, a complete nonstarter. Haydée, like many others including Yakelín and Nadia, dismissed the question altogether. It was Mariela's final words to me that made this click for me: "You can't tell me I'm building a bomb, because I'm not going to accept it."

This form of resistance does not concern itself directly with *that kind* of politics; it does not seek to seize power, to transform the system in its own image, or to posit any kind of alternative vision for Cuba's future. It is not left or right. It does not challenge sovereign power. These young Cubans may not articulate a particular oppositional politics, then, but this in itself represents a challenge to biopolitical care: this form of resistance does not propose any new type of regime but simply refuses in a gesture of *pure negation* and proceeds to explore the possibilities of *being otherwise,* at personal risk, without the support or assistance of care. Thus practicing what Prozorov calls "radical autonomy in relation to one's existence" can constitute an *exit* of a kind, from "totalitarian public space" and the grasp of the overwhelming power of care.[80] This makes it, in my view, perhaps the most effective mode of resistance of all: pursuing and enjoying a life other than that intended by power.

CONCLUSION: REINHABITING THE WORLD

> Strolling down the streets
> Of the town where she was born,
> In her soulful way, she gives out flowers.
> With her robe tucked up,
> And her flip-flops clapping,
> Men go chasing after her,
> The pretty little mulata.
>
> Los Zafiros, "La Caminadora"

Two of the most commonly recurring remarks I heard during my time in Cuba from young women (as well as young men) who dated foreigners pertained to bodily autonomy and ethics: first, "This is *my* body," and second, "I'm not hurting anyone." These statements highlight a will to carve out a new kind of existence of their own choosing for themselves and their families. In using sexuality and sexual relationships as a means of creating a new life for themselves, young Cubans are working toward lives centered on relationships and personal happiness, completely outside the paradigm of state socialism. Whether these new lives are *better* or *worse* is beside the point—the truth, like all truths, is messier, more complicated, more interesting than that—but it is not inherently antisocialist, or antileftist, or anti anything. It entails a throwing off of the bonds of one life, even if incompletely, even as that means subjecting oneself to new, as yet unknown forms of power. Sexuality, as a site for rejecting the life prescribed by state institutions *as well as* a channel for creating a new way of living, is an affront to the functioning of pastoral power in Cuba: it is a form of resistance that counters power not only with its efficacy but also with its qualitative content, that of sexual deviation from prescriptive norms.

As a mode of resistance, of refusal and disinvestment from biopolitical governance, jineterismo-as-sexual-practice is distinct in its bodily focus and in its seemingly *apolitical* aesthetic of self-creation. The bodies of mulata women in particular, the objects of both sanction and illicit desire for so many years, become the site of these women's resistance to prescribed ways of being and their forging of new lives and identities. These young people are becoming the ethical subjects of their own actions through a process, as Halberstam put it, of *unbecoming*—of refusal, unmaking, undoing of normative power and imposed subjectivities. For Butler, this is the definition of agency: "the assumption of a purpose unintended by power."[81] The expression of this agency is, of course, not without risk. Violence has come to play an everyday role in the lives of virtually all of the so-called jineteras and jineteros whom I met, taking the form of arrests, incarceration, rehabilitation, abuse, and even simply the fear that accompanies them daily and restricts their movements. On this, Foucault notes that "sexual pleasure as an ethical substance continues to be governed by relations of force."[82]

This violence itself, as an overwhelmingly state-centered phenomenon, merits a moment of consideration here. As I have noted here and there throughout the preceding chapters, the Cuban state's own relation to the foreign is an ambivalent one today: the state needs the revenues that international tourism brings, but this aperture implies a compromise to its unflinching rhetorical commitment to socialism on the one hand and to its vehemently nationalist independence on the other. The Cuban government's range of motion is limited by the Soviet collapse and the U.S. embargo, forcing it to turn to international tourism and to capitalism. As I argued in the first chapter of this book, the state has granted itself space to reassess and soften some of its socialist goals in the name of alleviating economic strain—it allowed tourists and hotel developers to establish themselves and even created new state-owned shops and businesses to corral as much hard currency as possible, from foreigners and from Cubans—but it has not allowed ordinary Cubans, and especially women, the same breathing room.[83] This theme recurs in all of the stories presented here. Andre remarked that "everyone is jineteando" in Cuba, referring to owners of small business like casas particulares and paladares, but the same is true of the state. The Cuban government is in bed with international tourism, the "principal source of funds that we have," in Andre's words. It is for this reason that, as Haydée told me, tourism carries on despite these conflicts of interest. "The government lets the tourists come," she said frankly. "We all do what we have to do to get by."

The problem that gives rise to such violence is that when young women begin to engage in sexual-affective relations with tourists—when they begin to appear on sex tourism websites, *Glamour* magazine, and the *New York Times* all at once—then Cuba's compromise becomes visible. From there, it becomes a source of shame, or a "loss of prestige" in Mariela's words, and is readily interpreted as a dreaded sign that socialism is not working—and Cuba might be losing its coveted position as moral critic of a decadent capitalist empire. Mariela spoke of this anxiety about maintaining the moral high ground: "What do they [the government] have to fear from it? Well, you can't criticize the boy across the street for being a thief if you have a thief in your home as well, now can you?" In the early nineteenth century, Cuba regulated marriage to assuage fears of another Haitian Revolution. Later, following the tumult of the independence wars and then again in the wake of the 1959 Revolution, thousands of young women were rounded up as prostitutes. Now, in the throes of painful and ongoing economic adjustment, this tradition of state discipline—or better, rescue and rehabilitation—of sexualized bodies marked by gender and race in the name of social order and national virtue continues.

It is worth asking what this cyclical narrative of exploitation and rescue does. Giorgio Agamben may offer a possible answer: apparatuses like the Cuban state, which have the capacity to shape, govern, and determine human beings, he argues, "must always imply a process of subjectification, that is to say, they must produce their subject."[84] Uniquely Cuban women are continuously created as sexually desirable, at home and abroad, but then disciplined for their own inappropriate desires. The state needs the jineteras and the legions of tourists they draw, not just as sources of immediate income, but also as problems to be solved ideologically, socially, and politically. It creates them as a group of people to be helped, or a hole to be patched, and it must then enact a regime of disciplinary violence against them to preserve its own moral superiority, conceal its own ambiguous relation to tourism, and—perhaps—start the cycle anew.

Crucially, however, this is a violence that by and large does not stop young people from engaging in sex and love with foreign visitors. Despite the serious social, political, emotional, and physical risks, they continue to deny power of some of its positive content by maintaining an open and dynamic relationality with the world. By pursuing pleasure—their own as well as others'—they open up a new space for the self and for self-crafting. Pleasure as a form of resistance makes it easier to refuse the loving embrace of care. It establishes a *different form* of care, one that is more diffuse and more fluid, one that might flow from many places, both within the self and from others. In that sense, pleasure individualizes and autonomizes, but it also creates potential for connection and new forms of community, between people and across borders—a fact that surely goes beyond Cuba and jineterismo.

I argue that the jinetera posits a more damning critique, of the Cuban regime and of its embargo-born impoverishment, as well as a more effective mode of resistance than any political activism or direct challenge, all the more so in a setting where overtly political forms of protest and resistance have seemed to hold little sway with the public. It is not the fact of the Revolution but rather what it asks of them as citizens today that they seek to resist. Through bodily practices of sex, love, and pleasure that turn conventional notions of mulata sexuality back on themselves, the jinetera is carving out a new space, however incomplete or partial, for herself—or, as Veena Das has said, "a new way by which she could reinhabit the world."[85]

Conclusion

ON THE MALECÓN

Finally, the industry of the exotic has been reborn. And
here it is likely to stay, as well as the exporting of the mythical Cuban paradise, where mulattas, as personifications of
Ochún, reign in the nights of Havana and in the feverish
imaginations of its visitors.

Raquel Mendieta Costa, "Exotic Exports"

The Malecón on a weekday afternoon is a quiet place, for the most part.
On windy days, sea waves sometimes crash up and over the concrete
embankment, drawing tourists to take pictures of the spectacular spray
and children to play in it. I usually come to the spot where Calle 23 meets
the seafront, but the Malecón itself is a long esplanade comprising the
road and a seaside walkway that stretches from the mouth of the harbor in
Habana Vieja, the old city, to the mouth of the Río Almendares—nearly
ten kilometers. It was built in three phases, beginning during the heady,
aspirational period of the American occupation, when Cuba sought to
leave behind the colonial years and emerge a sophisticated new country.
Construction was only finally completed the year prior to the Castro
brothers' attack on the Moncada Barracks in 1953, widely considered the
opening salvo of the Cuban Revolution.

Since then it has been restored in sections so that some—in the tourist
neighborhoods—are smooth and bright, whereas other areas are pebbled
by the waves and sometimes too rough to walk comfortably. The seawall is
dotted with some of the most prominent landmarks of the city and with
Cuba's history through the years. The sixteenth-century Castillo de la Real

Figure 19. The Malecón, Havana, on a day with high wind, when the road was closed to cars, 23 February 2010. Photo by author.

Fuerza stands near the eastern end, in Habana Vieja. Farther along, there is a statue and park dedicated to el Titán de Bronce, General Antonio Maceo. The palatial Hotel Nacional stands on its cliff top just above me at Calle 23, in stark contrast to the gaudy neon of Café Bim Bom below. Nearby, the monument to the sinking the of USS *Maine,* once topped by an eagle statue that angry crowds destroyed after the Bay of Pigs invasion, is now a popular place for young people to meet and socialize. Just west of there, the U.S. Interests Section and the defiant forest of Cuban flags that faces it are a testament to more recent moments in Cuba's story.

Sitting on the seawall by myself on a day with calm seas and sunshine, it is surprisingly still, despite the cars whizzing by. I take my life firmly in my hands to cross that road and reach the seawall, but the only disturbances once I'm there are the taxis, which slow down as they pass so their drivers can shout prices at me. On hot days, children and teenagers swim and sun themselves on the jagged rocks below. People stroll along at a leisurely pace, in the tradition of the grand parks and boulevards of Europe.

At night, however, it's a completely different place, and especially on stifling and windless summer evenings. After the sun has gone down and the heat subsides slightly, the Malecón fills with people, standing in groups and perching on the low concrete wall. There are loud music, shouts and laughter, dancing, and carousing. The pavement is thick with people, and on a weekend evening near the junction with Calle 23, it can be impossible to see more than a few feet ahead. This section of the Malecón lies at the foot of La Rampa, the section of Calle 23 that is packed with tourist hotels and exclusive nightclubs, but anyone can come here, and so the crowd is diverse and happy. There are couples and small groups everywhere, and there are even full-fledged parties in swing with drinks, music, and dancing. I come here often to sit on the wall and people watch, and I've met many of my friends, contacts, and informants while walking along this long promenade. Looking out into the blackness of the sea and the night sky, I can easily convince myself that I see the tiniest glow of light from Key West, only ninety miles away, but my eyes are playing tricks on me. I start to understand how the balseros, the people who escaped to Florida en masse in the worst years of the Special Period, found the journey so tempting, many of them setting off from the Malecón in the dead of night—even if many never made it there.

Living in Havana, the Malecón is the waterfront edge of the city. I have heard it called a democratic space, with all the symbolic burden that implies in a socialist state, or more amusingly, the "great sofa" of Cuba.[1] There is no entry fee and no doorman to turn away those without money, style, or foreign friends. Elderly women make their way slowly along bearing little bags of popcorn, lollipops, bunches of artificial roses, and bottles of homemade pineapple wine, making it into yet another space of the emergent economy as they hawk their wares to the crowd. On any given night, there are groups of teenagers playing music and carousing, families with small children out for an evening walk, older people enjoying the night air—and everywhere there are couples of all ages, races, and nationalities, because the Malecón is also a space for romance and sexual adventures. Couples stroll hand in hand, but they also tuck themselves into the shadows of the wide pillars topped with pyramids that appear at intervals in the seawall to kiss, cuddle, and then some. Young men sit with their friends and make vulgar remarks to passing women, and here by Calle 23, there is a strong presence of gay and transgender Cubans who have come—as they do every weekend—to mingle, flirt, and hook up. There are also young women sitting on their own here and there, much like they do in the cafés along La Rampa. Sometimes they call out to tourists, who are here to meander along and take pictures, but other times they just sit and wait expectantly to be approached. As Raúl told me in this very place, many of these girls are not really alone, as one of the men in her vicinity is there to keep an eye on her—perhaps protecting her from the police, perhaps ensuring she doesn't slip away without his approval. It is these last two presences—those of gay and transgender people and of jineteras—that have made this part of the Malecón a part of *el mundo bajo*—Havana's underworld.[2]

The Malecón is a European-style feature of the city that has been repurposed as a social space for working-class Cubans and as a space for cuentapropismo and jineterismo. Taken at face value, the Malecón is fairly austere, with its pale and almost completely unadorned concrete facade, unlike places like Callejón de Hamel, with which I began this story. It is even mostly free of graffiti, but it also lacks the polished veneer applied to tourist areas of Havana. It isn't even very well lit. The life and color of the Malecón are in the dynamic social scene that convenes there. Stretching almost the entire waterfront of the city, the Malecón is an unobtrusive fixture of everyday life in Havana. It was not until I had left that I realized how central it was to my life there and that not everyone—and especially those who have never been to Cuba—thinks of it when they imagine Havana. I spent many of my days there, reading my notes, meeting up with friends, trolling for new contacts and informants, doing interviews— I even had my goodbye party there with a group of Cuban friends. The Malecón is like a silent character in the narrative I have tried to present in these pages. It seems as fitting a place as any to draw the story to a close.

GOVERNANCE OF BODIES IN CUBA

I began this book by looking at the way people of different races and genders have been constituted in the Cuban imaginary throughout history.

Figure 20. The Malecón, Havana, looking toward Capitolio on a busy afternoon, 14 March 2010. Photo by author.

From the colonial years to the Special Period, it is possible to trace images of the mulata and the mambí through time, as archetypes and emblems of cubanidad that inform present-day understandings of the jinetera. Throughout Cuba's history, Afro-Cuban women and especially mixed-race mulatas have been read as the embodiment of sex, continuously available and lascivious. An ongoing theme of a moralizing state discipline emerges from studying the Cuban ambiente, in the ways that the bodies of dissident sexual subjects have been treated over the years: the raced social stratification of the colonial period and the slave society, the casas de recogidas and reglamentación that proliferated in the wake of the wars of independence, the campaign to end prostitution as well as the UMAP camps in the 1960s, and finally in the phenomenon that is today called jineterismo. I argue that the way the state has addressed jineterismo-as-sexual-practice—that is, by criminalizing and pathologizing suspected jineteras—reveals a preoccupation with the sexual proclivities of women, and especially young Afro-Cuban and mulata women. It shows not just an in-built conviction that Cuban women belong with Cuban men but also racially charged constructions of gender, sexuality, and morality. In this way, nonwhite women are perceived as (potential) weak spots in Cuba's ideological edifice because of the very sensuality with which they have been inscribed through the years. Their desirability to foreign men and any (potential) sexual relationships with those men are read as a slight against Cuba's vehemently nationalist independence.

The ethnographic fieldwork for this project was a process of learning and exploring, and that narrative itself has become central to the telling of my interviewees' stories. It is not, nor is it meant to be, a comprehensive anthropological study. Rather, it is an attempt to draw methods and methodologies from other disciplines into the world of international politics, showing what can be gained from opening the door to ethnographic, interpersonal, reflective research. I began by trying to understand how young people who involve themselves in Cuba's tourist-oriented sexual-affective economy conceive of their relationships and their own identities. I interviewed young women and men about their motivations for seeking out non-Cuban partners for sex or for long-term romantic attachments and how it has affected their self-esteem, feelings about their futures, and standing within their social circles and families. What I found was a group of young people who saw the possibilities available to them in their lives severely truncated by the economic crisis and the ongoing U.S. embargo and their opportunities to circumvent poverty and austerity limited, often by both race and gender. By and large, they seemed to view liaisons with tourists as a convenient and even enjoyable way to get access to much-needed hard currency, leisure establishments like restaurants and hotels, travel and emigration, and goods including clothing, appliances, toiletries, and other luxuries of the dollar economy—not to mention love, affection, and solidarity. Jineterismo provided a means to a life that they wanted for themselves and their families.

My next set of interviews was of a markedly different kind, speaking to the way jineterismo-as-sexual-practice and the jinetera have been confronted by state institutions on the ground. These informants detailed experiences that showed how race and gender function as markers of deviance in the eyes of police officers on the street. White women could pass virtually unseen by the police, so great was their association with a more pure and wholesome sexuality, and young men—regardless of their race—could occasionally defer police attention by benefiting from posi-tive, even congratulatory readings of masculine sexuality. On the other hand, young Afro-Cuban women were routinely assessed on the basis of their sexual integrity and, by being in public and affluent areas, risked harassment, violence, sexual assault, and extortion, on top of possible arrest and rehabilitative incarceration. Youth living in the heavily tour-isted cities of Cuba (even those who do not participate in sexual-affective economies of tourism) have found a set of what Scott calls the weapons of the weak, or everyday micropractices that helped them subvert, avert, and co-opt the gaze of comparatively powerful police officers.[3] This phase of my research dealt with vulnerable informants who faced considerable danger speaking to me, but from these interviews, I learned that the pros-pect of an escape from austerity can be enough to overcome even these dangers and that the young people involved can be innovative and resil-ient in confronting the violence of the state response to jineterismo.

After that, when I turned to finding out what was behind such practices of repression at the street level, I found a collection of state institutions and policies that inform and enable policing practices. This was also a delicate stage of my research, because the people I met when I visited these institutions had the power to report my work to state security or flag me as suspicious for border controls as I left the country, to say little of their potential power over my many informants. Through interviews and archival research, I uncovered a discourse among state-centric institu-tions in Cuba that portrays relationships between economic unequals as always at least potentially prostitution—though in practice this only meant pairings of Cuban women and foreign men, all the more so when race made them visible. Remarkably unconcerned with *proving* that money changed hands for sex, institutions like the FMC rather focused on other indicators—such as perceived promiscuity or materialism—that it took to be indicators of prostitution as a *moral* condition. I began to be able to compile a composite image of the New Woman these institutions were advocating as a role model for Cuban women and a post-prostitution blueprint for love and sexual relationships, one that was both restrictive and unattainable.

Finally, it came time to ask what all of this means for Cuba, and what possibilities arise from all of this for resistance and self-creation. It seems to me that what Cabezas calls "tactical sex"[4] in Cuba today constitutes a practice of resistance to biopolitical power, which seeks through care and cultivation to form individual subjects into productive and obedient citizens. As an aesthetic practice of freedom, jineterismo is distinct in that it is located in the body—the very same one inscribed with meaning by Cuba's history of colonialism, slavery, and machismo. It entails not just an alternative source of income, but a fundamental indifference to (some or all of) the ideals of the socialist state. Young Cuban women of color are taking the image created of them, one of tropical sensuality and allure, and using it wherever they can to circumvent the strictures of a socialist system that locates virtue in austerity—and to resist the ways of being that such a system foists upon them, creating something new and different in their own images.

Even at this point, however, drawing conclusions is proving to be something of a challenge, but after all—as Cynthia Enloe notes—"conclusions shouldn't sound too satisfied, all the edges rounded off."[5] Cuba is still undergoing rapid and deep social and economic changes, and the meanings attached to social and sexual practices are intersubjectively constituted and constantly evolving. Perhaps, however, this is the point: the meanings given to any one sexual relationship or practice cannot be determined in advance or from the outside, and the mere fact that these young people are defying what they are incited to be and to do is significant in itself.

This defiance is also not entirely unidirectional: many of my informants still value many key elements of the Revolution even as they articulate or enact various forms of resistance. They vacillate, they accept some of the things that the Revolution asks of them and reject others. It is a messy, indeterminate, and incomplete business full of slippages, which only increases its relevance. Outright, confrontational, assertive resistance is not terribly attractive to most of the Cubans I met, whether because it is so likely to be put down with brute force and imprisonment or because they have no particular desire for a new regime to come to power. They prefer to opt out, to turn away, because it keeps them safer, it suits their aims, and it exemplifies the indifference they feel.

Amir Valle's key informant for his book on jineteras was a woman he called Loretta, whom he treated as a sort of muse in his quest to learn more about the world of jineterismo. She gave him contacts and guidance along the way, but more important, Loretta provided her own understanding of jineterismo from the inside.

> Soon it turned out that when a woman went to bed with all the men in her little town, only the old ladies bothered to call her immoral and a slut. It's different if one goes to bed with a foreigner, or a mountain of foreigners. Isn't it the same thing? The one who went to bed with the Cubans in the village always got some benefit from it: being the lover of a man in Cuba always had its dividends. What was the difference in going to bed with a yuma? Do we have to carry such chauvinist patriotism with us in our pussies too? Is it obligatory to make use of a mambí dick? Or they are trying to avoid alienating penetrations [*penetraciones rabológicas extranjerizantes*]? Why did they unleash this against those who used to wander around after tourists in the hotels, and yet they didn't pick up any of the mountains of cheap whores who swarmed around Avenue 51, or at Monte and Cienfuegos, or in Chinatown . . . ?[6]

Here, Loretta gets at the very crux of the matter. She highlights that it is not just promiscuity, not just tourism, and not just economies of sex and desire that render the jinetera a troublesome body; it is the "possession" of Cuban women by foreign men, made all the more visible and objectionable by the racial difference between them.

As I argued in the previous chapter, however, this ongoing and cyclical narrative of feminine exploitation and masculine rescue is useful for Cuba: it creates Afro-Cuban women as a problem to be solved, a space of foreign incursion, and positions the government as the one to shore up the country's moral integrity. Cuba's anxious state of "permanent crisis," continuously in opposition to U.S. imperialism and economic straitjacketing, makes this imagery all the more powerful.[7] The crisis narrative is productive and constitutive of further waves and incarnations of prostitution, which acts as a disciplinary device to control the sexualities and the sexual enjoyment of raced Cuban women as dissident subjects. The women I interviewed are repositioning themselves within the sexual-affective economy of Cuba as authors of their own subjectivities, values, and desires by pursuing their own pleasure and well-being. Cuban women need the space and the language to express their sexualities in ways that, as of now, are not permitted outside tropes of the committed, heterosexual wife and mother of a Cuban man.

FIELDWORK, TEXTWORK, HEADWORK

Looking back from where I sit now, years after leaving Cuba, I cannot help but find fault with what I have written and accomplished. There have been so many moments when I have kicked myself for not asking a particular question, not pressing for further information, or not seeing a connection when I still had time to follow it up. The process of writing was one of looking back, and it is easy to forget now, with some distance between myself and the field experience, how difficult the research was and how careful I had to be at the time. My work and my behavior were disciplined by the same system in which my informants have lived their entire lives, though to a much lesser degree, and I came to understand quickly that there were certain questions, or ways of asking questions, that would instantly end an interview. This is just one of several limitations of the book I have produced.

First, the stories I have presented are—due to restrictions on fieldwork in Cuba, the sensitivity of my research, and the nature of ethnography, among other factors—fragmentary and uncertain. They are not exhaustive life stories or verbatim narratives but rather brief glimpses of people whose company I shared for sometimes only a few hours. They are detailed reconstructions of conversations that often were not recorded but rather transcribed by hand, encoded, and carefully slipped out of Cuba. I cannot make any claim to understand my informants' motivations for speaking to me, for telling me the things they told me, or for leaving out the things that I am sure they must have omitted at times. I have tried, however, to give an account of the experience of meeting them, the kinds of people they were, and the stories they told, because in my view, it is the telling that matters. The way they choose to present themselves and their stories is as important, if not more, than any elusive truth to be found within.

Second, the problem of trying to identify Cuban/foreign pairings plagues this project, as it has others who have studied Cuba's sexual-affective economy.[8] In trying to make contact with Cubans who sought to date and hook up with foreigners, I ran the risk of engaging in exactly that which I was criticizing state institutions for doing: attempting to pick out jineteras from the crowd based on looks alone. In so doing, I ran the risk of limiting myself to "visible" transcultural relationships and pairings—that is, those where the partners were marked by obvious differences of race, age, and sometimes affluence. This is one of many reasons that I preferred to get interviews by word of mouth or through a network of contacts. That way, I could speak to a variety of people who had or sought relationships with tourists. Some did match the archetype of the jinetera in terms of their gender, race, personal style, or social standing, but others did not.

Third, perhaps the biggest silence in my work is the foreigners themselves, as only one foreigner plays a significant role: Evan, who appears in chapter 3. I have done this for one principal reason, and that is to foreground the experiences and practices of my Cuban informants. As I moved through the research, I spoke to several of my informants' foreign partners and dates (all men), and—much like their Cuban girlfriends—they truly seemed to run the gamut.[9] Some spoke of their Cuban lovers as partners in the truest sense, others were openly exploitative and condescending, but most fell somewhere in between. They showed varying degrees of intentionality, reflexivity, and sensitivity with regard to their place in these women's lives and the power relations between them. While many of them seemed to value the more traditional gender roles they found in Cuba, unlike in their home countries in North America and Western Europe, or lamented an inability to find a "good woman" at home, this was not true of all of them. Perhaps controversially, I came to think that, at least for the purposes of this book, it really did not matter on what terms these men engaged with the supposed jineteras, or whether they were "good" people. It was up to each of these young Cubans to pursue the best relationship possible for themselves, in their own estimation and under terms they could accept, and the vast majority expressed satisfaction and happiness with their lot. There is certainly room for further work on the perceptions and motivations of the foreigners who seek or find sexual partners in Cuba, as in other tourist destinations, but this kind of exploration was not within the scope of this project.

Leaving aside these limitations for the moment, this book has important things to add to conversations about Cuba's sexual-affective economy of tourism. First of all, this is the first explicitly political treatment of this subject. Most other studies come from anthropological and sociological perspectives, though there are those that begin from literature and performance studies. Many of these take a human rights, or even sexual rights, approach to the phenomenon, which can be interpreted as political, but none explore the implications that jineterismo-as-sexual-practice has for political life and subjectivity in Cuba. Bringing together discourses of sexuality, machismo, race, nationalism, and nation building is usually reserved for less controversial topics in the study of Cuba. The reverse is also true: this book presents a challenge to the way we think and write about politics. There are multiple elements here that are not commonly seen in books about international politics: sexuality, the body, storytelling, and ethnography, to name a few. These elements are not really *new* at all, but they are drawn from outside the usual boundaries of what *counts* as real, verifiable, serious research in international politics.

The stories, too, bring something different to the table. I set out to portray my research subjects as agents with complex lives, personalities, and relationships. This, I hope, has challenged the way these women have been depicted in far too much of what has been written about them—that is, as helpless in the face of economic crisis, pawns in a greater political game, or vapid and materialistic. This last description was likely most clearly evidenced by my interview with Julia, presented in chapter 4. I found that conversation very tense and uncomfortable, and I realized some time later that this was likely because I had found myself trying so hard to describe the feelings, motivations, and conflicts faced by the women I had met, to paint them as sympathetic and multifaceted, while Julia seemed totally invested in denying them any depth or complexity. In a way, this impasse speaks to this book's entire ethos, which, while it is certainly not unique in international politics, is rare. I wanted to be sure to leave the discomfort in, because it is just as much a part of this story. As I noted in my introductory chapter, this is not meant to be a "comfort text."[10]

My overarching aim with this book, however, has been to cast a critical eye on the Cuban political project, as someone with a keen interest in the country and its explicit commitments to ending discrimination. Cuba's real claim to uniqueness lies in the new society and social values that it purports to have created, which from its own perspective ought to have precluded the jinetera from existence. This depends on the notion that these new values could somehow erase the need for, or even the possibility of, economic support within sexual-affective relationships with its supposed liberation of Cuban women. The reality is that Cuban women are embedded in a history where women's value has been determined through raced markers of respectability and desirability, which seemed often to be mutually exclusive. Jineterismo-as-sexual-practice fits into this unfolding history, which sees the country engaging in a recurring narrative of condemnation and rescue of sexual deviants. The Revolution has changed only the language of this script. Cuba's Revolution has not in itself transformed, or even done much to challenge, the social production of raced women as sexual objects whose value lies in their bodies themselves. In the face of great economic hardship and scarcity, not to mention persisting and even worsening gendered and raced forms of prejudice, it is not even surprising that this figure of the sensuous mulata has come to the fore once again to trouble Cuba's nationalist project, only in a new form—the jinetera.

It is in the context of this ostensibly humanist discourse of prostitution, and what is to be done about the jinetera, that these familiar tropes of the "Third World prostitute"[11] become a potential site of resistance to subjectifying power. Young people in Cuba are rapidly becoming disillusioned with politics in general. Their critique does not seek to topple the regime or replace it but rather to question its framing of the good life and the good citizen. They are building a barrier of a kind between themselves and the state machinery, ducking out of view even as they are rendered more and more visible. In a system that so explicitly demands all that each has to give, young women of color are using the identities created for them as tools to *opt out* to whatever extent they can. By rejecting the loving embrace of care and pursuing pleasure, young people engaged in Cuba's sexual-affective economy of tourism are opening up space for radical relationality between the self and the other—one that transcends borders, defies prescriptive norms, and raises the potential for new forms of community and care.

Against this backdrop, the jinetera is a specter that haunts Cuba's claims to a harmonious and well-fed society, liberated from the burdens of racist and gendered forms of discrimination, as well as its exhortations to women to work harder and be better, in order to achieve an unattainable ideal that many do not even seem to want. The young Afro-Cuban women engaged in Cuba's sexual-affective economy are actively spinning the image of the sensuous mulata in their own favor and deploying it in the name of a "better" future, though one that is completely different from the one intended for them by Cuba's powerful elites. In a system that would relegate them to being nothing more than victims of their own moral failings, the jineteras are reclaiming a measure of agency for themselves and, to return once more to Veena Das's phrase, finding "a new way [to] reinhabit the world."[12] Cuban youth—and especially young women of color, who have been the targets of so much disciplinary moralizing—deserve the space to express values, stories, sexualities, and ways of being other than those endorsed by a paternalist power.

Notes

INTRODUCTION

1. See Mason, *Living Santería*, p. 9.

2. Gonzalez, quoted in Romero-Cesareo, "Havana's Callejón de Hamel Celebrates Its 20th Anniversary"; see also Perez-Sarduy and Stubbs, *Afro-Cuban Voices*, p. 115.

3. Kapcia, *Cuba in Revolution*, p. 157; Pérez, *Cuba: Between Reform and Revolution*, p. 293.

4. See Anderson, "Island Socialism."

5. I also use this term to describe a kind of space, though not a physical one, where Cubans foreigners meet, and where relationships between them come into being and play out. "Sexual-affective economy" is a means of evoking not just the fact of such relationships, but the desire for them on both sides, and the collective, intersubjective meaning of them that can go beyond (but does not erase) individual meaning.

6. The words *mulata* (fem.) and *mulato* (masc.) are commonly used by Cubans to describe people of mixed white and Afro-Cuban heritage. I have chosen to use it here because many of my informants used it to identify themselves; however, the word does not adequately describe people who may also have indigenous or Chinese backgrounds, unlike *mestiza/o*, which is commonly heard across Latin America. See Hamilton, *Sexual Revolutions in Cuba*, pp. 12, 240 n. 34. This is not necessarily the case in other parts of the Latin America and the Caribbean;

for example, Dominicans do not generally use the term *mulata/o* to describe themselves. See Brennan, *What's Love Got to Do with It?*, p. 35.

7. Finn and Lukinbeal, "Musical Cartographies," p. 130.

8. Allen, *¡Venceremos?*, p. 40; Moore, *Music and Revolution*, p. 193.

9. See Fernandes, *Cuba Represent!*

10. Mason, *Living Santería*, p. 9.

11. Moore, *Music and Revolution*, p. 193.

12. Although the term *yuma* traditionally refers to U.S. Americans, it is increasingly used to refer to all non-Cubans, whether tourists, businesspeople, students, or others.

13. Sierra Madero, *Del otro lado del espejo*, p. 159. My translation.

14. Ian Lumsden and Jafari Allen also discuss this sexualized and male-dominated street culture in some detail. See Lumsden, *Machos, Maricones, and Gays;* Allen, *¡Venceremos?*

15. Cohen, "Cuba Libre," p. 69; see also Schwartz, *Pleasure Island*, p. 209.

16. Cabezas, *Economies of Desire*, p. 2.

17. Cohen, "Cuba Libre," p. 73.

18. Quoting Arturo Arango, Carrie Hamilton argues that the representation of jineteras in Cuban fiction may actually overstate their numbers due to intense international curiosity about them. See Hamilton, *Sexual Revolutions*, pp. 46–47, 260 n. 56.

19. Fernandes, *Cuba Represent!*, p. 20.

20. Fusco, "Hustling for Dollars," p. 154.

21. Pedro Juan Gutiérrez and Raquel Mendieta Costa link jineteras to Ochún, while Cabezas calls jineteras daughters of Yemayá, as some of her informants believe that foreign boyfriends are sent to them by the oricha. See Gutiérrez, *Dirty Havana Trilogy;* Mendieta Costa, "Exotic Exports," p. 45; Cabezas, *Economies of Desire*, pp. 112–17.

22. For more case studies on other locales, explorations of the concept of sex tourism, and encounters with the blurriness between sexual commerce and "real" affect, care, and love, see Allison, *Nightwork;* Brennan, *What's Love Got to Do with It?;* Hoefinger, *Sex, Love and Money in Cambodia;* Hunter, "The Materiality of Everyday Sex"; Kempadoo, *Sexing the Caribbean.*

23. Cabezas, "Discourses of Prostitution," p. 79.

24. Hoefinger, *Sex, Love and Money in Cambodia*, p. 7.

25. Stout, "Feminists, Queers, and Critics," p. 723.

26. Juline Koken observes a similar division in discussions of sex work outside of Cuba, which she labels the "anti-prostitution position," which conceives of all sex work as violence against women and seeks to rescue sex workers, as opposed to the "pro–sex work position," which recognizes sex work as legitimate work and advocates for sex workers' rights and decriminalization. See Koken, "The Meaning of the 'Whore.'"

27. Celia Sarduy Sánchez and Ada Alfonso Rodríguez edited a volume of essays, notably those of Natividad Guerrero Borrego and Ana Isabel Peñate Leiva, most of which take a strong socialist feminist stance toward jineterismo. See Sarduy Sánchez and Alfonso Rodríguez, *Género*. Rosa Miriam Elizalde's writing on the subject is nothing short of a polemic and is discussed in much greater detail in chapter 4. See in particular Elizalde, *Flores desechables*.

28. Strout, "Women, the Politics of Sexuality and Cuba's Economic Crisis"; Cabezas, "Discourses of Prostitution," pp. 82–83.

29. Stout, "Feminists, Queers, and Critics," p. 731.

30. Whitehead and Demirdirek, quoted in Stout, "Feminists, Queers, and Critics," p. 734.

31. Stout, "Feminists, Queers, and Critics," p. 734.

32. See Cabezas, "Between Love and Money"; Cabezas, *Economies of Desire*.

33. See García, "(Re)covering Women."

34. Zalewski, *Feminism after Postmodernism*, p. 134.

35. Van Maanen, "An End to Innocence: The Ethnography of Ethnography," p. 4.

36. Hamilton, *Sexual Revolutions*, p. 217.

37. Lawrence La Fountain-Stokes has written one of the few articles that mentions lesbian jineteras. See La Fountain-Stokes, "De un pájaro las dos alas: Travel Notes of a Queer Puerto Rican in Havana."

38. Cabezas, *Economies of Desire*, p. 8; see also Nencel, "Feeling Gender Speak."

39. Stern, *Naming In/security—Constructing Identity*, p. 84; Nencel, "Feeling Gender Speak."

40. See Zalewski, "Distracted Reflections on the Production, Narration, and Refusal of Feminist Knowledge in International Relations," p. 46.

41. Feldman, *Formations of Violence*, p. 12.

42. Scott, *Domination and the Arts of Resistance*, pp. 4–5.

43. Wahab, "Creating Knowledge Collaboratively with Female Sex Workers," p. 637; see also Nencel, "Feeling Gender Speak."

44. Patai, "U.S. Academics and Third World Women," pp. 139, 150.

45. Clifford, "Introduction: Partial Truths," p. 14.

46. Nencel, "Feeling Gender Speak," p. 348.

47. See Crapanzano, "Hermes' Dilemma."

48. See Mullings, "Insider or Outsider, Both or Neither"; Lerum, "Subjects of Desire."

49. Patai, "U.S. Academics and Third World Women," p. 140.

50. Nancy Wonders and Raymond Michalowski argue that "at some level, we remain global tourists ourselves. Given our research focus, however, we believe that this vantage point has its advantages." This is in reference to the very different (but still not entirely predictable) ways in which Cubans may respond to a

foreigner as opposed to a fellow Cuban. See Wonders and Michalowski, "Bodies, Borders and Sex Tourism in a Globalised World," p. 548.

51. Cabezas, *Economies of Desire*, p. 9. Nencel also discusses the unintelligibility of women who are not "prostitutes," and especially those who are foreigners, but who exist in and around the world of "prostitution." See Nencel, "Feeling Gender Speak," p. 351.

52. Stern, *Naming In/security*, p. 70. Clifford also argues, "Western texts conventionally come with authors attached. . . . But as ethnography's complex, plural *poesis* becomes more apparent—and politically charged—conventions begin, in small ways, to slip." Clifford, "Introduction: Partial Truths," p. 17.

53. Wahab, "Creating Knowledge Collaboratively," p. 637.

54. Deborah Green, quoted in Lather, "Postbook," p. 207.

55. Clifford, "Introduction: Partial Truths," p. 7.

56. Ibid.

57. Clifford refers to ethnographies and life stories as "fictions." Clifford, "Introduction: Partial Truths," p. 6.

58. Stern, *Naming In/security*, p. 66.

59. Patai also reflects on these issues. See Patai, "U.S. Academics and Third World Women," p. 141.

60. Lather, "Postbook," p. 205.

61. Zalewski, "Distracted Reflections," p. 44.

CHAPTER 1

1. U.N. Economic and Social Council, Commission on Human Rights, *Report of the Special Rapporteur on Violence against Women, Its Causes and Consequences. Addendum: Report on the Mission to Cuba*, pp. 6, 13–14. Hereafter cited as U.N. ECOSOC, *Report of the Special Rapporteur*.

2. Cabezas, *Economies of Desire*, pp. 144–46, 150–51.

3. The Varadero chief of police is quoted as saying he meant to undertake a "systematic effort to sanitize the spa town." See Elizalde, *Flores desechables*, p. 61. Numbers of arrests from García, "(Re)covering Women," p. 176.

4. Fusco, "Hustling for Dollars," p. 161; Stout, "Feminists, Queers, and Critics," p. 725.

5. U.N. ECOSOC, *Report of the Special Rapporteur*, p. 13.

6. Lumsden, *Machos, Maricones and Gays*, p. 103; Fusco, "Hustling for Dollars," p. 156.

7. Like several other countries, Cuba does not prohibit prostitution itself but rather acts such as facilitating or profiting from prostitution and running a house of prostitution.

8. Sierra Madero, *Del otro lado del espejo*, p. 13.

NOTES TO PAGES 28-39

9. Quoted in Valle, *Habana Babilonia*, p. 30.

10. de las Casas, quoted in Valle, *Habana Babilonia*, p. 36.

11. Beckles and Shepherd (2004) *Liberties Lost*, p. 4; Valle, *Habana Babilonia*, p. 30; Kempadoo, *Sexing the Caribbean*, p. 55.

12. Valle, *Habana Babilonia*, p. 75.

13. A census cited by Robert L. Scheina puts Cuba's population in 1817 at 630,980, of which 291,021 were white, 115,691 were free Afro-Cubans, and 224,268 were enslaved Afro-Cubans. See Scheina, *Latin America's Wars*, p. 352.

14. Puri, *Caribbean Postcolonial*, p. 46.

15. Martinez-Alier, *Marriage, Class and Colour in Nineteenth-Century Cuba*, p. 45; Kutzinski, *Sugar's Secrets*, p. 19.

16. Kutsinski, *Sugar's Secrets*, p. 20.

17. Lumsden, *Machos, Maricones, and Gays*, p. 31.

18. Tanco Armero, quoted in Pérez de la Riva, *La isla de Cuba en el siglo XIX vista por los extranjeros*, p. 112. My translation.

19. Pilon, *L'île de Cuba*, p. 25. My translation.

20. Sierra Madero, *Del otro lado del espejo*, p. 22.

21. Kutzinski, *Sugar's Secrets*, p. 48.

22. Allen describes how Fernando Ortiz, a seminal writer in the field of Cuban identity, pursues a series of "Manichean moves" that result in the taxonomy, "African is to European as male is to female as tobacco is to sugar." In this way, Allen argues, Ortiz is "expressing a Cuban race/color, gender, and sexual *common sense*" (emphasis in original). See Allen, *¡Venceremos?*, pp. 44–46; see also Fusco, "Hustling for Dollars," p. 155; Mendieta Costa, "Exotic Exports," p. 43.

23. Kutzinski, *Sugar's Secrets*, p. 86; García, "(Re)covering Women," p. 51.

24. Martinez-Alier, *Marriage, Class and Colour*, p. 118.

25. Marrero, "Scripting Sexual Tourism," p. 245.

26. Martínez-Alier, *Marriage, Class and Colour*, p. 118.

27. Villaverde, *Cecilia Valdés, o la loma del angel*; see also Kutzinski, *Sugar's Secrets*, p. 22.

28. Muñoz del Monte, quoted in Kutzinski, *Sugar's Secrets*, pp. 23, 28. Complete poem in Morales, *Poesía afroantillana y negrista*, pp. 195–200. Kutzinski's translation.

29. Kutzinski, *Sugar's Secrets*, p. 28.

30. Ibid., pp. 62–63.

31. Ibid., pp. 66–67.

32. Ibid., pp. 59–78.

33. Ortiz, *Hampa afro-cubana*.

34. Museo Nacional de Bellas Artes, *Guía de arte cubano*, p. 106.

35. Pichardo Moya, quoted in Morales, *Poesía afroantillana y negrista*, pp. 165–66; and in Williams, *Charcoal and Cinnamon*, pp. 90–91. Williams's translation.

36. For more on the representation of Afro-Cuban men, see the works of art curated in de la Fuente, *Queloides*.

37. Sierra Madero, *Del otro lado del espejo*, pp. 53–54.

38. Fernández Retamar, quoted in Loomba, *Colonialism/Postcolonialism*, pp. 146–47.

39. Martí, *Our America*, pp. 93–94.

40. Puri, *Caribbean Postcolonial*, p. 53.

41. Martí, *Our America*, p. 91; see also Puri, *Caribbean Postcolonial*, p. 55; Allen, *¡Venceremos?*, p. 48.

42. José Canalejas, quoted in Cantón Navarro, *History of Cuba*, p. 66.

43. Puri, *Caribbean Postcolonial*, p. 54.

44. Allen argues that "the celebration of mestizáje is a celebration of black holocaust"; see Allen, *¡Venceremos?*, p. 48. Martinez-Alier also discusses the racist implications of mestizaje and whitening; see Martinez-Alier, *Marriage, Class and Colour*, p. 35.

45. Kutzinski and de la Fuente both discuss increasing racial discrimination, including the segregation of the armed forces during the U.S. occupation of Cuba; see Kutzinski, *Sugar's Secrets*, p. 139; de la Fuente, *A Nation for All*, p. 5.

46. García, "(Re)covering Women," pp. 101, 105.

47. Kutzinski, *Sugar's Secrets*, pp. 4, 5.

48. Fernandes, *Cuba Represent!*, p. 69. Puri also argues that Martí's notion of mestizaje was "deeply concerned with asserting a regional identity that could provide a viable alternative to U.S.-satellite status." See Puri, *Caribbean Postcolonial*, p. 53.

49. Sierra Madero, *Del otro lado del espejo*, p. 61. My translation.

50. Smith and Padula, *Sex and Revolution*, p. 10. See also Fusco, "Hustling for Dollars," p. 52; Schwartz, *Pleasure Island*, p. 86; Horta Mesa, "Recodo sentencioso," p. 13.

51. See Valle, *Habana Babilonia*; Horta Mesa, "Recodo Sentencioso."

52. Thomas, *Cuba, or, The Pursuit of Freedom*, p. 12.

53. See Agustín, *Sex at the Margins*, p. 101.

54. For a description of the casas de citas, see Valle, *Habana Babilonia*, pp. 79–80.

55. Helg, "Race in Argentina and Cuba, 1880–1930."

56. Alfonso y García, *La prostitución*, p. 14.

57. De Céspedes, *La prostitucion en la ciudad de la Habana*, p. 66.

58. Beers, "Murder in San Isidro," p. 103. Sierra Madero notes the existence of a newspaper titled *La Cebolla* (The Onion) as an official mouthpiece for women who engaged in commercial sex, published for just one month in September 1888. Beatriz Calvo Peña, however, argues that *La Cebolla* was actually written by a Spanish journalist named Victorino Reineri, to suit Reineri's own political objectives at the time. I was unable to locate a copy of *La Cebolla* during my time

in Cuba to investigate this issue further. See Sierra Madero, *Del otro lado del espejo*, p. 35; Calvo Peña, "Prensa, política y prostitución en La Habana finisecular," pp. 23–49.

59. Federación de Mujeres Cubanas, *Programa a la atención a la problemática de la prostitución*, p. 10. Quoted in García, "(Re)covering Women," p. 67.

60. According to studies cited by Valle, before 1868 prostitutes in Cuba were 80 percent black and mulata, 12 percent Spanish, 6 percent "campesina" (peasant), and 2 percent "other." Between 1879 and 1895, these numbers changed to 35 percent black and mulata, 3 percent Spanish, 47 percent "campesina," and 15 percent "other." See Valle, *Habana Babilonia*, p. 120.

61. Wright, quoted in Beers, "Murder in San Isidro," p. 103; see also Díaz Canals and González Olmedo, "Cultura y prostitución," p. 68.

62. García, "(Re)covering Women," pp. 68–69.

63. The word *fletera* refers to a lower-class prostitute who works in and around the freighters (*fletes*) of the seaport. See Elizalde, "¿Crimen o castigo?"

64. García, "(Re)covering Women," 57.

65. Valle, *Habana Babilonia*, p. 125. My translation.

66. Schwartz, *Pleasure Island*, pp. 14–15.

67. Cabezas, *Economies of Desire*, pp. 43–44.

68. Schwartz, *Pleasure Island*, pp. 15, 86.

69. See Schwartz's discussion of the 1946 mob conference in Schwartz, *Pleasure Island*.

70. Schwartz, *Pleasure Island*, pp. 140–45.

71. Smith and Padula, *Sex and Revolution*, p. 21; Schwartz, *Pleasure Island*, p. 126.

72. Wonders and Michalowski, "Bodies, Borders and Sex Tourism in a Globalised World," p. 560; Cabezas, *Economies of Desire*, p. 44; Díaz and Gonzalez, "Cultura y prostitución," p. 168; Valle, *Habana Babilonia*, p. 166.

73. García, "Continuous Moral Economies," p. 177.

74. See César, *Mujer y política social en Cuba*; Lutjens, "Reading between the Lines."

75. De la Fuente, quoted in Fernandez, *Revolutionizing Romance*, p. 78.

76. See Federación de Mujeres Cubanas, "Programa a la atención."

77. See Valle, *Habana Babilonia*; Lumsden, *Machos, Maricones and Gays*, p. 58; Bejel, *Gay Cuban Nation*, p. 97.

78. See Federación de Mujeres Cubanas, "Programa a la atención"; Armando Torres, in 1970 interview with Oscar Lewis, quoted in Lewis, Lewis, and Rigdon, *Four Women*, p. 279 n. 7.

79. Díaz and Gonzalez, "Cultura y prostitución," p. 169; Elizalde, *Flores desechables*, p. 37; Lutjens, "Remaking the Public Sphere"; Torres, quoted in Lewis, Lewis, and Rigdon, *Four Women*, p. 279 n. 7.

80. Torres, quoted in Lewis, Lewis, and Rigdon, *Four Women,* p. 279 n. 7.

81. Díaz and Gonzalez, "Cultura y prostitución," p. 168. My translation.

82. Federación de Mujeres Cubanas, "Programa a la atención"; quoted in García, "(Re)covering Women," pp. 152–55.

83. Wonders and Michalowski, "Bodies, Borders and Sex Tourism," p. 560; Cabezas, *Economies of Desire,* pp. 47–48.

84. De la Torre Mulhare, "Sexual Ideology in Pre-Castro Cuba," pp. 60–64; quoted in Hamilton, *Sexual Revolutions,* p. 25.

85. Domínguez, *Cuba: Order and Revolution,* pp. 253–56.

86. Former sex worker Pilar López Gonzales, quoted in Lewis, Lewis, and Rigdon, *Four Women,* p. 277.

87. For a detailed discussion of the *Código de Familia,* see Lutjens, "Reading between the Lines."

88. César, *Mujer y politica social,* p. 95. My translation.

89. Lumsden, *Machos, Maricones, and Gays,* p. 75; see also Lutjens, "Reading between the Lines."

90. See an extensive discussion of the UMAP camps and their significance in Lumsden, *Machos, Maricones, and Gays.*

91. Hillson, "La política sexual de Reinaldo Arenas." My translation.

92. Kapcia, *Cuba in Revolution,* pp. 134–35.

93. César, *Mujer y política social,* p. 93. My translation.

94. Valle, *Habana Babilonia,* pp. 190–92, 187; Díaz and González, "Cultura y prostitución," pp. 173–74.

95. Fernández-Mouré, cited in Valle, *Habana Babilonia,* p. 214. My translation.

96. Valle, *Habana Babilonia;* Fusco, "Hustling for Dollars," pp. 153–54. See also Domínguez, *Cuba: Order and Revolution,* p. 498.

97. Smith and Padula, *Sex and Revolution,* pp. 66, 179.

98. *La titimanía* is the subject of a song by the same name by the famous Cuban salsa band Los Van Van. See Los Van Van, "La titimanía."

99. Valle, *Habana Babilonia,* pp. 190–92, 216–17, 222–23.

100. Fusco, "Hustling for Dollars," pp. 153–54. For Castro's denunciation of convenios sexuales, see Valle, *Habana Babilonia,* p. 221.

101. Elizalde, *Flores desechables,* p. 70; among those who disagree are Fusco, "Hustling for Dollars," pp. 153–54; and Valle, *Habana Babilonia,* pp. 15–16.

102. Allen, *¡Venceremos?,* p. 3.

103. Wonders and Michalowski, "Bodies, Borders and Sex Tourism," p. 561; Kapcia, *Cuba in Revolution,* p. 157; Pérez, *Cuba: Between Reform and Revolution,* pp. 292–293.

104. Symmes, "Thirty Days as a Cuban"; Kapcia, *Cuba in Revolution,* pp. 157–58.

105. Cabezas, *Economies of Desire,* pp. 67–73, 76–79.

106. Pérez, *Cuba: Between Reform and Revolution,* pp. 297, 311.

107. Cabezas, *Economies of Desire,* pp. 73-74.

108. In 1974 tourists numbered close to 8,400; by 1981 there were 132,900; and in 1990, just before the crisis, Cuba had 340,300 tourists. See Cabezas, *Economies of Desire,* pp. 47-48; Schwartz, *Pleasure Island,* p. 205.

109. Wonders and Michalowski, "Bodies, Borders and Sex Tourism," pp. 560-61; Schwartz, *Pleasure Island,* p. 205.

110. Wonders and Michalowski, "Bodies, Borders and Sex Tourism," p. 561.

111. Mesa-Lago, "Growing Economic Social Disparities in Cuba," pp. i, 1; Lutjens, "Reading between the Lines," p. 118.

112. Lutjens, "Reading between the Lines," p. 117; Cabezas, *Economies of Desire,* p. 77.

113. Among Cuban Americans, 83.5 percent identify themselves as white, according to 1990 U.S. Census data discussed in de la Fuente, *A Nation for All,* pp. 319, 321.

114. Cabezas, *Economies of Desire,* p. 98.

115. Sierra Madero, "Códigos en movimiento"; see also Fusco, "Hustling for Dollars"; Lumsden, *Machos, Maricones, and Gays.* See also Guerrero and Alonso, "La sexualidad en los jóvenes."

116. Fusco, "Hustling for Dollars," p. 154.

117. Guevara, quoted in Wonders and Michalowski, "Bodies, Borders and Sex Tourism," p. 559.

118. Stout, "Feminists, Queers, and Critics," pp. 725-26.

119. Pope, cited in Stout, "Feminists, Queers, and Critics," pp. 725-26.

120. Cabezas, "Between Love and Money," p. 1005; Cabezas, *Economies of Desire,* pp. 147-49.

121. Cabezas, *Economies of Desire,* p. 151.

122. Wilkinson, "Cuba Lay-Offs Reveal Evolving Communism."

123. Orsi, "Cuba Unveils Loan Program"; BBC News, "Cuba to Scrap Two-Currency System in Latest Reform."

124. BBC News, "Cuba Shuts Down Private Cinemas and Video-Game Salons."

125. Zurbano, "For Blacks in Cuba, the Revolution Hasn't Begun."

126. Lumsden, *Machos, Maricones, and Gays,* p. 103; Fusco, "Hustling for Dollars," 156.

127. Valle, *Habana Babilonia,* p. 16.

128. Cabezas, *Economies of Desire,* pp. 2-3.

129. Fusco, "Hustling for Dollars," p. 155.

130. Cabezas, *Economies of Desire,* p. 1; Gosse, *Where the Boys Are.*

131. Fanon, *The Wretched of the Earth,* p. 36.

132. Fusco, "Hustling for Dollars," p. 162.

133. Fanon, *Black Skin, White Masks,* pp. 41-62.

CHAPTER 2

1. Kempadoo, "Freelancers, Temporary Wives, and Beach-Boys," pp. 48–49; Cabezas, "Between Love and Money," p. 1010; Hermansen, "Jineteras, Luchadoras and the Awkward Tourist-Anthropologist in Havana," p. 50; García, "(Re) covering Women," p. 204.

2. See Cabezas, "Between Love and Money"; Cabezas, *Economies of Desire.*

3. Zelizer, *The Purchase of Intimacy*, p. 28. For more on authenticity of emotion and the intersections of affect and money, see Hochschild, *The Managed Heart;* Rebhun, *The Heart Is Unknown Country.*

4. Jineteras are commonly described this way in state-run newspapers and academic studies; for example, see Torres and Morales, "Asedio, prostitución y delincuencia."

5. Cabezas, *Economies of Desire*, p. 125.

6. Derrick Hodge, quoted in Cabezas, *Economies of Desire*, p. 123.

7. Cabezas, "Between Love and Money," p. 1002.

8. Los Aldeanos are a subversive Cuban rap group. Lili is referring to their song "Mangos bajitos" from their 2009 album, *El Atropello.*

9. Zelizer, *Purchase of Intimacy*, p. 33.

10. Kelley, quoted in Allen, *¡Venceremos?*, p. 182.

11. Kempadoo, "Freelancers," pp. 48–49.

12. Lumsden, *Machos, Maricones, and Gays*, pp. 21–24.

13. Valle, *Habana Babilonia*, p. 152.

14. Ibid., pp. 150–58.

15. Cabezas, "Discourses of Prostitution," p. 1009.

16. Fosado, "The Exchange of Sex for Money in Contemporary Cuba." For more on how gendered and sexualized roles in homosexual and queer relationships are constituted in Cuba, as well as other parts of Latin America, in terms of dominant/subordinate and hetero/homosexual binaries and identities, see Sierra Madero, *Del otro lado del espejo;* Stout, "Feminists, Queers, and Critics."

17. Fusco, *Corpus Delecti.*

18. Zelizer, *Purchase of Intimacy*, p. 18; Brennan, *What's Love Got to Do with It?*, p. 175.

19. Halley, "The Construction of Heterosexuality."

20. Conversely, and tellingly, what increasingly seems to be the standard global terminology, *sex worker,* has never taken root in Cuba—a side note but an interesting one nonetheless. This is first because it would require sex work to be broadly accepted as a form of labor in the Cuban setting—both its socialist paradigm and its deep-seated ideas about gender—which is highly unlikely to occur, and second, at the individual level, because it forecloses the possibility for other types of relationships to evolve out of these interactions. According to Cabezas, "There is no justification for imposing the term *sex worker* on people who do not

identify as such. In fact, within this context, the term *sex worker* imposes an arbitrarily derogatory and racist label" ("Between Love and Money," pp. 1002–3). Since the women interviewed for this project do not identify as such, not seeing their activities as in any way related to waged employment and not seeking any kind of rights as workers, this term will be discarded for my purposes.

21. Lumsden, *Machos, Maricones, and Gays*, p. 140. See chapter 1 for a brief discussion of the UMAP camps. For greater detail, see Lumsden's book.

22. Elizalde, *Flores desechables*, p. 70; Valle, *Habana Babilonia*, pp. 14–16.

23. Díaz Canals and González Olmedo, "Cultura y prostitución," p. 173. My translation.

24. Stout, "Feminists, Queers and Critics," p. 738; see also Cabezas, *Economies of Desire*, pp. 120–21.

25. Marrero, "Scripting Sexual Tourism," p. 238.

26. Fusco, "Hustling for Dollars," p. 154.

27. García, "(Re)covering Women," p. 178.

28. Cabezas, *Economies of Desire*, p. 129.

29. Ibid., pp. 112–17.

30. Puri, *The Caribbean Postcolonial*, p. 3.

31. Hall et al., *Policing the Crisis*, p. 190.

32. Foucault, *The History of Sexuality, Volume I*, p. 43.

33. Goldberg, "Sodomy in the New World," p. 3.

34. Ibid., p. 11.

35. There have been efforts to establish general trends for jineteras, but the results have been predictably unhelpful for such a fuzzy category. For example, a 1996 study found that most jineteras were white, while Domínguez, in his 1998 study, "La mujer joven en los 90," found that the majority were mixed race. See Díaz, discussed in Fernandez, "Back to the Future?"

36. Among others, Teresa Marrero argues that "disproportionate relations of economic power strip the situation of its possible amorous, rosy and seductive allure, grounding it within the stark black and white realm of economic disparity." See Marrero, "Scripting Sexual Tourism," p. 244.

37. Urry, *The Tourist Gaze*, pp. 74, 139, 145, 151.

38. Wonders and Michalowski, "Bodies, Borders and Sex Tourism in a Globalised World."

39. See Agustín, *Sex at the Margins*.

40. See discussion in Stout, "Feminists, Queers, and Critics," p. 741.

41. Lézama Lima, quoted in Soto, "Performance in Cuba in the 1980s," p. 266.

CHAPTER 3

1. Scott, *Weapons of the Weak*.

2. García, "(Re)covering Women," p. 212.

3. For other sources that corroborate the mass arrests, see Valle, *Habana Babilonia;* Elizalde, *Flores desechables;* Cabezas, *Economies of Desire;* Díaz Canals and González Olmedo, "Cultura y prostitución"; Facio, Toro-Morn, and Roschelle, "Tourism, Gender, and Globalization"; García, "(Re)covering Women"; Fusco, "Hustling for Dollars," p. 161.

4. De la Fuente, *A Nation for All,* p. 327.

5. Kruger, "Community-Based Crime Control in Cuba," p. 104.

6. Sierra Madero, *Del otro lado del espejo,* pp. 179-80.

7. Horta Mesa, "Recodo sentencioso de la prostitución en la colonia cubana," p. 51.

8. Valle, *Habana Babilonia,* pp. 42-43, 46-48, 51-59.

9. Allen, *¡Venceremos?,* p. 34; see also Clealand, "When Ideology Clashes with Reality."

10. Gámez Torres, "Hearing the Change," 238. Gámez Torres's translation.

11. This practice is also described in the report filed to the ECOSOC in February 2000 by the U.N. Special Rapporteur on Women's Rights. See U.N. ECOSOC, *Report of the Special Rapporteur,* p. 13.

12. U.N. ECOSOC, *Report of the Special Rapporteur,* p. 13.

13. Cabezas, "Between Love and Money," p. 1004.

14. Leiner, *Sexual Politics in Cuba,* p. 43.

15. The complete text of the relevant articles reads as follows: "ARTICLE 72. A dangerous state is considered the special proclivity in which a person is found to commit crimes, demonstrated by their conduct which is seen to be in manifest contradiction with the norms of socialist morality. ARTICLE 73. 1) The dangerous state can be seen when the individual takes part in one of the following indices of dangerousness: a) habitual inebriation and alcoholism; b) drug addiction; c) antisocial conduct; 2) An individual is considered to be in the dangerous state by virtue of antisocial conduct when he/she habitually disturbs the rules of social coexistence through acts of violence, or by other provocative acts, which violate the rights of others, or by their general behaviour which harms the rules of coexistence or perturbs the order of the community, or who lives, as a social parasite, off the work of another or exploits or practices socially reprehensible vices. ARTICLE 74. Also considered to be in the dangerous state are the mentally deranged and persons of retarded mental development if, because of this fact, they do not possess the faculty to comprehend the impact of their actions, nor to control their behaviour, as long as these represent a threat to the security of people or to the social order." Código Penal de Cuba, Articles 72-74. Translation of Article 72 from Cabezas, "Between Love and Money," p. 1006; translation of Articles 73 and 74 is mine. Further information follows in Articles 75-84.

16. Código Penal de Cuba, Articles 78-84. My translation.

17. Quoted in Elizalde, *Flores desechables,* p. 65. My translation.

18. Díaz and González, "Cultura y prostitución," p. 175.

19. The text of the article reads as follows: "ARTICLE 62. None of the recognized rights of citizens may be exercised against . . . the existence and the ends of the socialist State, nor against the decision of the Cuban people to construct socialism and communism" (Constitución de la República de Cuba). For another English translation, see Appendix 3 of Human Rights Watch, "New Castro, Same Cuba."

20. Cabezas, *Economies of Desire*, p. 147.

21. Hall et al., *Policing the Crisis*, p. 40.

22. Kempadoo, "Freelancers, Temporary Wives, and Beach-Boys," p. 57.

23. Cabezas, "Between Love and Money," p. 993.

24. Fosado, "The Exchange of Sex for Money in Contemporary Cuba."

25. Elizalde, *Flores desechables*, p. 62; Cabezas, "Between Love and Money," p. 1006.

26. U.N. ECOSOC, *Report of the Special Rapporteur*, pp. 14–15.

27. Quoted in Cabezas, *Economies of Desire*, pp. 148–49.

28. Quoted in Cabezas, *Economies of Desire*, p. 148.

29. Cabezas, *Economies of Desire*, pp. 147–48.

30. Quoted in Valle, *Habana Babilonia*, p. 128.

31. In an internal study of young women institutionalized for "conducta prostituida" (prostituted conduct) commissioned by MININT, 83.3 percent indicated they were unhappy with the way in which they had been treated by the police and the judicial process. See Mazola Fiallo et al., *Estudio sobre algunos valores morales de jóvenes con conducta sexual prostituida*, p. 21.

32. See Hamilton, *Sexual Revolutions*, p. 44; Sierra Madero, *Del otro lado del espejo;* Lumsden, *Machos, Maricones, and Gays*.

33. Cabezas, *Economies of Desire*, p. 143.

34. Kempadoo, "Freelancers."

35. The open space facing the U.S. Interests Section is a focal point for propaganda between the United States and Cuba. The 138 flagpoles mentioned here were erected in 2006 in order to hide an electronic billboard that the Interests Section had installed, displaying messages supporting democratic reform in Cuba. Each pole was hung with a black flag bearing a single white star, and the square was dubbed Plaza Anti-Imperialista (Anti-Imperialist Square) and used for concerts and rallies. The billboard has since been removed, but the flagpoles remain and are used to display Cuban flags during national holidays. See Carroll, "US Pulls the Plug on Ticker in Cuba."

36. Cabezas, *Economies of Desire*, p. 161.

37. Valle's book discusses the role and character of chulos at length throughout his work on jineterismo as sexual practice in Cuba. See Valle, *Habana Babilonia*.

38. César, *Mujer y política social en Cuba*, pp. 105–6, 108.

39. Scott, *Weapons of the Weak*, pp. 25–26. "Small arms in a cold war" is another way Scott commonly describes this phenomenon in *Weapons of the Weak*.

40. Ibid., p. 36.

41. Ibid., p. 242.

42. See Valle's numerous interviews with chulos in *Habana Babilonia*.

43. Quoted in Valle, *Habana Babilonia*, pp. 318–19.

44. Scott, *Weapons of the Weak*, p. 29.

45. Ibid., p. 36.

46. Sierra Madero, *Del otro lado del espejo*, p. 190. My translation.

CHAPTER 4

1. Stout, "Feminists, Queers, and Critics," pp. 726–27.

2. This fact is also noted by Allen, *¡Venceremos?*, pp. 90–92.

3. Quoted in Valle, *Habana Babilonia*, p. 21.

4. Valle, *Habana Babilonia*, p. 277.

5. The title is taken from a song by the Cuban folk singer Silvio Rodríguez, "Flores nocturnas" (Flowers of the Night).

6. Elizalde, *Flores desechables*, p. 11. My translation.

7. Elizalde, *Jineteros en La Habana*, pp. 6–7; also quoted in García, "(Re)covering Women," p. 170. García's translation.

8. Elizalde, *Flores desechables*, pp. 25–26, 28. My translation.

9. Torres and Morales, "Asedio, prostitución y delincuencia," p. 324.

10. Ibid., p. 313. My translation here and in the following quotations from this work.

11. Ibid., p. 325.

12. Ibid., pp. 313, 320, 324–25.

13. Oddly, Mirta Rodríguez Calderón was also a member of Magín, which had a notably more liberal view of jineterismo as an organization.

14. Strout, "Women, the Politics of Sexuality, and Cuba's Economic Crisis," p. 15.

15. Rodríguez Calderón, quoted in Strout, "Women, the Politics of Sexuality, and Cuba's Economic Crisis," pp. 16–17.

16. Elizalde, *Flores desechables*, p. 60. My translation here and in the following quotations from this work.

17. Ibid., pp. 19–20.

18. Ibid., p. 57.

19. Ibid., pp. 19–20.

20. Ibid., p. 71.

21. CENESEX, "Misión."

22. Quoted in Rowe, "The New Cuban Revolución."

23. Peñate Leiva, "Género y prostitución," p. 192. My translation here and in the following quotations from this work.

24. Ibid., p. 195.

25. Ibid., pp. 193–94, 200–203.

26. Ibid.

27. Fusco, "Hustling for Dollars," p. 156.

28. "Fidel Castro Takes Blame for 1960s Gay Persecution."

29. Hamilton, *Sexual Revolutions*, p. 48.

30. Sierra Madero, *Del otro lado del espejo.*

31. Federación de Mujeres Cubanas, *Memoria del 1er Congreso de la Federación de Mujeres Cubanas*, p. 6. My translation.

32. Stout, "Feminists, Queers, and Critics," p. 729.

33. Lutjens, "Reading between the Lines," p. 102.

34. Nazzari, "The 'Woman Question' in Cuba," p. 247.

35. Comité Provincial de Ciudad de La Habana de la Federación de Mujeres Cubanas, "Casas de Orientación a la Mujer y la Familia."

36. Federación de Mujeres Cubanas, "¿Quiénes somos?" My translation.

37. Federación de Mujeres Cubanas, "Cuban Women in Figures 2010" (in English).

38. Lutjens, "Reading between the Lines," pp. 110–15; Lumsden, *Machos, Maricones, and Gays*, pp. 118–19.

39. Arenas, "Los cubanos y el homosexualismo," p. 8; quoted in Hamilton, *Sexual Revolutions*, p. 45.

40. Herrera, quoted in Fernandes, "Transnationalism and Feminist Activism in Cuba," p. 445.

41. There has been some talk in the recent years of resurrecting Magín. See Acosta, "Women Journalists in Cuba Revive Transgressive Group."

42. Espín, "Anticipos de un congreso femenino," quoted in Holgado Fernandez, *¡No es fácil!*, p. 252.

43. Fusco, "Hustling for Dollars," p. 161.

44. Cabezas, "Between Love and Money," p. 1005; Fusco, "Hustling for Dollars"; Stout, "Feminists, Queers, and Critics"; García, "(Re)covering Women."

45. Quoted in Stout, "Feminists, Queers, and Critics," p. 737; Cabezas, "Between Love and Money," pp. 1005–6.

46. Rodríguez Calderón, in Strout, "Women, the Politics of Sexuality and Cuba's Economic Crisis," p. 16–17; see also pp. 16–18.

47. Stout, "Feminists, Queers, and Critics," p. 729.

48. Federación de Mujeres Cubanas, *Memoria del 2º Congreso de la Federación de Mujeres Cubanas*, p. 112. My translation here and for the following quotations from the FMC's memorias.

49. Federación de Mujeres Cubanas, *Memoria del 6º Congreso de la Federación de Mujeres Cubanas*, pp. 54–55.

50. Ibid.

51. Ibid., p. 56. The tourism offices, Yuris told me, quickly capitulated and removed the offending images; she cited this as an example of how social and ideological change at an individual and community level often lags behind structural and legal changes.

52. Ibid., pp. 140–41.

53. Federación de Mujeres Cubanas, *Memoria del 7º Congreso de la Federación de Mujeres Cubanas*, p. 8.

54. Ibid., p. 9.

55. Ibid.

56. Federación de Mujeres Cubanas, *Memoria del 8º Congreso de la Federación de Mujeres Cubanas*, p. 26.

57. Ibid., pp. 25–27.

58. Beretervide, quoted in Lotti, "Despejando horizontes," p. 8. My translation.

59. Beretervide, quoted in Lotti, "Despejando horizontes," p. 9. My translation.

60. U.N. ECOSOC, *Report of the Special Rapporteur*, p. 12.

61. The Instituto de Medicina Legal operates under the auspices of MININT, which jointly runs the Centros de Rehabilitación with the FMC. See Mazola Fiallo et al., *Estudio sobre algunos valores morales de jóvenes con conducta sexual prostituida*, p. 27.

62. García also makes this point in her work; see "(Re)covering Women," p. 195.

63. Johnson, "Introduction: Señoras . . . no ordinarias," pp. 4–5.

64. Beretervide, quoted in Lotti, "Despejando horizontes," p. 9; See Mazola Fiallo et al., "Estudio sobre algunos valores morales."

65. Quoted in Cabezas, *Economies of Desire*, pp. 148–49.

66. Lumsden, *Machos, Maricones, and Gays*, p. 7.

67. Fernandez, *Revolutionizing Romance*, pp. 20–23.

68. Foucault, *The History of Sexuality, Volume I*, p. 27.

69. De la Fuente, *A Nation for All*, p. 4.

70. Alejandro de la Fuente notes an organization called la Cofradía de la Negritud, an Afro-Cuban solidarity group founded in the late 1990s and then revived more recently as a mouthpiece for Afro-Cubans. He cites the organization's manifesto, but I could find no further mentions of it, so I hesitate to include it here. See de la Fuente, "The New Afro-Cuban Cultural Movement and the Debate on Race in Contemporary Cuba."

71. De la Fuente, *A Nation for All*.

72. Sawyer, quoted in Fernandez, *Revolutionizing Romance*, p. 24.

73. De la Fuente, "New Afro-Cuban Cultural Movement," p. 698.

74. Parker, "Unthinking Sex," p. 21.

75. Stout, "Feminists, Queers, and Critics," p. 729.

76. Rose and Miller, "Political Power beyond the State," p. 183.

77. Foucault, *History of Sexuality, Volume I*, p. 25.

78. Guerrero and Alonso, "La sexualidad en los jóvenes," p. 197.

79. The historian Louis A. Pérez writes that since the early 1990s the Cuban government has redoubled its rhetorical and symbolic use of ideas of struggle and rebellion as a show of defiance against the U.S. embargo and its own economic difficulties. The term *eterno Baraguá* recurs in Cuban propaganda and political rhetoric of this kind. It refers to General Antonio Maceo, who issued a statement at the end of the Guerra de los Diez Años in 1878 in which he vowed never to capitulate to Spain. See Pérez, *Cuba: Between Reform and Revolution*, p. 303.

80. Butler, *Gender Trouble*, p. 33.

CHAPTER 5

1. Deleuze, *Foucault*, pp. 92–93.

2. See chapter 2 for more discussion of the terms *candelero* and *el fuego*.

3. Foucault, *Security, Territory, Population*, p. 1.

4. Foucault, *Society Must Be Defended*, p. 241.

5. Foucault, *The Birth of Biopolitics*, p. 21.

6. Prozorov, *Foucault, Freedom and Sovereignty*, p. 103.

7. Prozorov, "Unrequited Love of Power," p. 67.

8. Scott, *Weapons of the Weak*.

9. See the discussion of the black market and *cuentapropismo* in the contemporary Cuban economy in Mesa-Lago, "Growing Economic Social Disparities in Cuba." Noelle Stout also discusses justifications and perceptions of extralegal activity, with some youth arguing that those who engage sexually with tourists just do not "have a head for" making money in other ways; see Stout, "Feminists, Queers, and Critics."

10. Scott, *Domination and the Arts of Resistance*, p. 20.

11. Valle, *Habana Babilonia*, pp. 318–19.

12. See Scott, *Domination and the Arts of Resistance*.

13. Ibid., pp. 14, 21.

14. Ibid., p. 14.

15. Symmes, "Thirty Days as a Cuban."

16. Bhabha, "Of Mimicry and Man," p. 86.

17. Ibid., pp. 86, 88.

18. Prozorov, "Unrequited Love of Power," p. 58.

19. Ibid., p. 56.

20. Prozorov, *Foucault, Freedom and Sovereignty*, pp. 110–11.

21. Prozorov, "Unrequited Love of Power," p. 59; Dillon, "Cared to Death."

22. Prozorov, "Unrequited Love of Power," p. 62. Emphasis in original.

23. Prozorov, *Foucault, Freedom and Sovereignty*, p. 144.

24. García, "(Re)covering Women," p. 195.

25. Prozorov, *Foucault, Freedom and Sovereignty*, p. 111.

26. Halberstam, "Going Gaga." This keynote lecture delivered at the conference "Love, Sex, Desire and the (Post)colonial," 28 October 2011, at Senate House, London, was derived in part from new research and in part from Halberstam's book, *The Queer Art of Failure*. See also Stern and Zalewski, "Feminist Fatigue(s)"; Ziarek, *The Rhetoric of Failure*.

27. Several feminist theorists have explored the idea of the nation-as-body, or the body politic. These include Yuval-Davis, *Gender and Nation;* Nelson, *A Finger in the Wound;* Anzaldúa, *Borderlands/La Frontera*.

28. García, "(Re)covering Women," p. 2; Heras León, quoted in García, "(Re)covering Women," p. 2.

29. Fanon, *Black Skin, White Masks*, p. 3.

30. Sierra Madero, *Del otro lado del espejo*, p. 71. My translation.

31. Rubin, "Thinking Sex," p. 10.

32. See Kutzinski, *Sugar's Secrets*.

33. "La chingada" is derived from the Spanish verb *chingarse*, which is variously used across Central and South America to indicate notions of failure (Chile and Argentina), disappointment (Colombia), damage (Argentina), and humiliation, aggression, and violence (everywhere). It implies a lack of consent when used to denote sexual activities. "La chingada" and, in turn, "hijo de la chingada" (son of the fucked woman) are common cultural tropes and insults in Mexico. See Paz, *Labyrinth of Solitude*, pp. 67–68.

34. Paz, *Labyrinth of Solitude*, pp. 67–77.

35. Weber, *Faking It*, p. 2.

36. Ibid.

37. Editorial in the *Louisville Daily Courier*, 11 January 1859, quoted in May, *The Southern Dream of a Caribbean Empire, 1854–1861*, p. 7.

38. Williams, *Empire as a Way of Life*, p. 117.

39. Gosse, *Where the Boys Are*, pp. 46–47.

40. "From the other side of the mirror" is the English translation of Sierra Madero's book, *Del otro lado del espejo*, about sexuality and Cuban nationhood.

41. Aradau, "The Perverse Politics of Four-Letter Words,"pp. 261, 274.

42. This is a common joke in Cuba, which Raquel Mendieta Costa mentions. See Mendieta Costa, "Exotic Exports," p. 43.

43. Elizalde, *Flores desechables*, p. 27.

44. Karl Marx, quoted in Parker, "Unthinking Sex," p. 36.

45. Sara, quoted in Valle, *Habana Babilonia*, p. 108. My translation.

46. Paz, *Labyrinth of Solitude*, pp. 77–78.

47. Scarry, *The Body in Pain*, pp. 22, 280; Mehta, "Circumcision, Body, Masculinity," p. 94.

48. Foucault, "Nietzsche, Genealogy, History," p. 83; quoted in Oksala, *Foucault on Freedom*, p. 112.

49. Foucault, *History of Sexuality, Volume I*, p. 145.

50. Feldman, *Formations of Violence*, p. 8.

51. Foucault, *History of Sexuality, Volume I*, p. 157.

52. Scarry, *The Body in Pain*, p. 12.

53. Ibid., pp. 1–23.

54. Scarry, "'The Body in Pain': An Interview," p. 226; Scarry, *The Body in Pain*, p. 12.

55. Scarry, *The Body in Pain*, p. 14.

56. Ibid., p. 162.

57. Deleuze understands desire in a similar way—as not *for*, *by*, or *to* any outside element; for my purposes, however, I prefer Foucault's separation of pleasure and desire. Quoted in Oksala, *Foucault on Freedom*, pp. 128–29.

58. Scarry, "'The Body in Pain: An Interview," p. 224.

59. Scarry, *The Body in Pain*, p. 326.

60. See an additional discussion of these trends in Lumsden, *Machos, Maricones, and Gays*.

61. Sierra Madero, "Códigos en movimiento," p. 72.

62. Fusco, "Hustling for Dollars," p. 156.

63. Scarry, *The Body in Pain*, p. 22. Emphasis in original.

64. See Butler, *Psychic Life of Power*.

65. Foucault, *History of Sexuality, Volume I*, p. 85.

66. Butler, *Psychic Life of Power*, p. 3.

67. Ibid., p. 28.

68. See Foucault, "Technologies of the Self."

69. Foucault, *History of Sexuality, Volume III*, pp. 51, 240.

70. Foucault, *The Government of the Self and Others*, p. 43.

71. O'Leary, quoted in Oksala, *Foucault on Freedom*, p. 169; see also Pickett, "Foucault and the Politics of Resistance," p. 462.

72. Foucault, "Technologies of the Self," p. 228; see also Foucault, "Ethics of Concern for the Self," p. 284.

73. Foucault, quoted in Pickett, "Foucault and the Politics of Resistance," p. 462; see also Hofmeyr, "The Power Not to Be (What We Are)," p. 217; Foucault, "Ethics of Concern for Self."

74. Weeks, "History, Desire and Identities," p. 38.

75. Foucault, "Technologies of the Self," p. 228.

76. Žižek, *For They Know Not What They Do*, p. 239.

77. Žižek, *The Parallax View*, pp. 309–10.

78. Žižek, *Interrogating the Real*, pp. 306–7, 176.

79. Edkins and Pin-Fat, "Through the Wire," p. 6; see also Feldman, *Formations of Violence;* Touraine, *Return of the Actor.*

80. Prozorov himself is unsatisfied with the notion of an "exit" from power, but I have included it here because in Cuba the notion of emigration is an extremely evocative one, in both the literal and the metaphoric sense. See Prozorov, "Unrequited Love of Power," pp. 71–74.

81. Butler, *Psychic Life of Power,* p. 17.

82. Foucault, *History of Sexuality, Volume III,* p. 67.

83. García, "(Re)covering Women," p. 188.

84. Agamben, *What Is an Apparatus? and Other Essays,* p. 11.

85. Das, "The Act of Witnessing," p. 223.

CONCLUSION

1. "Cuban Flotilla Irks Government, but Draws Few Spectators."

2. Larson, "Gay Space in Havana," p. 335.

3. See Scott, *Weapons of the Weak.*

4. Cabezas, *Economies of Desire,* p. 4.

5. Enloe, "Interview with Professor Cynthia Enloe," p. 660.

6. Loretta, quoted in Valle, *Habana Babilonia,* pp. 207–8. My translation.

7. Kapcia, *Cuba in Revolution,* p. 25.

8. Cabezas discusses this problem in the epilogue of *Economies of Desire,* pp. 166–68.

9. There are a number of authors who discuss the intentions and perspectives of tourists who seek out sex with locals in various tourism destinations. Perhaps predictably, they often find that they favor traditional gender roles. See, for example, Manderson and Jolly, *Sites of Desire, Economies of Pleasure;* Seabrook, *Travels in the Skin Trade;* Kempadoo, *Sexing the Caribbean.*

10. Lather, "Postbook," p. 205.

11. Doezema, "Ouch! Western Feminists' 'Wounded Attachment' to the 'Third World Prostitute.'"

12. Das, "The Act of Witnessing," p. 223.

Bibliography

Acosta, Daila. "Women Journalists in Cuba Revive Transgressive Group." *IPS News*, 29 February 2012, accessed 20 January 2014, www.ipsnews. net/2012/02/women-journalists-in-cuba-revive-transgressive-group/.

Agamben, Giorgio. *What Is an Apparatus? and Other Essays*. Trans. David Kishik and Stefan Pedatella. Stanford, CA: Stanford University Press, 2009.

Agustín, Laura María. *Sex at the Margins: Migration, Labour Markets and the Rescue Industry*. London: Zed Books, 2007.

Alfonso y García, Ramón María. *La prostitución en Cuba y especialmente en La Habana: Memoria de la comisión de higiene especial de la isla de Cuba elevada al secretario de Gobernación cumpliendo un precepto reglamentario*. Havana: Impr. P. Fernández, 1902.

Allen, Jafari S. *¡Venceremos? The Erotics of Black Self-Making in Cuba*. Durham, NC: Duke University Press, 2012.

Allison, Anne. *Nightwork: Sexuality, Pleasure, and Corporate Masculinity in a Tokyo Hostess Club*. Chicago: University of Chicago Press, 1994.

Amnesty International. "Repression of Cuban Dissidents Persists Despite Releases." *Amnesty International*, 16 March 2011, accessed 9 October 2011, www.amnesty.org/en/news-and-updates/repression-cuban-dissidents-persists-despite-releases-2011–03–16.

Anderson, Benedict. *Imagined Communities: Reflections on the Origin and Spread of Nationalism*. 2nd ed. London: Verso, 1991.

Anderson, Tim. "Island Socialism: Cuban Crisis and Structural Adjustment." *Australian Journal of Political Economy* 49 (2001): 56–86.

Anzaldúa, Gloria. *Borderlands/La Frontera: The New Mestiza.* San Francisco: Aunt Lute Books, 1987.

Aradau, Claudia. "The Perverse Politics of Four-Letter Words: Risk and Pity in the Securitisation of Human Trafficking." *Millennium* 33.2 (2004): 251–77.

Arenas, Reinaldo. "Los cubanos y el homosexualismo." *Mariel* (Spring 1984): 8.

Balzac, Honoré de. *Les paysans.* Paris: Pleiades, 1949.

BBC News. "Castro Ends State-Visit to South Africa." *BBC News,* 6 September 1998, accessed 9 October 2011, http://news.bbc.co.uk/1/hi/world/africa /165566.stm.

———. "Cuba Shuts Down Private Cinemas and Video-Game Salons." *BBC News,* 3 November 1013, accessed 18 January 2014, www.bbc.co.uk/news /world-latin-america-24790569.

———. "Cuba to Scrap Two-Currency System in Latest Reform." *BBC News,* 22 October 2013, accessed 18 January 2014, www.bbc.co.uk/news/ world-latin-america-24627620.

———. "EU Lifts Sanctions against Cuba." *BBC News,* 20 June 2008, accessed 9 October 2011, http://news.bbc.co.uk/1/hi/7463803.stm.

Beckles, Hilary, and Verene Shepherd. *Liberties Lost: Caribbean Indigenous Societies and Slave Systems.* Cambridge: Cambridge University Press, 2004.

Beers, Mayra. "Murder in San Isidro: Crime and Culture during the Second Cuban Republic." *Cuban Studies* 34 (2003): 97–129.

Bejel, Emilio. *Gay Cuban Nation.* Chicago: University of Chicago Press, 2001.

Bhabha, Homi K. "DissemiNation: Time, Narrative, and the Margins of the Modern Nation." In *Nation and Narration,* ed. Homi K. Bhabha, pp. 291–322. London: Routledge, 1990.

———. "Introduction: Narrating the Nation." In *Nation and Narration,* ed. Homi K. Bhabha, pp. 1–7. London: Routledge, 1990.

———. "Of Mimicry and Man: The Ambivalence of Colonial Discourse." In *The Location of Culture,* ed. Homi K. Bhabha, pp. 85–92. London: Routledge, 1994.

Brennan, Denise. "Love Work in Sex Work (and After): Performing at Love." In *Intimacies: Love and Sex across Cultures,* ed. William R. Jankowiak, pp. 174–93. New York: Columbia University Press, 2008.

———. *What's Love Got to Do with It? Transnational Desires and Sex Tourism in the Dominican Republic.* Durham, NC: Duke University Press, 2004.

Bruguera, Tania. "The Burden of Guilt." In *Corpus Delecti: Performance Art of the Americas,* ed. Coco Fusco, pp. 152–53. London: Routledge, 2000.

Butler, Judith. *Bodies That Matter: On the Discursive Limits of Sex.* New York: Routledge Classics, 1993.

———. *Gender Trouble: Feminism and the Subversion of Identity,* London: Routledge Classics, 1990.

———. *The Psychic Life of Power: Theories in Subjection,* Stanford: Stanford University Press, 1997.

Cabezas, Amalia L. "Between Love and Money: Sex, Tourism and Citizenship in Cuba and the Dominican Republic." *Signs* 29.4 (2004): 987–1015.

———. "Discourses of Prostitution: The Case of Cuba." In *Global Sex Workers: Rights, Resistance and Redefinition,* ed. Kamala Kempadoo and Jo Doezema, 79–86. London: Routledge, 1998.

———. *Economies of Desire: Sex and Tourism in Cuba and the Dominican Republic,* Philadelphia: Temple University Press, 2009.

Calvo Peña, Beatriz. "Prensa, política y prostitución en La Habana finisecular: El caso de La Cebolla y la 'polémica de las meretrices.'" *Cuban Studies* 36 (2005): 23–49.

Cantón Navarro, José. *History of Cuba: The Challenge of the Yoke and the Star.* Havana: Editoral SI-MAR, 1998.

Carroll, Rory. "US Pulls the Plug on Ticker in Cuba." *The Guardian,* 27 July 2009, accessed 28 November 2011, www.guardian.co.uk/world/2009/jul/27/us-mission-ticker-cuba.

Caulfield, Sueann. "El nacimiento de Mangue: La raza, la nación y la política de la prostitución en Río de Janeiro, 1850–1942." In *Sexo y sexualidades en América Latina,* ed. Daniel Balderston and Donna Guy, 139–61. Buenos Aires: Paídos, 1998.

CENESEX. "Misión." Centro Nacional de Educación Sexual, 2003, accessed 3 October 2011, www.cenesex.sld.cu/webs/cenesex_mision.htm.

César, Maria Auxiliadora. *Mujer y política social en Cuba: El contrapunto socialista al bienestar capitalista.* Ciudad de Panamá: Mercie Ediciones, 2005.

Clealand, Danielle P. "When Ideology Clashes with Reality: Racial Discrimination and Black Identity in Contemporary Cuba." *Ethnic and Racial Studies* 36.10 (May 2013): 1619–36.

Clifford, James. "Introduction: Partial Truths." In *Writing Culture: The Poetics and Politics of Ethnography,* 25th anniversary ed., ed. James Clifford and George E. Marcus, pp. 1–26. Berkeley: University of California Press, 2010.

Código Penal de Cuba. *Gaceta Oficial de la República de Cuba.* Ministerio de Justicia, 2008, accessed 26 November 2011, www.gacetaoficial.cu/html/codigo_penal.html.

Cohen, Jeff. "Cuba Libre." *Playboy* (March 1991): 68–74, 157–58.

Cole, Bankole A. "Post-Colonial Systems." In *Policing across the World: Issues for the Twenty-First Century,* ed. R. I. Mawby, pp. 88–108. London: University College London Press, 1999.

Comité Provincial de Ciudad de La Habana de la Federación de Mujeres Cubanas. "Casas de Orientación a la Mujer y la Familia." FMC brochure. Havana: FMC, n.d.

Constitución de la República de Cuba (n.d.). Cuba Portal, accessed 28 November 2011, www.cuba.cu/gobierno/cuba.htm.

Costa Vargas, João. "Hyperconsciousness of Race and Its Negation: The Dialectic of White Supremacy in Brazil." *Identities* 11.4 (2004): 443–70.

"Corruption in Cuba: The Cleanup Continues." *Economist Online,* 6 May 2011, accessed 9 May 2011, www.economist.com/blogs/americasview/2011/05/corruption_cuba.

Crapanzano, Vincent. "Hermes' Dilemma: The Masking of Subversion in Ethnographic Description." In *Writing Culture: The Poetics and Politics of Ethnography,* 25th anniversary ed., ed. James Clifford and George E. Marcus, pp. 51–76. Berkeley: University of California Press, 2010.

Daigle, Megan. "Love, Sex, Money and Meaning: Using Language to Create Identities and Challenge Categories in Cuba." *Alternatives* 38.1 (2013): 63–77.

Das, Veena. "The Act of Witnessing: Violence, Poisonous Knowledge, and Subjectivity." In *Violence and Subjectivity,* ed. Veena Das, Arthur Kleinman, Mamphela Ramphele, and Pamela Reynolds, pp. 205–25. Berkeley: University of California Press, 2000.

de Céspedes, Benjamín. *La prostitucion en la ciudad de la Habana.* Havana: O'Reilly, 1888.

de la Fuente, Alejandro. *A Nation for All.* Chapel Hill: University of North Carolina Press, 2001.

———. "The New Afro-Cuban Cultural Movement and the Debate on Race in Contemporary Cuba." *Journal of Latin American Studies* (Special Issue: 50th Anniversary of Cuban Revolution) 40 (2008): 697–720.

———. *Queloides: Race and Racism in Cuban Contemporary Art.* Pittsburgh: University of Pittsburgh Press, 2010.

de la Torre Mulhare, Mirta. "Sexual Ideology in Pre-Castro Cuba: A Cultural Analysis." PhD diss., University of Pittsburgh, 1969.

Deleuze, Gilles. *Foucault.* Minneapolis: University of Minnesota Press, 1988.

Díaz, Elena, Esperanza Fernández, and Tania Caram. "Turismo y prostitución en Cuba." Paper presented at the 21st Conference of the Caribbean Studies Association, San Juan, Puerto Rico, May 1996.

Díaz Canals, Teresa. "Laberintos feministas." In *Mirar de otra manera,* ed. Norma Vasallo Barrueta and Teresa Díaz Canals, pp. 9–16. Havana: Editorial de la Mujer, 2008.

Díaz Canals, Teresa, and Graciela González Olmedo. "Cultura y prostitución: Una solución posible." *Papers* 52 (1997): 167–75. Accessed 25 May 2011, http://ddd.uab.cat/pub/papers/02102862n52p167.pdf.

Dillon, Michael. "Cared to Death: The Biopoliticized Time of Your Life." *Foucault Studies* 2 (May 2005): 37–46.

Doezema, Jo. "Ouch! Western Feminists' 'Wounded Attachment' to the 'Third World Prostitute.'" *Feminist Review* 67 (Spring 2001): 16–38.

Domínguez, Jorge I. *Cuba: Order and Revolution*, Cambridge, MA: Belknap Press, 1978.

Domínguez, María Isabel, ed. "La mujer joven en los 90." *Temas* 5 (1996): 31–37.

Edkins, Jenny, and Véronique Pin-Fat. "Through the Wire: Relations of Power and Relations of Violence." *Millennium* 34.1 (2005): 1–24.

Escalona, María Elena. "She Is a Virgin and She Awaits You: An Excerpt." In *Corpus Delecti: Performance Art of the Americas*, ed. Coco Fusco, 55–57. London: Routledge, 2000.

Elizalde, Rosa Miriam. "¿Crimen o castigo?" *La Jiribilla* 122 (2003). Accessed 26 November 2011, www.lajiribilla.cu/2003/n122_09/122_09.html.

———. *Flores desechables: ¿Prostitución en Cuba?* Havana: Ediciones Abril, 1996.

———. *Jineteros en La Habana*. Havana: Editorial Pablo de la Torriente, 1996.

Enloe, Cynthia. "Interview with Professor Cynthia Enloe." *Review of International Studies* 27.4 (2001): 649–66.

Espín, Vilma. "Anticipos de un congreso femenino." *Granma* (undated cutting in file labeled 1995).

Facio, Elisa, Maura Toro-Morn, and Anne R. Roschelle. "Tourism, Gender, and Globalization: Tourism in Cuba during the Special Period." *Transnational Law and Contemporary Problems* 14 (Spring 2004): 119–42.

Fairley, Jan. "Dancing Back to Front: *Regetón*, Sexuality, Gender and Transnationalism in Cuba." *Popular Music* 25.3 (2006): 471–88.

Fanon, Frantz. *Black Skin, White Masks*. Trans. Charles Lam Markmann. London: Pluto, 1986.

———. *The Wretched of the Earth*. London: Penguin, 1963.

Federación de Mujeres Cubanas. *Memoria del 8º Congreso de la Federación de Mujeres Cubanas*. Havana: FMC, 2009.

———. *Memoria del 2º Congreso de la Federación de Mujeres Cubanas*. Havana: FMC, 1975.

———. *Memoria del 1er Congreso de la Federación de Mujeres Cubanas*. Havana: FMC, 1962.

———. *Memoria del 6º Congreso de la Federación de Mujeres Cubanas*, Havana: FMC, 1995.

———. *Memoria del 7º Congreso de la Federación de Mujeres Cubanas*, Havana: FMC, 2000.

———. *Programa a la Atención a la Problemática de la Prostitución*. Havana: FMC, 1993.

———. "¿Quiénes somos?" *Mujeres*, n.d., accessed 3 October 2011, www.mujeres. co.cu/revista.asp.

Federation of Cuban Women. "Cuban Women in Figures 2010." FMC brochure. Havana, 2010.

Feldman, Allen. *Formations of Violence: The Narrative of the Body and Political Terror in Northern Ireland*. Chicago: University of Chicago Press, 1991.

———. "Violence and Vision: The Prosthetics and Aesthetics of Terror." In *Violence and Subjectivity*, ed. Veena Das, Arthur Kleinman, Mamphela Ramphele, and Pamela Reynolds, pp. 46–78. Berkeley: University of California Press, 2000.

Fernandes, Sujatha. *Cuba Represent! Cuban Arts, State Power, and the Making of New Revolutionary Cultures*. Durham, NC: Duke University Press, 2006.

———. "Transnationalism and Feminist Activism in Cuba: The Case of Magín." *Politics and Gender* 1.3 (2005): 431–52.

Fernandez, Nadine T. "Back to the Future? Women, Race and Tourism in Cuba." In *Sun, Sex and Gold: Tourism and Sex Work in the Caribbean*, ed. Kamala Kempadoo, pp. 81–89. Lanham, MD: Rowman & Littlefield, 1999.

———. *Revolutionizing Romance: Interracial Couples in Contemporary Cuba*. New Brunswick, NJ: Rutgers University Press, 2010.

"Fidel Castro Takes Blame for 1960s Gay Persecution." *Globe and Mail*, 31 August 2010, accessed 29 November 2011, www.theglobeandmail.com/news /world/americas/fidel-castro-takes-blame-for-1960s-gay-persecution /article1691613/.

Finn, John, and Chris Lukinbeal. "Musical Cartographies: *Los ritmos de los barrios de la Habana*." In *Sound, Society and the Geography of Popular Music*, ed. Ola Johannson and Thomas L. Bell, pp. 127–44. Farnham: Ashgate, 2009.

Forrest, David. "Lenin, the *Pinguero*, and Cuban Imaginings of Maleness in Times of Scarcity." In *Masculinities Matter! Men, Gender and Development*, ed. Frances Cleaver, pp. 84–111. London: Zed Books, 2002.

Fosado, Gisela. "The Exchange of Sex for Money in Contemporary Cuba: Masculinity, Ambiguity and Love." PhD diss., University of Michigan, 2004.

Foucault, Michel. *The Birth of Biopolitics: Lectures at the Collège de France, 1978–1979*. Ed. Michel Senellart, trans. Graham Burchell. New York: Palgrave Macmillan, 2008.

———. "The Ethics of the Concern for Self as a Practice of Freedom." In *Essential Works of Michel Foucault, 1954–1984, Volume 1: Ethics*, ed. Paul Rabinow, trans. Robert Hurley, pp. 281–302. London: Penguin, 1994.

———. *The Government of the Self and Others: Lectures at the Collège de France, 1982–1983*. Ed. Frédéric Gros, trans. Graham Burchell. New York: Palgrave Macmillan, 2010.

———. *The History of Sexuality, Volume I: The Will to Knowledge*. Trans. Robert Hurley. London: Penguin Books, 1998.

———. *The History of Sexuality, Volume III: The Care of the Self.* Trans. Robert Hurley. London: Penguin, 1986.

———. "Nietzsche, Genealogy, History." In *The Foucault Reader*, ed. Paul Rabinow, 76–100. London: Penguin, 1991.

———. *Security, Territory, Population: Lectures at the Collège de France, 1977–1978*. Ed. Michel Senellart, trans. Graham Burchell. New York: Palgrave Macmillan, 2007.

———. *Society Must Be Defended: Lectures at the Collège de France, 1975–1976*. Trans. David Macey. New York: Picador, 2003.

———. "The Subject and Power." In *Michel Foucault: Beyond Structuralism and Hermeneutics*, ed. Hubert L. Dreyfus and Paul Rabinow, 208–26. Chicago: University of Chicago Press, 1983.

———. "Technologies of the Self." In *Essential Works of Michel Foucault, 1954–1984*, vol. 1: *Ethics*, ed. Paul Rabinow, trans. Robert Hurley, pp. 223–52. London: Penguin, 1994.

Fusco, Coco. "Hustling for Dollars: *Jineterismo* in Cuba." In *Global Sex Workers: Rights, Resistance and Redefinition*, ed. Kamala Kempadoo and Jo Doezema, pp. 151–66. London: Routledge, 1998.

———. "Introduction: Latin American Rerformance and the Reconquista of Civil Space." In *Corpus Delecti: Performance Art of the Americas*, ed. Coco Fusco, pp. 1–20. London: Routledge, 2000.

Fusco, Coco, and Nao Bustamente. "STUFF! An Excerpt." In *Corpus Delecti: Performance Art of the Americas*, ed. Coco Fusco, pp. 60–62. London: Routledge, 2000.

Gámez Torres, Nora. "Hearing the Change: Reggaeton and Emergent Values in Contemporary Cuba." *Latin American Music Review* 33.2 (Fall–Winter 2012): 227–60.

García, Alyssa. "Continuous Moral Economies: The State Regulation of Bodies and Sex Work in Cuba." *Sexualities* 13.2 (2010): 171–96.

———. "(Re)covering Women: The State, Morality, and Cultural Discourses of Sex-Work in Cuba." PhD dissertation, University of Illinois at Urbana-Champaign, 2008.

Goldberg, Jonathan. "Sodomy in the New World: Anthropologies Old and New." In *Fear of a Queer Planet: Queer Politics and Social Theory*, ed. Michael Warner, pp. 3–18. Minneapolis: University of Minnesota Press, 1990.

Gosse, Van. *Where the Boys Are: Cuba, Cold War America and the Making of a New Left*. London: Verso, 1993.

Guerrero, Natividad, and Josefina Alonso. "La sexualidad en los jóvenes." In *Cuba: Jóvenes en los 90*, ed. Centro de Estudios sobre Jóvenes, pp. 185–224. Havana: Editorial Abril, 1999.

Guerrero Borrego, Natividad. "Salud sexual y reproductiva: Reflexiones con los jóvenes." in (eds) In *Género: Salud y cotidianidad*, ed. Celia Sarduy Sánchez and Ada Alfonso Rodríguez, pp. 97–111. Havana: Editorial Científico-Técnica, 2000.

Gutiérrez, Pedro Juan. *Dirty Havana Trilogy: A Novel in Stories*. Trans. Natasha Wimmer. New York: HarperPerennial, 2002.

Halberstam, Judith. "Going Gaga: Dissent, Refusal and Postcolonial Desire." Paper presented at the conference "Love, Sex, Desire and the (Post)colonial," University of London, 28 October 2011.

———. *The Queer Art of Failure*. Durham, NC: Duke University Press, 2011.

Hall, Stuart, Chas Critcher, Tony Jefferson, John N. Clarke, and Brian Roberts. *Policing the Crisis: Mugging, the State and Law and Order*. London: Macmillan, 1978.

Halley, Janet E. "The Construction of Heterosexuality." In *Fear of a Queer Planet: Queer Politics and Social Theory*, ed. Michael Warner, pp. 82–102. Minneapolis: University of Minnesota Press, 1990.

Hamilton, Carrie. *Sexual Revolutions in Cuba: Passion, Politics, and Memory*. Chapel Hill: University of North Carolina Press, 2012.

Haney, Richard. *Celia Sanchez: The Legend of Cuba's Revolutionary Heart*. New York: Algora Publishing, 2005.

Helg, Aline. *Our Rightful Share: The Afro-Cuban Struggle for Equality, 1886–1912*. Durham, NC: Duke University Press, 1995.

———. "Race in Argentina and Cuba, 1880–1930: Theory, Politics, and Popular Reaction." In *The Idea of Race in Latin America, 1870–1940*, ed. Richard Graham, 37–69. Austin: University of Texas Press, 1990.

Hermansen, Anne-Mette. "Jineteras, Luchadoras and the Awkward Tourist-Anthropologist in Havana: People as Categories." *PlatForum* 10 (2009): 45–60.

Hillson, Jon. "La política sexual de Reinaldo Arenas: Realidad, ficción y el Archivo Real de la revolución cubana." *La Jiribilla* (April 2001), accessed 25 November 2011, www.lajiribilla.cu/2001/n1_abril/021_1.html.

Hochschild, Arlie Russell. *The Managed Heart: Commercialization of Human Feeling*. Berkeley: University of California Press, 1983.

Hodge, Derrick. "Colonization of the Cuban Body: The Growth of Male Sex Work in Havana." *NACLA* 34.5 (March–April 2001): 20–23.

Hoefinger, Heidi. *Sex, Love and Money in Cambodia: Professional Girlfriends and Transactional Relationships*. New York: Routledge, 2013.

Hofmeyr, Benda. "The Power Not to Be (What We Are): The Politics and Ethics of Self-Creation in Foucault." *Journal of Moral Philosophy* 3.2 (2006): 215–30.

Holgado Fernandez, Isabel. *No es fácil! Mujeres cubanas y la crisis revolucionaria*. Barcelona: Icaria Editorial, 2000.

Horta Mesa, Osmany. "Recodo sentencioso de la prostitución en la colonia cubana." Master's thesis, University of Havana, 1999.

Human Rights Watch. "New Castro, Same Cuba: Political Prisoners in the Post-Fidel Era." Report 1-56432-562-8, November 2009, accessed 17 September 2011, www.hrw.org/reports/2009/11/18/new-castro-same-cuba-0.

Hunter, Mark. "The Materiality of Everyday Sex: Thinking beyond 'Prostitu-tion.'" *African Studies* 61.1 (2002): 99–120.

Johnson, Sherry. "Introduction: Señoras . . . no ordinarias." *Cuban Studies* 34 (2003): 4–5.

Kapcia, Antoni. *Cuba in Revolution: A History since the Fifties*. London: Reaktion Books, 2008.

Kempadoo, Kemala. "Freelancers, Temporary Wives, and Beach-Boys: Researching Sex Work in the Caribbean." *Feminist Review* 67 (Spring 2001): 39–62.

———. "Introduction." In *Global Sex Workers: Rights, Resistance and Redefini-tion*, ed. Kamala Kempadoo and Jo Doezema, pp. 1–28. London: Routledge, 1998.

———. *Sexing the Caribbean: Gender, Race and Sexual Labor*. New York: Routledge, 2004.

Khan, Koushambhi Basu, Heather McDonald, Jennifer L. Baumbusch, Sheryl Reimer Kirkham, Elsie Tan, and Joan M. Anderson. "Taking Up Postcolonial Feminism in the Field: Working through a Method." *Women's Studies International Forum* 30 (2007): 228–42.

Koken, Juline A. "The Meaning of the 'Whore': How Feminist Theories on Prostitution Shape Research on Female Sex Workers." In *Sex Work Matters: Exploring Money, Power, and Intimacy in the Sex Industry*, ed. Melissa Hope Ditmore, Antonia Levy, and Alys Willman, pp. 28–64. London: Zed Books, 2010.

Kruger, Mark H. "Community-Based Crime Control in Cuba." *Contemporary Justice Review* 10.1 (March 2007): 101–14.

Kutzinski, Vera M. *Sugar's Secrets: Race and the Erotics of Cuban Nationalism*. Charlottesville: University of Virginia Press, 1993.

La Fountain-Stokes, Lawrence. "De un pajaro las dos alas: Travel Notes of a Queer Puerto Rican in Havana." *GLQ* 8.1 (2002): 7–33.

Lancaster, Roger N. "Sexual Positions: Caveats and Second Thoughts on 'Categories.'" *The Americas* 54.1 (July 1997): 1–16.

Larson, Scott. "Gay Space in Havana." In *The Politics of Sexuality in Latin America*, ed. Javier Corrales and Mario Pecheny, pp. 334–48. Pittsburgh: University of Pittsburgh Press, 2010.

Latell, Brian. *After Fidel: Raul Castro and the Future of Cuba's Revolution*. New York: Palgrave Macmillan, 2005.

Lather, Patti. "Postbook: Working the Ruins of Feminist Ethnography." *Signs* 27.1 (2001): 199–227.

Lauria, Carlos, Monica Campbell, and María Salazar. "Cuba's Long Black Spring." Report for Committee to Protect Journalists, 18 March 2008, accessed 3 August 2011, http://cpj.org/reports/2008/03/cuba-press-crackdown.php.

Leiner, Marvin. *Sexual Politics in Cuba: Machismo, Homosexuality, and AIDS.* Boulder, CO: Westview Press, 1994.

Lerum, Kari. "Subjects of Desire: Academic Armor, Intimate Ethnography, and the Production of Critical Knowledge." *Qualitative Inquiry* 7.4 (2001): 466–83.

Lewis, Oscar, Ruth M. Lewis, and Susan M. Rigdon. *Four Women: Living the Revolution. An Oral History of Contemporary Cuba.* Champaign: University of Illinois Press, 1977.

Loomba, Ania. *Colonialism/Postcolonialism.* 2nd ed. New York: Routledge, 2005.

Los Aldeanos. "Mangos Bajitos." In *El Atropello.* CD, independent release, 2009.

Los Van Van. "La titimanía." *Van Van 30 Aniversario, Vol. 1.* CD. Caribe Productions Inc., 2007.

Lotti, Alina M. "Despejando horizontes: Entrevista con Sonia Beretervide." *Mujeres* (n.d.): 8–9.

Lumsden, Ian. *Machos, Maricones, and Gays: Cuba and Homosexuality.* Philadelphia: Temple University Press, 1996.

Luna, Erik. "Cuban Criminal Justice and the Ideal of Good Governance." *Transnational Law and Contemporary Problems* 14 (Spring 2004): 529–654.

Lutjens, Sheryl L. "Reading between the Lines: Women, the State and Rectification in Cuba." *Latin American Perspectives* 89.22 (1995): 100–124.

———. "Remaking the Public Sphere." In *Women in Revolution in Africa, Asia, and the New World*, ed. Mary Ann Tetrault, pp. 366–93. Columbia: University of South Carolina Press, 1994.

Mabley, Robert. "Wanted: More Adult Commentary about Cuba, Less 'Adult' Commentary." *Cuba Update* (October 1995): 4.

Manderson, Lenore, and Margaret Jolly, eds. *Sites of Desire, Economies of Pleasure: Sexualities in Asia and the Pacific.* Chicago: University of Chicago Press, 1997.

Margaroni, Maria. "Care and Abandonment: A Response to Mika Ojakangas' 'Impossible Dialogue on Bio-power: Agamben and Foucault.'" *Foucault Studies* 2 (May 2005): 29–36.

Marrero, Teresa. "Scripting Sexual Tourism: Fusco and Bustamente's *STUFF*, Prostitution and Cuba's Special Period." *Theatre Journal* 55 (2003): 235–50.

Martí, José. *Our America: Writings on Latin America and the Struggle for Cuban Independence.* Ed. Philip S. Foner, trans. Elinor Randall. New York: Monthly Review Press, 1979.

Martinez-Alier, Verena. *Marriage, Class and Colour in Nineteenth-Century Cuba: A Study of Racial Attitudes and Sexual Values in a Slave Society.* London: Cambridge University Press, 1974.

Masiello, Francine. "Género, vestido y mercado: El comercio de la cuidadanía en América Latina." In *Sexo y sexualidades en América Latina*, ed. Daniel Balderston and Donna Guy, pp. 315–34. Buenos Aires: Paídos, 1998.

Mason, Michael Atwood. *Living Santería: Rituals and Experiences in an Afro-Cuban Religion*. Washington, DC: Smithsonian Institution Press, 2002.

May, Robert E. *The Southern Dream of a Caribbean Empire, 1854–1861*. Baton Rouge: University of Louisiana Press, 1973.

Mazola Fiallo, María Elena, Esperanza Fernández Zequeira, Marilyn Ramos Polanco, and Juan Carlos Rangel García. *Estudio sobre algunos valores morales de jóvenes con conducta sexual prostituida: Informe de investigación*. Havana: Instituto de Medicina Legal del Ministerio del Interior, 1996.

McRobbie, Angela. "The Politics of Feminist Research: Between Talk, Text and Action." *Feminist Review* 12 (October 1982): 47–57.

Mehta, Deepak. "Circumcision, Body, Masculinity: The Ritual Wound and Collective Violence." In *Violence and Subjectivity*, ed. Veena Das, Arthur Kleinman, Mamphela Ramphele, and Pamela Reynolds, pp. 79–101. Berkeley: University of California Press, 2000.

Mendieta Costa, Raquel. "Exotic Exports: The Myth of the Mulatta." Trans. Eduardo Aparicio. In *Corpus Delecti: Performance of the Americas*, ed. Coco Fusco, pp. 43–54. London: Routledge, 2000.

Menendez, Nina. "*Garzonas* y feministas cubanas en la década del 20." In *Sexo y sexualidades en América Latina*, ed. Daniel Balderston and Donna Guy, pp. 257–75. Buenos Aires: Paídos, 1998.

Mesa-Lago, Carmelo. "Growing Economic Social Disparities in Cuba: Impact and Recommendations for Change." Institute for Cuban and Cuban-American Studies, University of Miami, 2002, accessed 23 September 2009, http://ctp.iccas.miami.edu/research_studies/cmesalago.pdf.

Mohanty, Chandra Talpade. *Feminism without Borders: Decolonizing Theory, Practicing Solidarity*. Durham, NC: Duke University Press, 2003.

Moore, Robin. *Music and Revolution: Cultural Change in Socialist Cuba*. Berkeley: University of California Press, 2006.

Mullings, Beverly. "Globalization, Tourism, and the International Sex Trade." In *Sun, Sex and Gold: Tourism and Sex Work in the Caribbean*, ed. Kamala Kempadoo, pp. 55–80. Lanham, MD: Rowman & Littlefield, 1999.

———. "Insider or Outsider, Both or Neither: Some Dilemmas of Interviewing in a Cross-Cultural Setting." *Geoforum* 30.4 (November 1999): 337–50.

Muñoz del Monte, Francisco. "La mulata." In *Poesía afroantillana y negrista: Puerto Rico, República Dominicana, Cuba*, 2nd ed., ed. Jorge Luis Morales, pp. 195–200. San Juan: Editorial de la Universidad de Puerto Rico, 1981.

Museo Nacional de Bellas Artes. *Guía de arte cubano*. 90th anniversary ed. Córdoba: Impresa Provincial, Diputación de Córdoba, ca. 2003.

Nazzari, Muriel. "The 'Woman Question' in Cuba: An Analysis of Material Constraints on Its Solution." *Signs* 9.2 (Winter 1983): 246–63.

Nelson, Diane M. *A Finger in the Wound: Body Politics in Quincentennial Guatemala*. Berkeley: University of California Press, 1999.

Nencel, Lorraine. *Ethnography and Prostitution in Peru*. London: Pluto Press, 2001.

———. "Feeling Gender Speak: Intersubjectivity and Fieldwork Practice with Women Who Prostitute in Lima, Peru." *European Journal of Women's Studies* 12.3 (2005): 345–61.

O'Connell Davidson, Julia. *Prostitution, Power and Freedom*. Ann Arbor: University of Michigan Press, 1998.

———. "The Rights and Wrongs of Prostitution." *Hypatia* 17.2 (Spring 2002): 84–98.

Ojakangas, Mika. "Impossible Dialogue on Bio-power: Agamben and Foucault." *Foucault Studies* 2 (May 2005): 5–28.

Oksala, Johanna. *Foucault on Freedom*. Cambridge: Cambridge University Press, 2005.

Ortiz, Fernando. *Hampa afro-cubana: Los negros esclavos*. Havana: Revista Bimestre Cubana, 1916.

Parker, Andrew. "Unthinking Sex: Marx, Engels, and the Scene of Writing." In *Fear of a Queer Planet: Queer Politics and Social Theory*, ed. Michael Warner, pp. 19–41. Minneapolis: University of Minnesota Press, 1990.

Patai, Daphne. "U.S. Academics and Third World Women: Is Ethical Research Possible?" In *Women's Words: The Feminist Practice of Oral History*, ed. Sherna Berger Gluck and Daphne Patai, pp. 137–53. London: Routledge, 1991.

Paternoso, Silvana. "Sexual Revolution: Communism versus Prostitution." *New Republic* (10 July 2000): 18–22.

Paz, Octavio. *The Labyrinth of Solitude*. London: Penguin, 1967.

Peñate Leiva, Ana Isabel. "Género y prostitución: Algunos reflexiones a las puertas del tercer milenio." In *Género: Salud y cotidianidad*, ed. Celia Sarduy Sánchez and Ada Alfonso Rodríguez, pp. 189–204. Havana: Editorial Científico-Técnica, 2000.

Pérez, Louis A. *Cuba: Between Reform and Revolution*. 4th ed. New York: Oxford University Press, 2006.

———. *The War of 1898: The United States and Cuba in History and Historiography*. Chapel Hill: University of North Carolina Press, 1998.

Pérez de la Riva, Juan. *La isla de Cuba en el siglo XIX vista por los extranjeros*. Havana: Editorial Ciencias Sociales, 1981.

Perez-Sarduy, Pedro, and Jean Stubbs. *Afro-Cuban Voices: On Race and Identity in Contemporary Cuba*. Gainesville: University Press of Florida, 2000.

Phoenix, J. "Prostitution: Problematising the Definition." In *(Hetero)sexual Politics*, ed. M. Maynard and J. Purvis, 65–77. London: Taylor and Francis, 1995.

Pichardo Moya, Felipe. "Filosofía del bronce." In *Poesía afroantillana y negrista: Puerto Rico, República Dominicana, Cuba,* 2nd ed., ed. Jorge Luis Morales, pp. 165–66. San Juan: Editorial de la Universidad de Puerto Rico, 1981.

Pickett, Brent L. "Foucault and the Politics of Resistance." *Polity* 28.4 (Summer 1996): 445–66.

Piron, Hippolyte. *L'île de Cuba: Santiago, Puerto-Principe, Matanzas et La Havane.* Paris: E. Plon, 1876.

Prozorov, Sergei. *Foucault, Freedom and Sovereignty.* Aldershot: Ashgate, 2007.

———. "The Unrequited Love of Power: Biopolitical Investment and the Refusal of Care." *Foucault Studies* 4 (February 2007): 53–77.

Puri, Shalini. *The Caribbean Postcolonial: Social Equality, Post-Nationalism, and Cultural Hybridity.* New York: Palgrave Macmillan, 2004.

Quiroga, José. "Homosexualidades en el trópico de revolución." In *Sexo y sexualidades en América Latina,* ed. Daniel Balderston and Donna Guy, pp. 205–28. Buenos Aires: Paídos, 1998.

Ravelo, Aloyma. *Enigmas de la sexualidad femenina.* 2nd ed. Havana: Ediciones de la Mujer, 2010.

Rebhun, Linda-Anne. *The Heart Is Unknown Country: Love in the Changing Economy of Northeast Brazil.* Stanford, CA: Stanford University Press, 1999.

Romero-Cesareo, Ivette. "Havana's Callejón de Hamel Celebrates Its 20th Anniversary." *Repeating Islands,* 20 April 2010, accessed 16 November 2011, http://repeatingislands.com/2010/04/20/ havanas-callejon-de-hamel-celebrates-its-20th-anniversary/.

Rose, Nikolas, and Peter Miller. "Political Power beyond the State: Problematics of Government." *British Journal of Sociology* 43.2 (June 1992): 173–205.

Rosendahl, Mona. *Inside the Revolution: Everyday Life in Socialist Cuba.* Ithaca, NY: Cornell University Press, 1997.

Rowe, Michael. "The New Cuban Revolución." *The Advocate,* 14 September 2009, accessed 24 September 2011, www.advocate.com/News/World_News /The_New_Cuban_Revolucion/.

Rubin, Gayle S. "Thinking Sex: Notes for a Radical Theory of the Politics of Sexuality." In *The Lesbian and Gay Studies Reader,* ed. Henry Abelove, Michèle Aina Barale, and David M. Halperin, 3–44. New York: Routledge, 1993.

Rundle, Mette Louise B. (2001) "Tourism, Social Change and *Jineterismo* in Contemporary Cuba." In *Society for Caribbean Studies Annual Conference Papers Proceedings,* vol. 2, ed. Sandra Courtman. (PDF.)

Russell, Nelson Vance. "The Reaction in England and America to the Capture of Havana, 1762." *Hispanic American Historical Review* 9 (1929): 303–16.

Sarduy Sánchez, Celia, and Ada Alfonso Rodríguez, eds. *Género: Salud y cotidianidad.* Havana: Editorial Científico-Técnica, 2000.

Scarry, Elaine. "'The Body in Pain': An Interview with Elaine Scarry by Elizabeth Irene Smith." *Concentric: Literary and Cultural Studies* 32.2 (September 2006): 223–37.

———. *The Body in Pain: The Making and Unmaking of the World.* Oxford: Oxford University Press, 1985.

Scheina, Robert L. *Latin America's Wars: The Age of the Caudillo, 1791–1899.* Dulles, VA: Potomac Books, 2003.

Schrage, Laurie. *Moral Dilemmas of Feminism: Prostitution, Adultery and Abortion.* London: Routledge, 1994.

Schwartz, Rosalie. *Pleasure Island: Tourism and Temptation in Cuba.* Lincoln: University of Nebraska Press, 1997.

Scott, James C. *Domination and the Arts of Resistance: Hidden Transcripts.* New Haven, CT: Yale University Press, 1990.

———. *Weapons of the Weak: Everyday Forms of Peasant Resistance.* New Haven, CT: Yale University Press, 1985.

Seabrook, Jeremy. *Travels in the Skin Trade: Tourism and the Sex Industry.* London: Pluto, 1996.

Sedgwick, Eve Kosofsky. "Nationalisms and Sexualities in the Age of Wilde." In *Nationalisms and Sexualities,* ed. Andrew Parker, Mary Russo, Doris Sommer, and Patricia Yaeger, pp. 235–45. London: Routledge, 1992.

Seidman, Steven. "Identity and Politics in 'Postmodern' Gay Culture: Some Historical and Conceptual Notes." In *Fear of a Queer Planet: Queer Politics and Social Theory,* ed. Michael Warner, pp. 105–42. Minneapolis: University of Minnesota Press, 1990.

Shelley, Louise I. "Post-Socialist Policing: Limitations on Institutional Change." In *Policing across the World: Issues for the Twenty-First Century,* ed. R. I. Mawby, pp. 75–87. London: University College London Press, 1999.

Sierra Madero, Abel. "Códigos en movimiento: Masculinidad sobre ruedas." *La Siempreviva* 7 (2009): 70–81.

———. *Del otro lado del espejo: La sexualidad en la construcción de la nación cubana.* Havana: Casa de las Américas, 2006.

———. "Relaciones de género y sexo en Cuba, 1830–1855." Master's thesis, University of Havana, 2000.

Smith, Lois M., and Alfred Padula. *Sex and Revolution: Women in Socialist Cuba.* New York: Oxford University Press, 1996.

Soto, Leandro. "Performance in Cuba in the 1980s: A Personal Testimony." In *Corpus Delecti: Performance Art of the Americas,* ed. Coco Fusco, pp. 266–74. London: Routledge, 2000.

Stern, Maria. *Naming In/security—Constructing Identity: "Mayan Women" in Guatemala on the Eve of "Peace."* Gothenburg: Department of Peace and Development Research, Gothenburg University, 2001.

Stern, Maria, and Marysia Zalewski. "Feminist Fatigue(s): Reflections on Feminism and Familiar Fables of Militarisation." *Review of International Studies* 35 (2009): 611–30.

Stoler, Ann Laura. *Carnal Knowledge and Imperial Power: Race and the Intimate in Colonial Rule.* Berkeley: University of California Press, 2002.

Stout, Noelle M. "Feminists, Queers, and Critics: Debating the Cuban Sex Trade." *Journal of Latin American Studies* 40.4 (November 2008): 721–42.

Strout, Jan. "Women, the Politics of Sexuality and Cuba's Economic Crisis." *Cuba Update* 16 (30 June 1995): 15–18.

Suleri, Sara. "Woman Skin Deep: Feminism and the Postcolonial Condition." *Critical Inquiry* 18.4 (Summer 1992): 756–69.

Symmes, Patrick. "Thirty Days as a Cuban: Pinching Pesos and Dropping Pounds in Havana." *Harper's Magazine* (October 2010): 43–57.

Taylor, Jacqueline Sánchez. "Tourism and 'Embodied' Commodities: Sex Tourism and the Caribbean." In *Tourism and Sex: Culture, Commerce and Coercion,* ed. Stephen Clift and Simon Carter, pp. 41–53. London: Pinter, 2000.

Thomas, Hugh. *Cuba, or, The Pursuit of Freedom.* 2nd ed. New York: Da Capo Press, 1998.

Tickner, J. Ann. "Feminism Meets International Relations: Some Methodological Issues." In *Feminist Methodologies for International Relations,* ed. Brooke A. Ackerly, Maria Stern, and Jacqui True, pp. 19–41. Cambridge: Cambridge University Press, 2006.

Torres, Eduardo, and Elaine Morales. "Asedio, prostitución y delincuencia: Contextos y particularidades." In *Cuba: Jóvenes en los 90,* ed. Centro de Estudios sobre Jóvenes, pp. 311–32. Havana: Editorial Abril, 1999.

Touraine, Alain. *Return of the Actor: Social Theory in Postindustrial Society.* Minneapolis: University of Minnesota Press, 1988.

U.N. Economic and Social Council, Commission on Human Rights, 56th Session. *Note verbale dated 8 March 2000 from the Permanent Mission of Cuba to the United Nations Office at Geneva addressed to the Office of the High Commissioner on Human Rights* (E/CN.4/2000/131). 22 March 2000.

———. *Report of the Special Rapporteur on Violence against Women, Its Causes and Consequences. Addendum: Report on the Mission to Cuba* (E/CN.4/2000/68/Add.2). 8 February 2000.

Urry, John. *The Tourist Gaze.* 2nd ed. London: Sage, 2002.

Valle, Amir. *Habana Babilonia: La cara oculta de las jineteras.* Barcelona: Zeta Bolsillo, 2008.

Van Maanen, John. "An End to Innocence: The Ethnography of Ethnography." In *Representation in Ethnography,* ed. John Van Maanen, pp. 1–5. Thousand Oaks, CA: Sage, 1995.

Vasallo Barrueta, Norma. "Del feminismo al género: Un intento de romper estereotipos desde una relectura de las clásicas." In *Mirar de otra manera,* ed. Norma Vasallo Barrueta and Teresa Díaz Canals, pp. 17–38. Havana: Editorial de la Mujer, 2008.

Villaverde, Cirilo. *Cecilia Valdés, o la Loma del Angel.* Trans. Helen Lane. Oxford: Oxford University Press, 2005.

Voss, Michael. "Dissidents' Release Draws Line under Cuba Crackdown." *BBC News,* 23 March 2011, accessed 3 August 2011, www.bbc.co.uk/news/ world-latin-america-12842392.

Wahab, Stéphanie. "Creating Knowledge Collaboratively with Female Sex Workers: Insights from a Qualitative, Feminist, and Participatory Study." *Qualitative Inquiry* 9.4 (2003): 625–42.

Walkowitz, Judith. "Male Vice and Feminist Virtue: Feminist and the Politics of Prostitution in Nineteenth-Century Britain." *History Workshop Journal* 13 (Spring 1982): 79–93.

Weber, Cynthia. *Faking It: U.S. Hegemony in a "Post-Phallic" Era.* Minneapolis: University of Minnesota Press, 1999.

Weeks, Jeffrey. "History, Desire and Identities." In *Conceiving Sexuality,* ed. Richard G. Parker and John H. Gagnon, pp. 33–50. New York: Routledge, 1995.

Wilkinson, Stephen. "Cuba Lay-Offs Reveal Evolving Communism." *BBC News,* 14 September 2010, accessed 25 November 2011, www.bbc.co.uk/news/ world-latin-america-11302430.

Williams, Claudette M. *Charcoal and Cinnamon: The Politics of Color in Spanish Caribbean Literature.* Gainseville: University Press of Florida, 1999.

Williams, William Appleman. *Empire as a Way of Life: An Essay on the Causes and Character of America's Present Predicament along with a Few Thoughts about an Alternative.* Oxford: Oxford University Press, 1980.

Wonders, Nancy A., and Raymond Michalowski. "Bodies, Borders and Sex Tourism in a Globalised World: A Tale of Two Cities—Amsterdam and Havana." *Social Problems* 48.4 (November 2001): 545–71.

Wright, Irene A. *Cuba, Illustrated.* Norwood, MA: Macmillan, 1910.

Yáñez, Mirta. "We Blacks All Drink Coffee." In *Her True-True Story,* ed. P. Mordechai and B. Wilson, pp. 37–43. Oxford: Heinemann International.

Young, Allen. "The Cuban Revolution and Gay Liberation." In *Out of the Closets: Voices of Gay Liberation,* 20th anniversary ed., ed. Karla Jay and Allen Young, pp. 206–28. London: GMP Publishers, 1992.

Yuval-Davis, Nira. *Gender and Nation.* London: Sage, 1997.

Los Zafiros. *Bossa Cubana.* World Circuit Records, London, 1963–66 [1999].

Zalewski, Marysia. "Distracted Reflections on the Production, Narration, and Refusal of Feminist Knowledge in International Relations." In *Feminist Methodologies for International Relations,* ed. Brooke A. Ackerly, Maria Stern, and Jacqui True, pp. 42–61. Cambridge: Cambridge University Press, 2006.

———. *Feminism after Postmodernism: Theorising through Practice*. London: Routledge, 2000.

Zelizer, Viviana. *The Purchase of Intimacy*. Princeton, NJ: Princeton University Press, 2005.

Ziarek, Ewa Płonowska. *The Rhetoric of Failure: Deconstruction of Skepticism, Reinvention of Modernism*. Albany: State University of New York Press, 1996.

Žižek, Slavoj. *For They Know Not What They Do: Enjoyment as a Political Factor*. 2nd ed. London: Verso, 2002.

———. *Interrogating the Real*. London: Continuum, 2005.

———. *The Parallax View*. Cambridge, MA: MIT Press, 2006.

Zurbano, Roberto. "For Blacks in Cuba, the Revolution Hasn't Begun." *New York Times*, 23 March 2013, accessed 18 January 2014, www.nytimes.com/2013/03/24/opinion/sunday/for-blacks-in-cuba-the-revolution-hasnt-begun.html?_r = 2&.

Index

aesthetics, 181, 213–15, 217, 226–27. *See also* ethics

Afro-Cubans: culture, 1–3, 5–7, 115; and police, 62, 63, 112–15, 121; social conditions of, 9–10, 40, 51, 176. *See also* race

Agramonte, Ignacio, 40

Aldeanos, Los, 244n8; "Mangos bajitos," 84

Alma Mater, 197, 198 *fig*

arrest, 25, 92–96, 119–20, 143; forced gynecological examinations following, 26, 123, 141. *See also* mass arrest (*operativo*)

Article 72. *See* Código Penal de Cuba

Batista, Fulgencio, 47–50, 200

biopolitics, 204, 212–14, 227; as care, 181, 186–87, 190, 194–96, 206–7, 216, 219, 232; refusal of, 141, 187–88, 194–97, 217 (*see also* disinvestment); and sexuality, 204–5

biopower. *See* biopolitics

blanqueamiento, 31–32, 63. *See also* race

British occupation of Cuba, 28, 44

Callejón de Hamel, 1–4, 5–8, 223

carta de advertencia, 26, 121–22, 125, 138, 210

Casas de Orientación a la Mujer y la Familia, 159, 165, 170, 177

casas de recogidas, 45–46, 53, 62, 65, 205

Castro, Fidel, 50, 145, 188; on *convenios sexuales,* 56; on homosexuality, 55, 157; on racism, 175

Castro, Raúl, 50, 151, 188

Castro Espín, Mariela, 151–52

categorization, practices of, 23, 70, 85, 97–104, 133, 238n51. *See also* labeling

Catholicism. *See* Roman Catholicism

Cebolla, La, 240n58

Cecilia Valdés (Villaverde), 32, 43

CENESEX. *See* Centro Nacional de Educación Sexual

Central de Trabajadores Cubanos (CTC), 158

Centro de Estudios Sobre la Juventud (CESJ), 147, 149, 155–56, 179

Centro Nacional de Educación Sexual (CENESEX), 151–58, 177, 179, 180

CESJ. *See* Centro de Estudios Sobre la Juventud

chastity. See *pudor*

Chinese Cubans, 28, 175, 235n6

chulo(s), 109, 129–31, 142; and police, 132–34

Código de Familia, 54, 159

Código Penal de Cuba: *estado peligroso* in, 119, 143–44, 246n15; on interracial marriage, 29; on prostitution, 26, 46, 52, 120, 167, 238n7. See also *peligrosidad*